Criticism and Fiction

The Responsibilities
of the Novelist

Criticism and Fiction .

by

WILLIAM DEAN HOWELLS

and

The Responsibilities
of the Novelist

by

FRANK NORRIS .

American Century Series

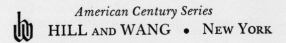 HILL AND WANG • NEW YORK

Manufactured in the United States of America
1234567890

C O N T E N T S

INTRODUCTION

INTRODUCTION

William Dean Howells, author of *The Rise of Silas Lapham* and *A Hazard of New Fortunes,* found great merit in Frank Norris' first naturalistic novel, *McTeague.* But Howells concluded his review of the book with, "His true picture of life is not true, because it leaves beauty out. Life is squalid, and cruel and vile and hateful, but it is noble and tender and pure and lovely, too. By and by he will put these traits in, and then his powerful scene will be a reflection of reality; by and by he will achieve something of the impartial fidelity of the photograph."

Norris' grateful letter in reply reveals the determined effort of both writers to seek clarification in a confusion of critical values and terms. Norris wrote Howells that his review "encouraged me more than anything that has ever been said of my work. I believe, too, you were quite right in saying that it was not the whole truth, and that the novel that is true to life cannot afford to ignore the finer things." The generosity and respect of these men for each other never led them to compromise their intellectual positions. But their two books of critical essays show how they were brought together when the dispute opened out into issues much larger than the success or failure of particular kinds of writing.

Criticism and Fiction was first published in 1891. Howells selected the chapters for it from articles he had written between 1886 and 1891 for "The Editor's Study" in *Harper's Monthly Magazine.* Norris wrote his essays in 1901 and 1902 for *The Critic, World's Work,* and syndicated newspaper columns. They were collected and published as *The Responsibilities of the Novelist* in 1903. The two books are well known to students of American literature as the central statements in the argument between realism and naturalism as the most suitable technique for American fiction.

When read together these critical essays present a dialogue that is sometimes in opposition but often in agreement on major principles. Although Norris was eager to free the novel from limitations imposed by Howell's prudery, it must be remembered that Howells regarded Norris as his successor. The differences in the theories of the two writers are not so great as they have been made to appear. A novel of realism written along lines suggested by Howells' example of the real and ideal grasshopper would not very much differ from one guided by Norris' naturalistic propositions. The concern for the role of the critic, the extended passages on the techniques of fiction, and the speculation about the objectives of the novel are all aspects of a deeper concern shared by both writers.

The appearance toward the end of the nineteenth century of books on the theory and craft of fiction by Hamlin Garland, Howells, and Norris, reflects the desire of serious writers in the post-romantic period to order the world in which they found themselves. We read them today because of their courage in facing up to the realities of the life Utopian idealists and Genteel Traditionalists were hard at work to deny. Howells and Norris were members of a generation beginning to count the cost in terms of American life of a "century of progress." They were eager to put to use what that century had taught and they were aware that new ways of thinking about problems old and new would be useless until set on firm foundations.

The frequent references to French, English, Spanish, and Russian literature appear at first a naive attempt to raise the stature of American writing by forcing it into the context of the continental tradition. But by 1890 life in America resembled more and more that of the industrial nations of Europe. It was increasingly clear that writers everywhere shared the same preoccupations. The frontier in the American West had closed. The growth of the cities, the consolidation of the middle classes, and increasing pressures toward conformity gave fiction new problems and themes that were as vital in New York as in Paris and London. Howells and Norris early recognized the growing power of the moral force of art in the largest sense and this led them both to deal critically with the age-old problem of how to tell the truth about life and still hold a large audience by legitimate means.

Together with Theodore Dreiser and Henry James, Howells and Norris gave the twentieth-century American novel its specific shape and substance. *Criticism and Fiction* and *The Responsibilities of the Novelist* can be used as yardsticks to measure the fiction of others but inevitably one will judge these writers against their own practice. Their failure to write the books they called for does not take away the naked honesty of their courage to assert a point of view and to stand by it with conviction to ease the way for others. It is always too easy to attack another's position so long as you have none of your own to defend. If the work of Howells and Norris seems provincial or limited in comparison with that of present day authors, Eliot reminds us, "Someone said: 'The dead writers are remote from us because we *know* so much more than they did.' Precisely, and they are that which we know."

Realism and Naturalism fail in a purified state as a technique for fiction because writers had yet to discover that the perfect reproduction of a *mise en scene* does not guarantee emotional sincerity. But these men greatly extended the range of the novel in subject matter and in new attitudes with which to organize and, ultimately, to value experience. These two books of critical essays touch a new sense of reality which demanded new terms for its expression. Howells and Norris fought for this expression in American literature and behind the debate about character and theme one realizes that, in the end, what they sought and what they achieved was the freedom to write more openly about their own inner perceptions. And it is here, in the struggle for enlarged sensibility and understanding that these writers mean most to us. They discovered new ways to tell us more of the truth about ourselves.

Eliot House
Cambridge, Mass.
January, 1962

WALKER COWEN

CRITICISM

AND

FICTION

CRITICISM AND FICTION

THE question of a final criterion for the appreciation of art is one that perpetually recurs to those interested in any sort of æsthetic endeavor. Mr. John Addington Symonds, in a chapter of The Renaissance in Italy treating of the Bolognese school of painting, which once had so great cry, and was vaunted the supreme exemplar of the grand style, but which he now believes fallen into lasting contempt for its emptiness and soullessness, seeks to determine whether there can be an enduring criterion or not; and his conclusion is applicable to literature as to the other arts. "Our hope," he says, "with regard to the unity of taste in the future then is, that all sentimental or academical seekings after the ideal having been abandoned, momentary theories founded upon idiosyncratic or temporary partialities exploded, and nothing accepted but what is solid and positive, the scientific spirit shall make men progressively more and more conscious of these bleibende Verhältnisse, more and more capable of living in the whole ; also, that in proportion as we gain a firmer hold upon our own place in the world, we shall come to comprehend with more instinctive certitude what is simple, natural, and honest, welcoming with gladness all artistic products that exhibit these qualities. The perception of the enlightened man will then be the task of a healthy person who has made himself acquainted with the laws of evolution in art and in society, and is able to test the excellence of work in any stage from immaturity to decadence by discerning what there is of truth, sincerity, and natural vigor in it."

I

THAT is to say, as I understand, that moods and tastes and fashions change; people fancy now this and now that; but what is unpretentious and what is true is always beautiful and good, and nothing else is so. This is not saying that fantastic and monstrous and artificial things do not please; everybody knows that they do please immensely for a time, and then, after the lapse of a much longer time, they have the charm of the rococo. Nothing is more curious than the charm that fashion has. Fashion in women's dress, almost every fashion, is somehow delightful, else it would never have been the fashion; but if any one will look through a collection of old fashion plates, he must own that most fashions have been ugly. A few, which could be readily instanced, have been very pret·

ty, and even beautiful, but it is doubtful
if these have pleased the greatest number of people. The ugly delights as well
as the beautiful, and not merely because
the ugly in fashion is associated with the
young loveliness of the women who wear
the ugly fashions, and wins a grace from
them, not because the vast majority of
mankind are tasteless, but for some cause
that is not perhaps ascertainable. It is
quite as likely to return in the fashions
of our clothes and houses and furniture,
and poetry and fiction and painting, as the
beautiful, and it may be from an instinctive or a reasoned sense of this that some
of the extreme naturalists have refused
to make the old discrimination against it,
or to regard the ugly as any less worthy
of celebration in art than the beautiful;
some of them, in fact, seem to regard it
as rather more worthy, if anything. Possibly there is no absolutely ugly, no absolutely beautiful; or possibly the ugly contains always an element of the beautiful
better adapted to the general appreciation than the more perfectly beautiful.
This is a somewhat discouraging conject-

ure, but I offer it for no more than it is worth; and I do not pin my faith to the saying of one whom I heard denying, the other day, that a thing of beauty was a joy forever. He contended that Keats's line should have read, "Some things of beauty are sometimes joys forever," and that any assertion beyond this was too hazardous.

I SHOULD, indeed, prefer another line of Keats's, if I were to profess any formulated creed, and should feel much safer with his "Beauty is Truth, Truth Beauty," than even with my friend's reformation of the more quoted verse. It brings us back to the solid ground taken by Mr. Symonds, which is not essentially different from that taken in the great Mr. Burke's Essay on the Sublime and the Beautiful—a singularly modern book, considering how long ago it was wrote (as the great Mr. Steele would have written the participle a little longer ago), and full of a certain well-mannered and agreeable instruction. In some things it is of that droll little eighteenth-century world, when philosophy had got the neat little universe into the hollow of its hand, and knew just what

it was, and what it was for; but it is
quite without arrogance. "As for those
called critics," the author says, "they
have generally sought the rule of the arts
in the wrong place; they have sought
among poems, pictures, engravings, statues, and buildings; but art can never give
the rules that make an art. This is, I believe, the reason why artists in general,
and poets principally, have been confined
in so narrow a circle; they have been
rather imitators of one another than of
nature. Critics follow them, and therefore can do little as guides. I can judge
but poorly of anything while I measure it
by no other standard than itself. The
true standard of the arts is in every man's
power; and an easy observation of the
most common, sometimes of the meanest
things, in nature will give the truest
lights, where the greatest sagacity and industry that slights such observation must
leave us in the dark, or, what is worse,
amuse and mislead us by false lights."

If this should happen to be true—and
it certainly commends itself to acceptance
—it might portend an immediate danger

to the vested interests of criticism, only
that it was written a hundred years ago;
and we shall probably have the "sagacity
and industry that slights the observation"
of nature long enough yet to allow most
critics the time to learn some more useful trade than criticism as they pursue
it. Nevertheless, I am in hopes that the
communistic era in taste foreshadowed
by Burke is approaching, and that it will
occur within the lives of men now over-
awed by the foolish old superstition that
literature and art are anything but the
expression of life, and are to be judged
by any other test than that of their fidelity to it. The time is coming, I hope,
when each new author, each new artist,
will be considered, not in his proportion
to any other author or artist, but in his
relation to the human nature, known to
us all, which it is his privilege, his high
duty, to interpret. "The true standard
of the artist is in every man's power"
already, as Burke says; Michelangelo's
"light of the piazza," the glance of the
common eye, is and always was the best
light on a statue; Goethe's "boys and

blackbirds" have in all ages been the real connoisseurs of berries; but hitherto the mass of common men have been afraid to apply their own simplicity, naturalness, and honesty to the appreciation of the beautiful. They have always cast about for the instruction of some one who professed to know better, and who browbeat wholesome common-sense into the self-distrust that ends in sophistication. They have fallen generally to the worst of this bad species, and have been "amused and misled" (how pretty that quaint old use of amuse is!) "by the false lights" of critical vanity and self-righteousness. They have been taught to compare what they see and what they read, not with the things that they have observed and known, but with the things that some other artist or writer has done. Especially if they have themselves the artistic impulse in any direction they are taught to form themselves, not upon life, but upon the masters who became masters only by forming themselves upon life. The seeds of death are planted in them, and they can produce only the still-born, the academic

They are not told to take their work into the public square and see if it seems true to the chance passer, but to test it by the work of the very men who refused and decried any other test of their own work The young writer who attempts to report the phrase and carriage of every-day life, who tries to tell just how he has heard men talk and seen them look, is made to feel guilty of something low and unworthy by the stupid people who would like to have him show how Shakespeare's men talked and looked, or Scott's, or Thackeray's, or Balzac's, or Hawthorne's, or Dickens's; he is instructed to idealize his personages, that is, to take the life-likeness out of them, and put the book-likeness into them. He is approached in the spirit of the wretched pedantry into which learning, much or little, always decays when it withdraws itself and stands apart from experience in an attitude of imagined superiority, and which would say with the same confidence to the scientist: "I see that you are looking at a grasshopper there which you have found in the grass, and I suppose you intend to describe it. Now don't waste your time and sin against culture in that way. I've got a grasshopper here, which has been evolved at considerable pains and expense out of the grasshopper in general; in fact, it's a type. It's made up of wire and card-board, very prettily painted in a conventional tint, and it's perfectly indestructible. It isn't very much like a real grasshopper, but it's a great deal nicer, and it's served to represent the notion of a grasshopper ever since man emerged from barbarism. You may say that it's artificial. Well, it is artificial; but then it s ideal too; and what you want to do is to cultivate the ideal. You'll find the books full of my kind of grasshopper, and scarcely a trace of yours in any of them. The thing that you are proposing to do is commonplace; but if you say that it isn't commonplace, for the very reason that it hasn't been done before, you'll have to admit that it's photographic."

As I said, I hope the time is coming when not only the artist, but the common, average man, who always " has the standard of the arts in his power," will have also the courage to apply it, and will reject the ideal grasshopper wherever he finds it, in science, in literature, in art, because it is not "simple, natural, and honest," because it is not like a real grasshopper. But I will own that I think the time is yet far off, and that the people who have been brought up on the ideal grasshopper, the heroic grasshopper, the impassioned grasshopper, the self-devoted, adventureful, good old romantic cardboard grasshopper, must die out before the simple, honest, and natural grasshopper can have a fair field. I am in no haste to compass the end of these good people, whom I find in the mean time very amusing. It is delightful to meet one of them, either in print or out of it—some sweet elderly lady or excellent gentleman whose youth was pastured on the literature of thirty or forty years ago—and to witness the confidence with which they preach their favorite authors as all the law and the prophets. They have commonly read little or nothing since, or, if they have, they have judged it by a standard taken from these authors, and never dreamed of judging it by nature; they are destitute of the documents in the case of the later writers; they suppose that Balzac was the beginning of realism, and that Zola is its wicked end ; they are quite ignorant, but they are ready to talk you down, if you differ from them, with an assumption of knowledge sufficient for any occasion. The horror, the resentment, with which they receive any question of their literary saints is genuine; you descend at once very far in the moral and social scale, and anything short of offensive personality is too good for you; it is expressed to you that you are one to be avoided, and put down even a little lower than you have naturally fallen.

These worthy persons are not to blame ; it is part of their intellectual mission to represent the petrifaction of taste, and to preserve an image of a smaller and cruder and emptier world than we now live in, a world which was feeling its way towards the simple, the natural, the honest, but was a good deal "amused and misled" by lights now no longer mistakable for heavenly luminaries. They belong to a time, just passing away, when certain authors were considered authorities in certain kinds, when they must be accepted entire and not questioned in any particular. Now we are beginning to see and to say that no author is an authority except in those moments when he held his ear close to Nature's lips and caught her very accent. These moments are not continuous with any authors in the past, and they are rare with all. Therefore I am not afraid to say now that the greatest classics are sometimes not at all great, and that we can profit by them only when we hold them, like our meanest contemporaries, to a strict accounting, and verify their work by the standard of the arts which we all have in our power, the simple, the natural, and the honest.

Those good people, those curious and interesting if somewhat musty back-numbers, must always have a hero, an idol of some sort, and it is droll to find Balzac, who suffered from their sort such bitter scorn and hate for his realism while he was alive, now become a fetich in his turn, to be shaken in the faces of those who will not blindly worship him. But it is no new thing in the history of literature: whatever is established is sacred with those who do not think. At the beginning of the century, when romance was making the same fight against effete classicism which realism is making to-day against effete romanticism,the Italian poet Monti declared that "the romantic was the cold grave of the Beautiful," just as the realistic is now supposed to be. The romantic of that day and the real of this are in certain degree the same. Romanticism then sought, as realism seeks now, to widen the bounds of sympathy, to level every barrier against æsthetic freedom, to escape from the paralysis of tradition. It exhausted itself in this impulse ; and it remained for realism to assert that fidelity to experience and probability of motive are essential conditions of a great imaginative literature. It is not a new theory, but it has never before universally characterized literary endeavor. When realism becomes false to itself, when it heaps up facts merely, and maps life in-

stead of picturing it, realism will perish too. Every true realist instinctively
knows this, and it is perhaps the reason
why he is careful of every fact, and feels
himself bound to express or to indicate
its meaning at the risk of over-moraliz-
ing. In life he finds nothing insignificant; all tells for destiny and character;
nothing that God has made is contemptible. He cannot look upon human life
and declare this thing or that thing unworthy of notice, any more than the scientist can declare a fact of the material
world beneath the dignity of his inquiry.
He feels in every nerve the equality of
things and the unity of men; his soul is
exalted, not by vain shows and shadows
and ideals, but by realities, in which alone
the truth lives. In criticism it is his business to break the images of false gods
and misshapen heroes, to take away the
poor silly toys that many grown people
would still like to play with. He cannot
keep terms with Jack the Giant-killer or
Puss in Boots, under any name or in any
place, even when they reappear as the
convict Vautrec, or the Marquis de Mon-

trivaut, or the Sworn Thirteen Noblemen. He must say to himself that Balzac, when he imagined these monsters, was not Balzac, he was Dumas; he was not realistic, he was romantic.

SUCH a critic will not respect Balzac's good work the less for contemning his bad work. He will easily account for the bad work historically, and when he has recognized it, will trouble himself no further with it. In his view no living man is a type, but a character; now noble, now ignoble; now grand, now little; complex, full of vicissitude. He will not expect Balzac to be always Balzac, and will be perhaps even more attracted to the study of him when he was trying to be Balzac than when he had become so. In César Birotteau, for instance, he will be interested to note how Balzac stood at the beginning of the great things that have followed since in fiction. There is an interesting likeness between his work in this and Nicolas Gogol's in Dead Souls, which serves to illustrate the simultaneity of the literary movement in men of such widely separated civilizations and conditions. Both represent their characters with the touch of exaggeration which typifies; but in bringing his story to a close, Balzac employs a beneficence unknown to the Russian, and almost as universal and as apt as that which smiles upon the fortunes of the good in the Vicar of Wakefield. It is not enough to have rehabilitated Birotteau pecuniarily and socially; he must make him die triumphantly, spectacularly, of an opportune hemorrhage, in the midst of the festivities which celebrate his restoration to his old home. Before this happens, human nature has been laid under contribution right and left for acts of generosity towards the righteous bankrupt; even the king sends him six thousand francs. It is very pretty; it is touching, and brings the lump into the reader's throat; but it is too much, and one perceives that Balzac lived too soon to profit by Balzac. The later men, especially the Russians, have known how to forbear the excesses of analysis, to withhold the weakly recurring descriptive and caressing epithets, to let the characters suffice for themselves. All this does not mean that César Birotteau is not a beautiful and pathetic story, full of shrewdly considered knowledge of men, and of a good art struggling to free itself from self-consciousness. But it does mean that Balzac, when he wrote it, was under the burden of the very traditions which he has helped fiction to throw off. He felt obliged to construct a mechanical plot, to surcharge his characters, to moralize openly and baldly; he permitted himself to "sympathize" with certain of his people, and to point out others for the abhorrence of his readers. This is not so bad in him as it would be in a novelist of our day. It is simply primitive and inevitable, and he is not to be judged by it.

N the beginning of any art even the most gifted worker must be crude in his methods, and we ought to keep this fact always in mind when we turn, say, from the purblind worshippers of Scott to Scott himself, and recognize that he often wrote a style cumbrous and diffuse; that he was tediously analytical where the modern novelist is dramatic, and evolved his characters by means of long-winded explanation and commentary; that, except in the case of his lower-class personages, he made them talk as seldom man and never woman talked; that he was tiresomely descriptive; that on the simplest occasions he went about half a mile to express a thought that could be uttered in ten paces across lots; and that he trusted his readers' intuitions so little that he was apt to

rub in his appeals to them. He was probably right : the generation which he wrote
for was duller than this; slower-witted, æsthetically untrained, and in maturity not
so apprehensive of an artistic intention
as the children of to-day. All this is not
saying Scott was not a great man ; he was
a great man, and a very great novelist as
compared with the novelists who went
before him. He can still amuse young
people, but they ought to be instructed
how false and how mistaken he often
is, with his mediæval ideals, his blind
Jacobitism, his intense devotion to aristocracy and royalty ; his acquiescence in
the division of men into noble and ignoble, patrician and plebeian, sovereign
and subject, as if it were the law of God ;
for all which, indeed, he is not to blame
as he would be if he were one of our contemporaries. Something of this is true
of another master, greater than Scott in
being less romantic, and inferior in being
more German, namely, the great Goethe
himself. He taught us, in novels otherwise now antiquated, and always full of
German clumsiness, that it was false to

good art—which is never anything but the reflection of life—to pursue and round the career of the persons introduced, whom he often allowed to appear and disappear in our knowledge as people in the actual world do. This is a lesson which the writers able to profit by it can never be too grateful for; and it is equally a benefaction to readers; but there is very little else in the conduct of the Goethean novels which is in advance of their time; this remains almost their sole contribution to the science of fiction. They are very primitive in certain characteristics, and unite with their calm, deep insight, an amusing helplessness in dramatization. "Wilhelm retired to his room, and indulged in the following reflections," is a mode of analysis which would not be practised nowadays; and all that fancifulness of nomenclature in Wilhelm Meister is very drolly sentimental and feeble. The adventures with robbers seem as if dreamed out of books of chivalry, and the tendency to allegorization affects one like an endeavor on the author's part to escape from the unrealities which he must have felt harassingly, German as he was. Mixed up with the shadows and illusions are honest, wholesome, every-day people, who have the air of wandering homelessly about among them, without definite direction; and the mists are full of a luminosity which, in spite of them, we know for common-sense and poetry. What is useful in any review of Goethe's methods is the recognition of the fact, which it must bring, that the greatest master cannot produce a masterpiece in a new kind. The novel was too recently invented in Goethe's day not to be, even in his hands, full of the faults of apprentice work.

V

IN fact, a great master may sin against the "modesty of nature" in many ways, and I have felt this painfully in reading Balzac's romance— it is not worthy the name of novel—L^e Père Goriot, which is full of a malarial restlessness, wholly alien to healthful art. After that exquisitely careful and truthful setting of his story in the shabby boarding-house, he fills the scene with figures jerked about by the exaggerated passions and motives of the stage. We cannot have a cynic reasonably wicked, disagreeable, egoistic; we must have a lurid villain of melodrama, a disguised convict, with a vast criminal organization at his command, and

"So dyèd double red"

in deed and purpose that he lights up the faces of the horrified spectators with his

glare. A father fond of unworthy children, and leading a life of self-denial for
their sake, as may probably and pathet-
ically be, is not enough; there must be
an imbecile, trembling dotard, willing to
promote even the liaisons of his daughters to give them happiness and to teach
the sublimity of the paternal instinct.
The hero cannot sufficiently be a selfish
young fellow, with alternating impulses
of greed and generosity; he must su-
perfluously intend a career of iniquitous
splendor, and be swerved from it by nothing but the most cataclysmal interposi-
tions. It can be said that without such
personages the plot could not be trans-
acted; but so much the worse for the
plot. Such a plot had no business to be;
and while actions so unnatural are imagined, no mastery can save fiction from
contempt with those who really think
about it. To Balzac it can be forgiven,
not only because in his better mood he
gave us such biographies as Eugénie Gran-
det, but because he wrote at a time when
fiction was just beginning to verify the
externals of life, to portray faithfully the

outside of men and things. It was still held that in order to interest the reader the characters must be moved by the old romantic ideals; we were to be taught that "heroes" and "heroines" existed all around us, and that these abnormal beings needed only to be discovered in their several humble disguises, and then we should see every-day people actuated by the fine frenzy of the creatures of the poets. How false that notion was few but the critics, who are apt to be rather belated, need now be told. Some of these poor fellows, however, still contend that it ought to be done, and that human feelings and motives, as God made them and as men know them, are not good enough for novel-readers.

This is more explicable than would appear at first glance. The critics—and in speaking of them one always modestly leaves one's self out of the count for some reason—when they are not elders ossified in tradition, are apt to be young people, and young people are necessarily conservative in their tastes and theories. They have the tastes and theories of their instructors, who perhaps caught the truth of their day, but whose routine life has been alien to any other truth. There is probably no chair of literature in this country from which the principles now shaping the literary expression of every civilized people are not denounced and confounded with certain objectionable French novels, or which teaches young men anything of the universal impulse which has given us the work, not only of Zola, but of Tourguéneff and Tolstoï in Russia, of Björnson and Ibsen in Norway, of Valdés and Galdós in Spain, of Verga in Italy. Till these younger critics have learned to think as well as to write for themselves they will persist in heaving a sigh, more and more perfunctory, for the truth as it was in Sir Walter, and as it was in Dickens and in Hawthorne. Presently all will have been changed; they will have seen the new truth in larger and larger degree; and when it shall have become the old truth, they will perhaps see it all.

VI

N the mean time the average of criticism is not wholly bad with us. To be sure, the critic sometimes appears in the panoply of the savages whom we have supplanted on this continent; and it is hard to believe that his use of the tomahawk and the scalping-knife is a form of conservative surgery. It is still his conception of his office that he should assail with obloquy those who differ with him in matters of taste or opinion; that he must be rude with those he does not like, and that he ought to do them violence as a proof of his superiority. It is too largely his superstition that because he likes a thing it is good, and because he dislikes a thing it is bad; the reverse is quite possibly the case, but he is yet indefinitely far from knowing that in affairs of taste his personal preference en-ters very little. Commonly he has no principles, but only an assortment of pre-possessions for and against; and this otherwise very perfect character is sometimes uncandid to the verge of dishonesty. He seems not to mind misstating the position of any one he supposes himself to disagree with, and then attacking him for what he never said, or even implied; the critic thinks this is droll, and appears not to suspect that it is immoral. He is not tolerant; he thinks it a virtue to be intolerant; it is hard for him to understand that the same thing may be admirable at one time and deplorable at another; and that it is really his business to classify and analyze the fruits of the human mind very much as the naturalist classifies the objects of his study, rather than to praise or blame them; that there is a measure of the same absurdity in his trampling on a poem, a novel, or an essay that does not please him as in the botanist's grinding a plant underfoot because he does not find it pretty. He does not conceive that it is his business rather to identify the species and then explain how and where the specimen is imperfect and irregular. If he could once acquire this simple idea of his duty he would be much more agreeable company than he now is, and a more useful member of society; though I hope I am not yet saying that he is not extremely delightful as he is, and wholly indispensable. He is certainly more ignorant than malevolent; and considering the hard conditions under which he works, his necessity of writing hurriedly from an imperfect examination of far more books, on a greater variety of subjects, than he can even hope to read, the average American critic—the ordinary critic of commerce, so to speak—is very well indeed. Collectively he is more than this; for the joint effect of our criticism is the pretty thorough appreciation of any book submitted to it.

 HE misfortune rather than the fault of our individual critic is that he is the heir of the false theory and bad manners of the English school. The theory of that school has apparently been that almost any person of glib and lively expression is competent to write of almost any branch of polite literature; its manners are what we know. The American, whom it has largely formed, is by nature very glib and very lively, and commonly his criticism, viewed as imaginative work, is more agreeable than that of the Englishman; but it is, like the art of both countries, apt to be amateurish. In some degree our authors have freed themselves from English models; they have gained some notion of the more serious work of the Continent; but it is still the ambi-

tion of the American critic to write like the English critic, to show his wit if not his learning, to strive to eclipse the author under review rather than illustrate him. He has not yet caught on to the fact that it is really no part of his business to display himself, but that it is altogether his duty to place a book in such a light that the reader shall know its class, its function, its character. The vast good-nature of our people preserves us from the worst effects of this criticism without principles. Our critic, at his lowest, is rarely malignant; and when he is rude or untruthful, it is mostly without truculence; I suspect that he is often offensive without knowing that he is so. If he loves a shining mark because a fair shot with mud shows best on that kind of target, it is for the most part from a boyish mischievousness quite innocent of malice. Now and then he acts simply under instruction from higher authority, and denounces because it is the tradition of his publication to do so. In other cases the critic is obliged to support his journal's repute for severity, or for wit, or for morality, though he may himself be entirely amiable, dull, and wicked; this necessity more or less warps his verdicts.

The worst is that he is personal, perhaps because it is so easy and so natural to be personal, and so instantly attractive. In this respect our criticism has not improved from the accession of numbers of ladies to its ranks, though we still hope so much from women in our politics when they shall come to vote. They have come to write, and with the effect to increase the amount of little-digging, which rather superabounded in our literary criticism before. They "know what they like" — that pernicious maxim of those who do not know what they ought to like—and they pass readily from censuring an author's performance to censuring him. They bring a lively stock of misapprehensions and prejudices to their work; they would rather have heard about than known about a book; and they take kindly to the public wish to be amused rather than edified. But neither have they so much harm in them: they, too, are more ignorant than malevolent.

VIII

UR criticism is disabled by the unwillingness of the critic to learn from an author, and his readiness to mistrust him. A writer passes his whole life in fitting himself for a certain kind of performance; the critic does not ask why, or whether the performance is good or bad, but if he does not like the kind, he instructs the writer to go off and do some other sort of thing—usually the sort that has been done already, and done sufficiently. If he could once understand that a man who has written the book he dislikes, probably knows infinitely more about its kind and his own fitness for doing it than any one else, the critic might learn something, and might help the reader to learn; but by putting himself in a false position, a position of superiority, he is of no use. He ought, in the first place,

to cast prayerfully about for humility, and especially to beseech the powers to preserve him from the sterility of arrogance and the deadness of contempt, for out of these nothing can proceed. He is not to suppose that an author has committed an offence against him by writing the kind of book he does not like; he will be far more profitably employed on behalf of the reader in finding out whether they had better not both like it. Let him conceive of an author as not in any wise on trial before him, but as a reflection of this or that aspect of life, and he will not be tempted to browbeat him or bully him.

The critic need not be impolite even to the youngest and weakest author. A little courtesy, or a good deal, a constant perception of the fact that a book is not a misdemeanor, a decent self-respect that must forbid the civilized man the savage pleasure of wounding, are what I would ask for our criticism, as something which will add sensibly to its present lustre.

IX

WOULD have my fellow-critics consider what they are really in the world for. It is not, apparently, for a great deal, because their only excuse for being is that somebody else has been. The critic exists because the author first existed. If books failed to appear, the critic must disappear, like the poor aphis or the lowly caterpillar in the absence of vegetation. These insects may both suppose that they have something to do with the creation of vegetation; and the critic may suppose that he has something to do with the creation of literature; but a very little reasoning ought to convince alike aphis, caterpillar, and critic that they are mistaken. The critic—to drop the others—must perceive, if he will question himself more carefully, that his office is mainly

to ascertain facts and traits of literature, not to invent or denounce them; to discover principles, not to establish them; to report, not to create.

It is so much easier to say that you like this or dislike that, than to tell why one thing is, or where another thing comes from, that many flourishing critics will have to go out of business altogether if the scientific method comes in, for then the critic will have to know something beside his own mind, which is often but a narrow field. He will have to know something of the laws of that mind, and of its generic history.

The history of all literature shows that even with the youngest and weakest author criticism is quite powerless against his will to do his own work in his own way; and if this is the case in the green wood, how much more in the dry! It has been thought by the sentimentalist that criticism, if it cannot cure, can at least kill, and Keats was long alleged in proof of its efficacy in this sort. But criticism neither cured nor killed Keats, as we all now very well know. It wounded, it cruelly hurt him, no doubt; and it is always in the power of the critic to give pain to the author — the meanest critic to the greatest author—for no one can help feeling a rudeness. But every literary movement has been violently opposed at the start, and yet never stayed in the least, or arrested, by criticism; every author has been condemned for his virtues, but in no wise changed by it. In the beginning he reads the critics; but presently perceiving that he alone makes or mars himself, and that they have no instruction for him, he mostly leaves off reading them, though he is always glad of their kindness or grieved by their harshness when he chances upon it. This, I believe, is the general experience, modified, of course, by exceptions.

Then, are we critics of no use in the world? I should not like to think that, though I am not quite ready to define our use. More than one sober thinker is inclining at present to suspect that æsthetically or specifically we are of no use, and that we are only useful historically; that we may register laws, but not enact them. I am not quite prepared to admit that æsthetic criticism is useless, though in view of its futility in any given instance it is hard to deny that it is so. It certainly seems as useless against a book that strikes the popular fancy, and prospers on in spite of condemnation by the best critics, as it is against a book which does not generally please, and which no critical favor can make acceptable. This is so common a phenomenon that I wonder it has never hitherto suggested to criticism that its point of view was altogether mistaken, and that it was really necessary to judge books not as dead things, but as living things—things which have an influence and a power irrespective of beauty and wisdom, and merely as expressions of actuality in thought and feeling. Perhaps criticism has a cumulative and final effect; perhaps it does some good we do not know of. It apparently does not affect the author directly, but it may reach him through the reader. It may in some cases enlarge or diminish his audience for a while, until he has thoroughly measured and tested his own powers. If criticism is to affect literature at all, it must be through the writers who have newly left the starting-point, and are reasonably uncertain of the race, not with those who have won it again and again in their own way. I doubt if it can do more than that; but if it can do that I will admit that it may be the toad of adversity, ugly and venomous, from whose unpleasant brow he is to snatch the precious jewel of lasting fame.

I employ this figure in all humility, and I conjure our fraternity to ask themselves, without rancor or offence, whether I am right or not. In this quest let us get together all the modesty and candor and impartiality we can; for if we should happen to discover a good reason for continuing to exist, these qualities will be of more use to us than any others in examining the work of people who really produce something.

OMETIMES it has seemed to me that the crudest expression of any creative art is better than the finest comment upon it. I have sometimes suspected that more thinking, more feeling certainly, goes to the creation of a poor novel than to the production of a brilliant criticism; and if any novel of our time fails to live a hundred years, will any censure of it live? Who can endure to read old reviews? One can hardly read them if they are in praise of one's own books.

The author neglected or overlooked need not despair for that reason, if he will reflect that criticism can neither make nor unmake authors; that there have not been greater books since criticism became an art than there were before; that in fact the greatest books seem to have come much earlier.

That which criticism seems most certainly to have done is to have put a literary consciousness into books unfelt in the early masterpieces, but unfelt now only in the books of men whose lives have been passed in activities, who have been used to employing language as they would have employed any implement, to effect an object, who have regarded a thing to be said as in no wise different from a thing to be done. In this sort I have seen no modern book so unconscious as General Grant's Personal Memoirs. The author's one end and aim is to get the facts out in words. He does not cast about for phrases, but takes the word, whatever it is, that will best give his meaning, as if it were a man or a force of men for the accomplishment of a feat of arms. There is not a moment wasted in preening and prettifying, after the fashion of literary men; there is no thought of style, and so the style is good as it is in the Book of Chronicles, as it is in the Pilgrim's Progress, with a peculiar, almost plebeian, plainness at times. There is no more attempt at dramatic effect than there is at ceremonious pose ; things happen in that tale of a mighty war as they happened in the mighty war itself, without setting, without artificial reliefs one after another, as if they were all of one quality and degree. Judgments are delivered with the same unimposing quiet ; no awe surrounds the tribunal except that which comes from the weight and justice of the opinions ; it is always an unaffected, unpretentious man who is talking ; and throughout he prefers to wear the uniform of a private, with nothing of the general about him but the shoulder-straps, which he sometimes forgets.

XI

ANON FARRAR'S opinions of literary criticism are very much to my liking, perhaps because when I read them I found them so like my own, already delivered in print. He tells the critics that " they are in no sense the legislators of literature, barely even its judges and police ; " and he reminds them of Mr. Ruskin's saying that " a bad critic is probably the most mischievous person in the world," though a sense of their relative proportion to the whole of life would perhaps acquit the worst among them of this extreme of culpability. A bad critic is as bad a thing as can be, but, after all, his mischief does not carry very far. Otherwise it would be mainly the conventional books and not the original books which would survive ; for the censor who imagines himself a law-giver can give law

only to the imitative and never to the
creative mind. Criticism has condemned
whatever was, from time to time, fresh
and vital in literature; it has always
fought the new good thing in behalf of
the old good thing; it has invariably fos-
tered and encouraged the tame, the trite,
the negative. Yet upon the whole it is
the native, the novel, the positive that
has survived in literature. Whereas, if
bad criticism were the most mischievous
thing in the world, in the full implication of the words, it must have been the
tame, the trite, the negative, that survived.

Bad criticism is mischievous enough,
however; and I think that much if
not most current criticism as practised
among the English and Americans is
bad, is falsely principled, and is conditioned in evil. It is falsely principled
because it is unprincipled, or without
principles; and it is conditioned in evil
because it is almost wholly anonymous.
At the best its opinions are not conclusions from certain easily verifiable
principles, but are effects from the wor-

ship of certain models. They are in so far quite worthless, for it is the very nature of things that the original mind cannot conform to models; it has its norm within itself; it can work only in its own way, and by its self-given laws. Criticism does not inquire whether a work is true to life, but tacitly or explicitly compares it with models, and tests it by them. If literary art travelled by any such road as criticism would have it go, it would travel in a vicious circle, and would arrive only at the point of departure. Yet this is the course that criticism must always prescribe when it attempts to give laws. Being itself artificial it cannot conceive of the original except as the abnormal. It must altogether reconceive its office before it can be of use to literature. It must reduce this to the business of observing, recording, and comparing; to analyzing the material before it, and then synthetizing its impressions. Even then, it is not too much to say that literature as an art could get on perfectly well without it. Just as many good novels, poems, plays, essays, sketches, would be written if there were no such thing as criticism in the literary world, and no more bad ones.

But it will be long before criticism ceases to imagine itself a controlling force, to give itself airs of sovereignty, and to issue decrees. As it exists it is mostly a mischief, though not the greatest mischief; but it may be greatly ameliorated in character and softened in manner by the total abolition of anonymity.

I think it would be safe to say that in no other relation of life is so much brutality permitted by civilized society as in the criticism of literature and the arts. Canon Farrar is quite right in reproaching literary criticism with the uncandor of judging an author without reference to his aims ; with pursuing certain writers from spite and prejudice, and mere habit ; with misrepresenting a book by quoting a phrase or passage apart from the context ; with magnifying misprints and careless expressions into important faults; with abusing an author for his opinions; with base and personal motives. Every writer of experience knows

that certain critical journals will condemn his work without regard to its
quality, even if it has never been his fortune to learn, as one author did from a
repentant reviewer, that in a journal pretending to literary taste his books were
given out for review with the caution,
" Remember that the Clarion is opposed
to Soandso's books." Any author is in
luck if he escapes without personal abuse;
contempt and impertinence as an author
no one will escape.

The final conclusion appears to be that
the man, or even the young lady, who is
given a gun, and told to shoot at some
passer from behind a hedge, is placed in
circumstances of temptation almost too
strong for human nature.

XII

S I have already intimated, I doubt the more lasting effects of unjust criticism. It is no part of my belief that Keats's fame was long delayed by it, or Wordsworth's, or Browning's. Something unwonted, unexpected, in the quality of each delayed his recognition; each was not only a poet, he was a revolution, a new order of things, to which the critical perceptions and habitudes had painfully to adjust themselves. But I have no question of the gross and stupid injustice with which these great men were used, and of the barbarization of the public mind by the sight of the wrong inflicted on them with impunity. This savage condition still persists in the toleration of anonymous criticism, an abuse that ought to be as extinct as the torture of witnesses. It is hard enough to

treat a fellow-author with respect even
when one has to address him, name to
name, upon the same level, in plain day;
swooping down upon him in the dark,
panoplied in the authority of a great
journal, it is impossible.

Every now and then some idealist
comes forward and declares that you
should say nothing in criticism of a man's
book which you would not say of it to
his face. But I am afraid this is asking
too much. I am afraid it would put an
end to all criticism ; and that if it were
practised literature would be left to purify
itself. I have no doubt literature would
do this ; but in such a state of things
there would be no provision for the critics. We ought not to destroy critics, we
ought to reform them, or rather trans-
form them, or turn them from the assumption of authority to a realization of
their true function in the civilized state.
They are no worse at heart, probably,
than many others, and there are probably good husbands and tender fathers,
loving daughters and careful mothers,
among them. I venture to suppose this

because I have read that Monsieur de Paris is an excellent person in all the relations of private life, and is extremely anxious to conceal his dreadful occupation from those dear to him.

It is evident to any student of human nature that the critic who is obliged to sign his review will be more careful of an author's feelings than he would if he could intangibly and invisibly deal with him as the representative of a great journal. He will be loath to have his name connected with those perversions and misstatements of an author's meaning in which the critic now indulges without danger of being turned out of honest company. He will be in some degree forced to be fair and just with a book he dislikes; he will not wish to misrepresent it when his sin can be traced directly to him in person; he will not be willing to voice the prejudice of a journal which is "opposed to the books" of this or that author; and the journal itself, when it is no longer responsible for the behavior of its critic, may find it interesting and profitable to give to an author his innings when he feels wronged by a reviewer and desires to right himself; it may even be eager to offer him the opportunity. We shall then, perhaps, frequently witness the spectacle of authors turning upon their reviewers, and improving their manners and morals by confronting them in public with the errors they may now commit with impunity. Many an author smarts under injuries and indignities which he might resent to the advantage of literature and civilization, if he were not afraid of being browbeaten by the journal whose nameless critic has outraged him.

The public is now of opinion that it involves loss of dignity to creative talent to try to right itself if wronged, but here we are without the requisite statistics. Creative talent may come off with all the dignity it went in with, and it may accomplish a very good work in demolishing criticism.

In any other relation of life the man who thinks himself wronged tries to right himself, violently, if he is a mistaken man, and lawfully if he is a wise man or a rich one, which is practically the same thing. But the author, dramatist, painter, sculptor, whose book, play, picture, statue, has been unfairly dealt with, as he believes, must make no effort to right himself with the public; he must bear his wrong in silence; he is even expected to grin and bear it, as if it were funny. Everybody understands that it is not funny to him, not in the least funny, but everybody says that he cannot make an effort to get the public to take his point of view without loss of dignity. This is very odd, but it is the fact, and I suppose that it comes from the feeling that the author, dramatist, painter, sculptor, has already said the best he can for his side in his book, play, picture, statue. This is partly true, and yet if he wishes to add something more to prove the critic wrong, we do not see how his attempt to do so should involve loss of dignity. The public, which is so jealous for his dignity, does not otherwise use him as if he were a very great and invaluable creature; if he fails, it lets him starve like any one else. I should say that he lost dignity or not

as he behaved, in his effort to right himself, with petulance or with principle. If
he betrayed a wounded vanity, if he im-
pugned the motives and accused the lives
of his critics, I should certainly feel that
he was losing dignity; but if he tem-
perately examined their theories, and
tried to show where they were mistaken,
I think he would not only gain dignity,
but would perform a very useful work.

The temptation for a critic to cut fantastic tricks before high heaven in the
full light of day is great enough, and for
his own sake he should be stripped of
the shelter of the dark. Even then it
will be long before the evolution is complete, and we have the gentle, dispassion-
ate, scientific student of current literature
who never imagines that he can direct literature, but realizes that it is a plant which
springs from the nature of a people, and
draws its forces from their life, that its
root is in their character, and that it
takes form from their will and taste.

XIII

N fine, I would beseech the literary critics of our country to disabuse themselves of the mischievous notion that they are essential to the progress of literature in the way critics have vainly imagined. Canon Farrar confesses that with the best will in the world to profit by the many criticisms of his books, he has never profited in the least by any of them ; and this is almost the universal experience of authors. It is not always the fault of the critics. They sometimes deal honestly and fairly by a book, and not so often they deal adequately. But in making a book, if it is at all a good book, the author has learned all that is knowable about it, and every strong point and every weak point in it, far more accurately than any one else can possibly learn them. He has learned to do better

than well for the future; but if his book
is bad, he cannot be taught anything
about it from the outside. It will perish;
and if he has not the root of literature in
him, he will perish as an author with it.

But what is it that gives tendency in
art, then? What is it makes people like
this at one time, and that at another?
Above all, what makes a better fashion
change for a worse; how can the ugly
come to be preferred to the beautiful; in
other words, how can an art decay?

This question came up in my mind
lately with regard to English fiction and
its form, or rather its formlessness. How,
for instance, could people who had once
known the simple verity, the refined perfection of Miss Austen, enjoy anything
less refined and less perfect?

With her example before them, why
should not English novelists have gone
on writing simply, honestly, artistically,
ever after? One would think it must
have been impossible for them to do
otherwise, if one did not remember, say,
the lamentable behavior of the actors
who support Mr. Jefferson, and their the-

atricality in the very presence of his beautiful naturalness.   It is very difficult, that
simplicity, and nothing is so hard as to
be honest, as the reader, if he has ever
happened to try it, must know.   " The big
bow-wow I can do myself, like any one
going," said Scott, but he owned that the
exquisite touch of Miss Austen was denied him ; and it seems certainly to have
been denied in greater or less measure to
all her successors.   But though reading
and writing come by nature, as Dogberry
justly said, a taste in them may be cultivated, or once cultivated, it may be pre-
served ; and why was it not so among
those poor islanders ?   One does not ask
such things in order to be at the pains
of answering them one's self, but with
the hope that some one else will take the
trouble to do so, and I propose to be
rather a silent partner in the enterprise,
which I shall leave mainly to Señor
Armando Palacio Valdés.   This delightful author will, however, only be able to
answer my question indirectly from the
essay on fiction with which he prefaces
one of his novels, the charming story of

The Sister of San Sulphizo, and I shall have some little labor in fitting his saws to my instances. It is an essay which I wish every one intending to read, or even to write, a novel, might acquaint himself with ; for it contains some of the best and clearest things which have been said of the art of fiction in a time when nearly all who practise it have turned to talk about it.

Señor Valdés is a realist, but a realist according to his own conception of realism ; and he has some words of just censure for the French naturalists, whom he finds unnecessarily, and suspects of being sometimes even mercenarily, nasty. He sees the wide difference that passes between this naturalism and the realism of the English and Spanish ; and he goes somewhat further than I should go in condemning it. "The French naturalism represents only a moment, and an insignificant part of life. . . . It is characterized by sadness and narrowness. The prototype of this literature is the Madame Bovary of Flaubert. I am an admirer of this novelist, and especially of this novel ;

but often in thinking of it I have said,
How dreary would literature be if it were
no more than this! There is something
antipathetic and gloomy and limited in
it, as there is in modern French life;"
but this seems to me exactly the best
possible reason for its being. I believe
with Señor Valdés that "no literature
can live long without joy," not because of
its mistaken æsthetics, however, but because no civilization can live long without joy. The expression of French life
will change when French life changes;
and French naturalism is better at its
worst than French unnaturalism at its
best. "No one," as Señor Valdés truly
says, "can rise from the perusal of a naturalistic book . . . without a vivid desire
to escape" from the wretched world de-
picted in it, "and a purpose, more or
less vague, of helping to better the lot
and morally elevate the abject beings
who figure in it. Naturalistic art, then,
is not immoral in itself, for then it would
not merit the name of art; for though it
is not the business of art to preach morality, still I think that, resting on a divine

and spiritual principle, like the idea of the beautiful, it is perforce moral. I hold much more immoral other books which, under a glamour of something spiritual and beautiful and sublime, portray the vices in which we are allied to the beasts. Such, for example, are the works of Octave Feuillet, Arséne Houssaye, Georges Ohnet, and other contemporary novelists much in vogue among the higher classes of society."

But what is this idea of the beautiful which art rests upon, and so becomes moral? "The man of our time," says Señor Valdés, "wishes to know everything and enjoy everything: he turns the objective of a powerful equatorial towards the heavenly spaces where gravitate the infinitude of the stars, just as he applies the microscope to the infinitude of the smallest insects; for their laws are identical. His experience, united with intuition, has convinced him that in nature there is neither great nor small; all is equal. All is equally grand, all is equally just, all is equally beautiful, because all is equally divine." But beauty, Señor Valdés explains, exists in the human spirit, and is the beautiful effect which it receives from the true meaning of things; it does not matter what the things are, and it is the function of the artist who feels this effect to impart it to others. I may add that there is no joy in art except this perception of the meaning of things and its communication; when you have felt it, and portrayed it in a poem, a symphony, a novel, a statue, a picture, an edifice, you have fulfilled the purpose for which you were born an artist.

The reflection of exterior nature in the individual spirit, Señor Valdés believes to be the fundamental of art. "To say, then, that the artist must not copy but create is nonsense, because he can in no wise copy, and in no wise create. He who sets deliberately about modifying nature, shows that he has not felt her beauty, and therefore cannot make others feel it. The puerile desire which some artists without genius manifest to go about selecting in nature, not what seems to them beautiful, but what they think will seem beautiful to others, and rejecting what may displease them, ordinarily produces cold and insipid works. For, instead of exploring the illimitable fields of reality, they cling to the forms invented by other artists who have succeeded, and they make statues of statues, poems of poems, novels of novels. It is entirely false that the great romantic, symbolic, or classic poets modified nature ; such as they have expressed her they felt her; and in this view they are as much realists as ourselves. In like manner if in the realistic tide that now bears us on there are some spirits who feel nature in another way, in the romantic way, or the classic way, they would not falsify her in expressing her so. Only those falsify her who, without feeling classic wise or romantic wise, set about being classic or romantic, wearisomely reproducing the models of former ages; and equally those who, without sharing the sentiment of realism, which now prevails, force themselves to be realists merely to follow the fashion."

The pseudo-realists, in fact, are the worse offenders, to my thinking, for they sin against the living ; whereas those who continue to celebrate the heroic adventures of Puss in Boots and the hairbreadth escapes of Tom Thumb, under various aliases, only cast disrespect upon the immortals who have passed beyond these noises.

XIV

"THE principal cause," our Spaniard says, "of the decadence of contemporary literature is found, to my thinking, in the vice which has been very graphically called effectism, or the itch of awaking at all cost in the reader vivid and violent emotions, which shall do credit to the invention and originality of the writer. This vice has its roots in human nature itself, and more particularly in that of the artist; he has always something feminine in him, which tempts him to coquet with the reader, and display qualities that he thinks will astonish him, as women laugh for no reason, to show their teeth when they have them white and small and even, or lift their dresses to show their feet when there is no mud in the street. . . . What many writers nowadays wish, is to produce an effect, grand and immediate, to play the part of geniuses. For this they have learned that it is only necessary to write exaggerated works in any sort, since the vulgar do not ask that they shall be quietly made to think and feel, but that they shall be startled; and among the vulgar, of course, I include the great part of those who write literary criticism, and who constitute the worst vulgar, since they teach what they do not know. . . . There are many persons who suppose that the highest proof an artist can give of his fantasy is the invention of a complicated plot, spiced with perils, surprises, and suspenses; and that anything else is the sign of a poor and tepid imagination. And not only people who seem cultivated, but are not so, suppose this, but there are sensible persons, and even sagacious and intelligent critics, who sometimes allow themselves to be hoodwinked by the dramatic mystery and the surprising and fantastic scenes of a novel. They own it is all false; but they admire the imagination, what they call the 'power' of the author. Very well;

all I have to say is that the 'power' to
dazzle with strange incidents, to entertain with complicated plots and impossible characters, now belongs to some hundreds of writers in Europe; while there
are not much above a dozen who know
how to interest with the ordinary events
of life, and with the portrayal of characters truly human. If the former is a talent, it must be owned that it is much
commoner than the latter. . . . If we are
to rate novelists according to their fe-
cundity, or the riches of their invention,
we must put Alexander Dumas above
Cervantes. Cervantes wrote a novel with
the simplest plot, without belying much
or little the natural and logical course of
events. This novel, which was called
Don Quixote, is perhaps the greatest work
of human wit. Very well; the same Cervantes, mischievously influenced after-
wards by the ideas of the vulgar, who
were then what they are now and always
will be, attempted to please them by a
work giving a lively proof of his invent-
ive talent, and wrote the Persiles and
Sigismunda, where the strange incidents,

the vivid complications, the surprises, the
pathetic scenes, succeed one another so
rapidly and constantly that it really fa-
tigues you. . . . But in spite of this flood
of invention, imagine," says Señor Valdés,
"the place that Cervantes would now occupy in the heaven of art, if he had never
written Don Quixote," but only Persiles
and Sigismunda !

From the point of view of modern
English criticism, which likes to be melt-
ed, and horrified, and astonished, and
blood-curdled, and goose-fleshed, no less
than to be "chippered up" in fiction,
Señor Valdés were indeed incorrigible.
Not only does he despise the novel of
complicated plot, and everywhere prefer
Don Quixote to Persiles and Sigismunda,
but he has a lively contempt for another
class of novels much in favor with the
gentilities of all countries. He calls their
writers "novelists of the world," and he
says that more than any others they have
the rage of effectism. "They do not seek
to produce effect by novelty and invention in plot . . . they seek it in character.
For this end they begin by deliberately

falsifying human feelings, giving them a
paradoxical appearance completely inad-
missible. . . . Love that disguises itself
as hate, incomparable energy under the
cloak of weakness, virginal innocence under the aspect of malice and impudence,
wit masquerading as folly, etc., etc. By
this means they hope to make an effect
of which they are incapable through the
direct, frank, and conscientious study of
character." He mentions Octave Feuillet as the greatest offender in this sort
among the French, and Bulwer among
the English; but Dickens is full of it
(Boffin in Our Mutual Friend will suffice
for all example), and the present loathsome artistic squalor of the English drama is witness of the result of this effectism when allowed full play.

But what, then, if he is not pleased
with Dumas, or with the effectists who
delight genteel people at all the theatres,
and in most of the romances, what, I ask,
will satisfy this extremely difficult Spanish
gentleman? He would pretend, very little. Give him simple, life-like character;
that is all he wants. "For me, the only

condition of character is that it be human, and that is enough. If I wished to know what was human, I should study humanity."

But, Señor Valdés, Señor Valdés! Do not you know that this small condition of yours implies in its fulfilment hardly less than the gift of the whole earth, with a little gold fence round it? You merely ask that the character portrayed in fiction be human; and you suggest that the novelist should study humanity if he would know whether his personages are human. This appears to me the cruelest irony, the most sarcastic affectation of humility. If you had asked that character in fiction be superhuman, or subterhuman, or preterhuman, or intrahuman, and had bidden the novelist go, not to humanity, but the humanities, for the proof of his excellence, it would have been all very easy. The books are full of those "creations," of every pattern, of all ages, of both sexes; and it is so much handier to get at books than to get at men; and when you have portrayed "passion" instead of feeling, and used "power" instead of common-sense, and shown yourself a "genius" instead of an artist, the applause is so prompt and the glory so cheap, that really anything else seems wickedly wasteful of one's time. One may not make one's reader enjoy or suffer nobly, but one may give him the kind of pleasure that arises from conjuring, or from a puppetshow, or a modern stage play, and leave him, if he is an old fool, in the sort of stupor that comes from hitting the pipe; or if he is a young fool, half crazed with the spectacle of qualities and impulses like his own in an apotheosis of achievement and fruition far beyond any earthly experience.

But apparently Señor Valdés would not think this any great artistic result. "Things that appear ugliest in reality to the spectator who is not an artist, are transformed into beauty and poetry when the spirit of the artist possesses itself of them. We all take part every day in a thousand domestic scenes, every day we see a thousand pictures in life, that do not make any impression upon us, or if they make any it is one of repugnance;

but let the novelist come, and without betraying the truth, but painting them as they appear to his vision, he produces a most interesting work, whose perusal enchants us. That which in life left us indifferent, or repelled us, in art delights us. Why? Simply because the artist has made us see the idea that resides in it. Let not the novelists, then, endeavor to add anything to reality, to turn it and twist it, to restrict it. Since nature has endowed them with this precious gift of discovering ideas in things, their work will be beautiful if they paint these as they appear. But if the reality does not impress them, in vain will they strive to make their work impress others."

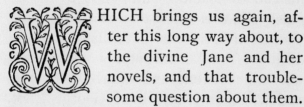HICH brings us again, after this long way about, to the divine Jane and her novels, and that troublesome question about them. She was great and they were beautiful, because she and they were honest, and dealt with nature nearly a hundred years ago as realism deals with it to-day. Realism is nothing more and nothing less than the truthful treatment of material, and Jane Austen was the first and the last of the English novelists to treat material with entire truthfulness. Because she did this, she remains the most artistic of the English novelists, and alone worthy to be matched with the great Scandinavian and Slavic and Latin artists. It is not a question of intellect, or not wholly that. The English have mind enough; but they have not taste

enough; or, rather, their taste has been perverted by their false criticism, which is based upon personal preference, and not upon principle; which instructs a man to think that what he likes is good, instead of teaching him first to distinguish what is good before he likes it. The art of fiction, as Jane Austen knew it, declined from her through Scott, and Bulwer, and Dickens, and Charlotte Brontë, and Thackeray, and even George Eliot, because the mania of romanticism had seized upon all Europe, and these great writers could not escape the taint of their time; but it has shown few signs of recovery in England, because English criticism, in the presence of the Continental masterpieces, has continued provincial and special and personal, and has expressed a love and a hate which had to do with the quality of the artist rather than the character of his work. It was inevitable that in their time the English romanticists should treat, as Señor Valdés says, "the barbarous customs of the Middle Ages, softening and disfiguring them, as Walter Scott and his kind did;"

that they should " devote themselves to
falsifying nature, refining and subtilizing
sentiment, and modifying psychology
after their own fancy," like Bulwer and
Dickens, as well as like Rousseau and
Madame de Staël, not to mention Balzac,
the worst of all that sort at his worst.
This was the natural course of the disease; but it really seems as if it were
their criticism that was to blame for the
rest : not, indeed, for the performance of
this writer or that, for criticism can never
affect the actual doing of a thing; but
for the esteem in which this writer or
that is held through the perpetuation of
false ideals. The only observer of English middle-class life since Jane Austen
worthy to be named with her was not
George Eliot, who was first ethical and
then artistic, who transcended her in
everything but the form and method
most essential to art, and there fell hopelessly below her. It was Anthony Trollope who was most like her in simple
honesty and instinctive truth, as unphi-
losophized as the light of common day;
but he was so warped from a wholesome

ideal as to wish at times to be like the
caricaturist Thackeray, and to stand
about in his scene, talking it over with
his hands in his pockets, interrupting the
action, and spoiling the illusion in which
alone the truth of art resides. Mainly,
his instinct was too much for his ideal,
and with a low view of life in its civic
relations and a thoroughly bourgeois soul,
he yet produced works whose beauty is
surpassed only by the effect of a more
poetic writer in the novels of Thomas
Hardy. Yet if a vote of English criticism even at this late day, when all continental Europe has the light of æsthetic truth, could be taken, the majority
against these artists would be overwhelm-
ingly in favor of a writer who had so
little artistic sensibility, that he never
hesitated on any occasion, great or small,
to make a foray among his characters,
and catch them up to show them to the
reader and tell him how beautiful or ugly
they were ; and cry out over their amazing properties.

Doubtless the ideal of those poor islanders will be finally changed. If the

truth could become a fad it would be accepted by all their "smart people," but truth is something rather too large for that; and we must await the gradual advance of civilization among them. Then they will see that their criticism has misled them; and that it is to this false guide they owe, not precisely the decline of fiction among them, but its continued debasement as an art.

XVI

"HOW few materials," says Emerson, "are yet used by our arts! The mass of creatures and of qualities are still hid and expectant," and to break new ground is still one of the uncommonest and most he roic of the virtues. The artists are not alone to blame for the timidity that keeps them in the old furrows of the worn-out fields; most of those whom they live to please, or live by pleasing, prefer to have them remain there; it wants rare virtue to appreciate what is new, as well as to invent it; and the "easy things to understand" are the conventional things. This is why the ordinary English novel, with its hackneyed plot, scenes, and figures, is more comfortable to the ordinary American than an American novel, which deals, at its worst, with comparatively new in-

terests and motives. To adjust one's self
to the enjoyment of these costs an intellectual effort, and an intellectual effort is
what no ordinary person likes to make.
It is only the extraordinary person who
can say, with Emerson: "I ask not for
the great, the remote, the romantic. . . .
I embrace the common; I sit at the feet
of the familiar and the low. . . . Man is
surprised to find that things near are not
less beautiful and wondrous than things
remote. . . . The perception of the worth
of the vulgar is fruitful in discoveries. . . .
The foolish man wonders at the unusual.
but the wise man at the usual. . . . To-day
always looks mean to the thoughtless; but
to-day is a king in disguise. . . . Banks
and tariffs, the newspaper and caucus,
Methodism and Unitarianism, are flat
and dull to dull people, but rest on the
same foundations of wonder as the town
of Troy and the temple of Delphos."

Perhaps we ought not to deny their
town of Troy and their temple of Delphos to the dull people; but if we ought,
and if we did, they would still insist upon
having them. An English novel, full of

titles and rank, is apparently essential to the happiness of such people; their weak and childish imagination is at home in its familiar environment; they know what they are reading; the fact that it is hash many times warmed over reassures them; whereas a story of our own life, honestly studied and faithfully represented, troubles them with varied misgiving. They are not sure that it is literature; they do not feel that it is good society; its characters, so like their own, strike them as commonplace; they say they do not wish to know such people.

Everything in England is appreciable to the literary sense, while the sense of the literary worth of things in America is still faint and weak with most people, with the vast majority who "ask for the great, the remote, the romantic," who cannot "embrace the common," cannot "sit at the feet of the familiar and the low," in the good company of Emerson. We are all, or nearly all, struggling to be distinguished from the mass, and to be set apart in select circles and upper classes like the fine people we have read about.

We are really a mixture of the plebeian ingredients of the whole world ; but that is not bad ; our vulgarity consists in trying to ignore " the worth of the vulgar," in believing that the superfine is better.

XVII

NOTHER Spanish novelist of our day, whose books have given me great pleasure, is so far from being of the same mind of Señor Valdés about fiction that he boldly declares himself, in the preface to his Pepita Ximenez, "an advocate of art for art's sake." I heartily agree with him that it is "in very bad taste, always impertinent and often pedantic, to attempt to prove theses by writing stories," and yet I fancy that no reader whom Señor Valera would care to please could read his Pepita Ximenez without finding himself in possession of a great deal of serious thinking on a very serious subject, which is none the less serious because it is couched in terms of delicate irony. If it is true that "the object of a novel should be to charm through a faithful represen-

tation of human actions and human passions, and to create by this fidelity to
nature a beautiful work," and if " the creation of the beautiful " is solely "the object of art," it never was and never can
be solely its effect as long as men are men
and women are women. If ever the race
is resolved into abstract qualities, perhaps this may happen; but till then the
finest effect of the "beautiful" will be
ethical and not æsthetic merely. Morality penetrates all things, it is the soul of
all things. Beauty may clothe it on,
whether it is false morality and an evil
soul, or whether it is true and a good
soul. In the one case the beauty will cor-
rupt, and in the other it will edify, and in
either case it will infallibly and inevitably
have an ethical effect, now light, now
grave, according as the thing is light or
grave. We cannot escape from this; we
are shut up to it by the very conditions
of our being. What is it that delights us
in this very Pepita Ximenez, this exquisite masterpiece of Señor Valera's? Not
merely that a certain Luis de Vargas,
dedicated to the priesthood, finds a cer-

tain Pepita Ximenez lovelier than the priesthood, and abandons all his sacerdotal hopes and ambitions, all his poetic dreams of renunciation and devotion, to marry her. That is very pretty and very true, and it pleases; but what chiefly appeals to the heart is the assertion, however delicately and adroitly implied, that their right to each other through their love was far above his vocation. In spite of himself, without trying, and therefore without impertinence and without pedantry, Señor Valera has proved a thesis in his story. They of the Church will acquiesce with the reservation of Don Luis's uncle the Dean that his marriage was better than his vocation, because his vocation was a sentimental and fancied one; we of the Church-in-error will accept the result without any reservation whatever; and I think we shall have the greater enjoyment of the delicate irony, the fine humor, the amusing and unfailing subtlety, with which the argument is enforced. In recognizing these, however, in praising the story for the graphic skill with which Southern characters and passions are por-

trayed in the gay light of an Andalusian
sky, for the charm with which a fresh and
unhackneyed life is presented, and the
fidelity with which novel conditions are
sketched, I must not fail to add that the
book is one for those who have come to
the knowledge of good and evil, and to
confess my regret that it fails of the
remoter truth, "the eternal amenities"
which only the avowed advocates of "art
for art's sake" seem to forget. It leaves
the reader to believe that Vargas can be
happy with a woman who wins him in
Pepita's way; and that is where it is false
both to life and to art. For the moment,
it is charming to have the story end happily, as it does, but after one has lived a
certain number of years, and read a certain number of novels, it is not the prosperous or adverse fortune of the characters that affects one, but the good or
bad faith of the novelist in dealing with
them. Will he play us false or will he
be true in the operation of this or that
principle involved? I cannot hold him
to less account than this: he must be
true to what life has taught me is the

truth, and after that he may let any fate betide his people; the novel ends well that ends faithfully. The greater his power, the greater his responsibility before the human conscience, which is God in us. But men come and go, and what they do in their limited physical lives is of comparatively little moment; it is what they say that really survives to bless or to ban; and it is the evil which Wordsworth felt in Goethe, that must long survive him. There is a kind of thing—a kind of metaphysical lie against righteousness and common-sense — which is called the Unmoral, and is supposed to be different from the Immoral; and it is this which is supposed to cover many of the faults of Goethe. His Wilhelm Meister, for example, is so far removed within the region of the " ideal " that its unprincipled, its evil-principled, tenor in regard to women is pronounced " unmorality," and is therefore inferably harmless. But no study of Goethe is complete without some recognition of the qualities which caused Wordsworth to hurl the book across the room with an indignant perception of its sensuality. For the sins of his life Goethe was perhaps sufficiently punished in his life by his final marriage with Christiane; for the sins of his literature many others must suffer. I do not despair, however, of the day when the poor honest herd of mankind shall give universal utterance to the universal instinct, and shall hold selfish power in politics, in art, in religion, for the devil that it is; when neither its crazy pride nor its amusing vanity shall be flattered by the puissance of the "geniuses" who have forgotten their duty to the common weakness, and have abused it to their own glory. In that day we shall shudder at many monsters of passion, of self-indulgence, of heartlessness, whom we still more or less openly adore for their "genius," and shall account no man worshipful whom we do not feel and know to be good. The spectacle of strenuous achievement will then not dazzle or mislead; it will not sanctify or palliate iniquity; it will only render it the more hideous and pitiable.

In fact, the whole belief in "genius"

seems to me rather a mischievous superstition, and if not mischievous always, still always a superstition. From the account of those who talk about it, "genius" appears to be the attribute of a sort of very potent and admirable prodigy which God has created out of the common for the astonishment and confusion of the rest of us poor human beings. But do they really believe it? Do they mean anything more or less than the Mastery which comes to any man according to his powers and diligence in any direction? If not, why not have an end of the superstition which has caused our race to go on so long writing and reading of the difference between talent and genius? It is within the memory of middle-aged men that the Maelstrom existed in the belief of the geographers, but we now get on perfectly well without it; and why should we still suffer under the notion of "genius" which keeps so many poor little authorlings trembling in question whether they have it, or have only "talent?"

One of the greatest captains who ever lived—a plain, taciturn, unaffected soul—

has told the story of his wonderful life as unconsciously as if it were all an every-day affair, not different from other lives, except as a great exigency of the human race gave it importance. So far as he knew, he had no natural aptitude for arms, and certainly no love for the call-ing. But he went to West Point be-cause, as he quaintly tells us, his father "rather thought he would go;" and he fought through one war with credit, but without glory. The other war, which was to claim his powers and his science, found him engaged in the most prosaic of peace-ful occupations; he obeyed its call because he loved his country, and not because he loved war. All the world knows the rest, and all the world knows that greater military mastery has not been shown than his campaigns illustrated. He does not say this in his book, or hint it in any way; he gives you the facts, and leaves them with you. But the Personal Me-moirs of U. S. Grant, written as simply and straightforwardly as his battles were fought, couched in the most unpreten-tious phrase, with never a touch of gran-

diosity or attitudinizing, familiar, homely
in style, form a great piece of literature,
because great literature is nothing more
nor less than the clear expression of
minds that have something great in them,
whether religion, or beauty, or deep experience. Probably Grant would have said
that he had no more vocation to literature than he had to war. He owns, with
something like contrition, that he used
to read a great many novels; but we
think he would have denied the soft im-
peachment of literary power. Nevertheless, he shows it, as he showed military
power, unexpectedly, almost miraculous-
ly. All the conditions here, then, are
favorable to supposing a case of "genius."
Yet who would trifle with that great heir
of fame, that plain, grand, manly soul,
by speaking of "genius" and him together? Who calls Washington a genius?
or Franklin, or Bismarck, or Cavour, or
Columbus, or Luther, or Darwin, or Lincoln? Were these men second-rate in
their way? Or is "genius" that indefinable, preternatural quality, sacred to the
musicians, the painters, the sculptors, the

actors, the poets, and above all, the poets? Or is it that the poets, having most of the say in this world, abuse it to shameless self-flattery, and would persuade the inarticulate classes that they are on peculiar terms of confidence with the deity?

XVIII

IN General Grant's confession of novel-reading there is a sort of inference that he had wasted his time, or else the guilty conscience of the novelist in me imagines such an inference. But however this may be, there is certainly no question concerning the intention of a correspondent who once wrote to me after reading some rather bragging claims I had made for fiction as a mental and moral means. "I have very grave doubts," he said, "as to the whole list of magnificent things that you seem to think novels have done for the race, and can witness in myself many evil things which they have done for me. Whatever in my mental make-up is wild and visionary, whatever is untrue, whatever is injurious, I can trace to the perusal of some work of fiction. Worse

than that, they beget such high - strung
and supersensitive ideas of life that plain
industry and plodding perseverance are
despised, and matter-of-fact poverty, or
every-day, commonplace distress, meets
with no sympathy, if indeed noticed at
all, by one who has wept over the impossibly accumulated sufferings of some gaudy hero or heroine."

I am not sure that I had the controversy with this correspondent that he
seemed to suppose; but novels are now
so fully accepted by every one pretending
to cultivated taste—and they really form
the whole intellectual life of such immense numbers of people, without question of their influence, good or bad, upon
the mind—that it is refreshing to have
them frankly denounced, and to be invited to revise one's ideas and feelings in
regard to them. A little honesty, or a
great deal of honesty, in this quest will
do the novel, as we hope yet to have it,
and as we have already begun to have it,
no harm ; and for my own part I will
confess that I believe fiction in the past
to have been largely injurious, as I be-

lieve the stage play to be still almost wholly injurious, through its falsehood, its folly, its wantonness, and its aimlessness. It may be safely assumed that most of the novel-reading which people fancy an intellectual pastime is the emptiest dissipation, hardly more related to thought or the wholesome exercise of the mental faculties than opium-eating; in either case the brain is drugged, and left weaker and crazier for the debauch. If this may be called the negative result of the fiction habit, the positive injury that most novels work is by no means so easily to be measured in the case of young men whose character they help so much to form or deform, and the women of all ages whom they keep so much in ignorance of the world they misrepresent. Grown men have little harm from them, but in the other cases, which are the vast majority, they hurt because they are not true—not because they are malevolent, but because they are idle lies about human nature and the social fabric, which it behooves us to know and to understand, that we may deal justly with ourselves and with

one another. One need not go so far as
our correspondent, and trace to the fiction habit "whatever is wild and visionary, whatever is untrue, whatever is injurious," in one's life ; bad as the fiction
habit is it is probably not responsible for
the whole sum of evil in its victims, and
I believe that if the reader will use care
in choosing from this fungus-growth with
which the fields of literature teem every
day, he may nourish himself as with the
true mushroom, at no risk from the poisonous species.

The tests are very plain and simple, and
they are perfectly infallible. If a novel
flatters the passions, and exalts them
above the principles, it is poisonous ; it
may not kill, but it will certainly injure ;
and this test will alone exclude an entire
class of fiction, of which eminent exam-
ples will occur to all. Then the whole
spawn of so-called unmoral romances,
which imagine a world where the sins of
sense are unvisited by the penalties following, swift or slow, but inexorably sure,
in the real world, are deadly poison :
these do kill. The novels that merely

tickle our prejudices and lull our judgment, or that coddle our sensibilities or
pamper our gross appetite for the marvellous are not so fatal, but they are innutri-
tious, and clog the soul with unwholesome vapors of all kinds. No doubt they
too help to weaken the moral fibre, and
make their readers indifferent to "plodding perseverance and plain industry,"
and to "matter-of-fact poverty and commonplace distress."

Without taking them too seriously, it
still must be owned that the "gaudy hero
and heroine" are to blame for a great
deal of harm in the world. That heroine
long taught by example, if not precept,
that Love, or the passion or fancy she
mistook for it, was the chief interest of a
life, which is really concerned with a great
many other things; that it was lasting
in the way she knew it; that it was worthy of every sacrifice, and was altogether
a finer thing than prudence, obedience,
reason; that love alone was glorious and
beautiful, and these were mean and ugly
in comparison with it. More lately she
has begun to idolize and illustrate Duty,

and she is hardly less mischievous in this new role, opposing duty, as she did love, to prudence, obedience, and reason. The stock hero, whom, if we met him, we could not fail to see was a most deplorable person, has undoubtedly imposed himself upon the victims of the fiction habit as admirable. With him, too, love was and is the great affair, whether in its old romantic phase of chivalrous achievement or manifold suffering for love's sake, or its more recent development of the "virile," the bullying, and the brutal, or its still more recent agonies of self-sacrifice, as idle and useless as the moral experiences of the insane asylums. With his vain posturings and his ridiculous splendor he is really a painted barbarian, the prey of his passions and his delusions, full of obsolete ideals, and the motives and ethics of a savage, which the guilty author of his being does his best—or his worst—in spite of his own light and knowledge, to foist upon the reader as something generous and noble. I am not merely bringing this charge against that sort of fiction which is beneath lit-

erature and outside of it, "the shoreless
lakes of ditch-water," whose miasms fill
the air below the empyrean where the
great ones sit ; but I am accusing the
work of some of the most famous, who
have, in this instance or in that, sinned
against the truth, which can alone exalt
and purify men. I do not say that they
have constantly done so, or even commonly done so ; but that they have done
so at all marks them as of the past, to be
read with the due historical allowance
for their epoch and their conditions. For
I believe that, while inferior writers will
and must continue to imitate them in
their foibles and their errors, no one here-
after will be able to achieve greatness
who is false to humanity, either in its
facts or its duties. The light of civilization has already broken even upon the
novel, and no conscientious man can now
set about painting an image of life without perpetual question of the verity of
his work, and without feeling bound to
distinguish so clearly that no reader of
his may be misled, between what is right
and what is wrong, what is noble and

what is base, what is health and what
is perdition, in the actions and the characters he portrays.

The fiction that aims merely to entertain—the fiction that is to serious fiction
as the opera-bouffe, the ballet, and the
pantomime are to the true drama—need
not feel the burden of this obligation
so deeply; but even such fiction will not
be gay or trivial to any reader's hurt, and
criticism will hold it to account if it
passes from painting to teaching folly.

More and more not only the criticism
which prints its opinions, but the infinitely vaster and powerfuler criticism which
thinks and feels them merely, will make
this demand. I confess that I do not
care to judge any work of the imagination without first of all applying this test
to it. We must ask ourselves before we
ask anything else, Is it true?—true to the
motives, the impulses, the principles that
shape the life of actual men and wom-
en? This truth, which necessarily includes the highest morality and the highest artistry—this truth given, the book
cannot be wicked and cannot be weak;

and without it all graces of style and feats of invention and cunning of construction are so many superfluities of naughtiness. It is well for the truth to have all these, and shine in them, but for falsehood they are merely meretricious, the bedizenment of the wanton ; they atone for nothing, they count for nothing. But in fact they come naturally of truth, and grace it without solicitation ; they are added unto it. In the whole range of fiction we know of no true picture of life—that is, of human nature—which is not also a masterpiece of literature, full of divine and natural beauty. It may have no touch or tint of this special civilization or of that ; it had better have this local color well ascertained ; but the truth is deeper and finer than aspects, and if the book is true to what men and women know of one another's souls it will be true enough, and it will be great and beautiful. It is the conception of literature as something apart from life, superfinely aloof, which makes it really unimportant to the great mass of mankind, without a message or a meaning for them ; and it is the notion that a novel may be false in its portrayal of causes and effects that makes literary art contemptible even to those whom it amuses, that forbids them to regard the novelist as a serious or right-minded person. If they do not in some moment of indignation cry out against all novels, as my correspondent does, they remain besotted in the fume of the delusions purveyed to them, with no higher feeling for the author than such maudlin affection as the habitué of an opium-joint perhaps knows for the attendant who fills his pipe with the drug.

Or, as in the case of another correspondent who writes that in his youth he "read a great many novels, but always regarded it as an amusement, like horse-racing and card-playing," for which he had no time when he entered upon the serious business of life, it renders them merely contemptuous. His view of the matter may be commended to the brotherhood and sisterhood of novelists as full of wholesome if bitter suggestion; and we urge them not to dismiss it with high literary scorn as that of some Bœotian dull to the beauty of art. Refuse it as we may, it is still the feeling of the vast majority of people for whom life is earnest, and who find only a distorted and misleading likeness of it in our books. We may fold ourselves in our scholars' gowns, and close the doors of our studies, and affect to despise this rude voice; but we cannot shut it out. It comes to us from wherever men are at work, from wherever they are truly living, and accuses us of unfaithfulness, of triviality, of mere stage-play; and none of us can escape conviction except he prove himself worthy of his time—a time in which the great masters have brought literature back to life, and filled its ebbing veins with the red tides of reality. We cannot all equal them; we need not copy them; but we can all go to the sources of their inspiration and their power; and to draw from these no one need go far—no one need really go out of himself.

Fifty years ago, Carlyle, in whom the truth was always alive, but in whom it was then unperverted by suffering, by celebrity, and by despair, wrote in his study of Diderot: "Were it not reasonable to

prophesy that this exceeding great multitude of novel-writers and such like must,
in a new generation, gradually do one of
two things : either retire into the nurser-
ies, and work for children, minors, and
semi-fatuous persons of both sexes, or
else, what were far better, sweep their
novel-fabric into the dust-cart, and betake
themselves with such faculty as they have
to understand and record what is true, of
which surely there is, and will forever be,
a whole infinitude unknown to us of infinite importance to us? Poetry, it will
more and more come to be understood,
is nothing but higher knowledge; and
the only genuine Romance (for grown
persons), Reality."

If, after half a century, fiction still
mainly works for " children, minors, and
semi-fatuous persons of both sexes," it is
nevertheless one of the hopefulest signs of
the world's progress that it has begun to
work for "grown persons," and if not exactly in the way that Carlyle might have
solely intended in urging its writers to
compile memoirs instead of building the
" novel-fabric," still it has, in the highest

and widest sense, already made Reality its Romance. I cannot judge it, I do not even care for it, except as it has done this; and I can hardly conceive of a literary self-respect in these days compatible with the old trade of make-believe, with the production of the kind of fiction which is too much honored by classification with card-playing and horse-racing. But let fiction cease to lie about life; let it portray men and women as they are, actuated by the motives and the passions in the measure we all know; let it leave off painting dolls and working them by springs and wires; let it show the different interests in their true proportions; let it forbear to preach pride and revenge, folly and insanity, egotism and prejudice, but frankly own these for what they are, in whatever figures and occasions they appear; let it not put on fine literary airs; let it speak the dialect, the language, that most Americans know—the language of unaffected people everywhere — and there can be no doubt of an unlimited future, not only of delightfulness but of usefulness, for it.

XIX

THIS is what I say in my severer moods, but at other times I know that, of course, no one is going to hold all fiction to such strict account. There is a great deal of it which may be very well left to amuse us, if it can, when we are sick or when we are silly, and I am not inclined to despise it in the performance of this office. Or, if people find pleasure in having their blood curdled for the sake of having it uncurdled again at the end of the book, I would not interfere with their amusement, though I do not desire it. There is a certain demand in primitive natures for the kind of fiction that does this, and the author of it is usually very proud of it. The kind of novels he likes, and likes to write, are intended to take his reader's mind, or what that reader would probably call his mind, off himself ; they make one forget life and all its cares and duties; they are not in the least like the novels which make you think of these, and shame you into at least wishing to be a helpfuler and wholesomer creature than you are. No sordid details of verity here, if you please; no wretched being humbly and weakly struggling to do right and to be true, suffering for his follies and his sins, tasting joy only through the mortification of self, and in the help of others ; nothing of all this, but a great, whirling splendor of peril and achievement, a wild scene of heroic adventure and of emotional ground and lofty tumbling, with a stage "picture" at the fall of the curtain, and all the good characters in a row, their left hands pressed upon their hearts, and kissing their right hands to the audience, in the good old way that has always charmed and always will charm, Heaven bless it !

In a world which loves the spectacular drama and the practically bloodless sports of the modern amphitheatre the author of this sort of fiction has his place, and we must not seek to destroy him because he fancies it the first place. In fact, it is a condition of his doing well the kind of work he does that he should think it important, that he should believe in himself; and I would not take away this faith of his, even if I could. As I say, he has his place. The world often likes to forget itself, and he brings on his heroes, his goblins, his feats, his hair-breadth escapes, his imminent deadly breaches, and the poor, foolish, childish old world renews the excitements of its nonage. Perhaps this is a work of beneficence; and perhaps our brave conjurer in his cabalistic robe is a philanthropist in disguise.

Within the last four or five years there has been throughout the whole English-speaking world what Mr. Grant Allen happily calls the "recrudescence" of taste in fiction. The effect is less noticeable in America than in England, where effete Philistinism, conscious of the dry-rot of its conventionality, is casting about for cure in anything that is wild and strange and unlike itself. But the recrudescence has been evident enough here, too; and a writer in one of our periodicals has put into convenient shape some common errors concerning popularity as a test of merit in a book. He seems to think, for instance, that the love of the marvellous and impossible in fiction, which is shown not only by "the unthinking multitude clamoring about the book counters" for fiction of that sort, but by the "literary elect" also, is proof of some principle in human nature which ought to be respected as well as tolerated. He seems to believe that the ebullition of this passion forms a sufficient answer to those who say that art should represent life, and that the art which misrepresents life is feeble art and false art. But it appears to me that a little carefuler reasoning from a little closer inspection of the facts would not have brought him to these conclusions. In the first place, I doubt very much whether the "literary elect" have been fascinated in great numbers by the fiction in question ; but if I supposed them to have really fallen under that spell, I should still be able to account for their fondness and that of the "unthinking multitude" upon the same grounds, without honoring either very much. It is the habit of hasty casuists

to regard civilization as inclusive of all
the members of a civilized community ;
but this is a palpable error.   Many persons in every civilized community live in
a state of more or less evident savagery
with respect to their habits, their morals,
and their propensities ; and they are held
in check only by the law.   Many more
yet are savage in their tastes, as they
show by the decoration of their houses
and persons, and by their choice of books
and pictures ; and these are left to the
restraints of public opinion.   In fact, no
man can be said to be thoroughly civilized or always civilized ; the most refined, the most enlightened person has
his moods, his moments of barbarism, in
which the best, or even the second best,
shall not please him.   At these times the
lettered and the unlettered are alike primitive and their gratifications are of the
same simple sort ; the highly cultivated
person may then like melodrama, impossible fiction, and the trapeze as sincerely
and thoroughly as a boy of thirteen or a
barbarian of any age.

I do not blame him for these moods ; I

find something instructive and interesting in them; but if they lastingly established themselves in him, I could not help deploring the state of that person. No one can really think that the "literary elect," who are said to have joined the "unthinking multitude" in clamoring about the book counters for the romances of no-man's land, take the same kind of pleasure in them as they do in a novel of Tolstoï, Tourguéneff, George Eliot, Thackeray, Balzac, Manzoni, Hawthorne, Henry James, Thomas Hardy, Palacio Valdés, or even Walter Scott. They have joined the "unthinking multitude," perhaps because they are tired of thinking, and expect to find relaxation in feeling—feeling crudely, grossly, merely. For once in a way there is no great harm in this; perhaps no harm at all. It is perfectly natural; let them have their innocent debauch. But let us distinguish, for our own sake and guidance, between the different kinds of things that please the same kind of people; between the things that please them habitually and those that please them occasionally; between the pleasures that edify them and those that amuse them. Otherwise we shall be in danger of becoming permanently part of the "unthinking multitude," and of remaining puerile, primitive, savage. We shall be so in moods and at moments; but let us not fancy that those are high moods or fortunate moments. If they are harmless, that is the most that can be said for them. They are lapses from which we can perhaps go forward more vigorously; but even this is not certain.

My own philosophy of the matter, however, would not bring me to prohibition of such literary amusements as the writer quoted seems to find significant of a growing indifference to truth and sanity in fiction. Once more, I say, these amusements have their place, as the circus has, and the burlesque and negro minstrelsy, and the ballet, and prestidigitation. No one of these is to be despised in its place; but we had better understand that it is not the highest place, and that it is hardly an intellectual delight. The lapse of all the "literary elect" in the world could not dignify unreality; and their present mood, if it exists, is of no more weight against that beauty in literature which comes from truth alone, and never can come from anything else, than the permanent state of the "unthinking multitude."

Yet even as regards the "unthinking multitude," I believe I am not able to take the attitude of the writer I have quoted. I am afraid that I respect them more than he would like to have me, though I cannot always respect their taste, any more than that of the "literary elect." I respect them for their good sense in most practical matters; for their laborious, honest lives; for their kindness, their good-will; for that aspiration towards something better than themselves which seems to stir, however dumbly, in every human breast not abandoned to literary pride or other forms of self-righteousness. I find every man interesting, whether he thinks or unthinks, whether he is savage or civilized; for this reason I cannot thank the novelist who teaches us not to know but to unknow our kind.

Yet I should by no means hold him to such strict account as Emerson, who felt the absence of the best motive, even in the greatest of the masters, when he said of Shakespeare that, after all, he was only master of the revels. The judgment is so severe, even with the praise which precedes it, that one winces under it ; and if one is still young, with the world gay before him, and life full of joyous promise, one is apt to ask, defiantly, Well, what is better than being such a master of the revels as Shakespeare was ? Let each judge for himself. To the heart again of serious youth uncontaminate and exigent of ideal good, it must always be a grief that the great masters seem so often to have been willing to amuse the leisure and vacancy of meaner men, and leave their mission to the soul but partially fulfilled. This, perhaps, was what Emerson had in mind ; and if he had it in mind of Shakespeare, who gave us, with his histories and comedies and problems, such a searching homily as " Macbeth," one feels that he scarcely recognized the limitations of the dramatist's art. Few consciences, at times, seem so enlightened as that of this personally unknown person, so withdrawn into his work, and so lost to the intensest curiosity of after-time; at other times he seems merely Elizabethan in his coarseness, his courtliness, his imperfect sympathy.

XX

F the finer kinds of romance, as distinguished from the novel, I would even encourage the writing, though it is one of the hard conditions of romance that its personages starting with a parti pris can rarely be characters with a living growth, but are apt to be types, limited to the expression of one principle, simple, elemental, lacking the God-given complexity of motive which we find in all the human beings we know.

Hawthorne, the great master of the romance, had the insight and the power to create it anew as a kind in fiction ; though I am not sure that The Scarlet Letter and the Blithedale Romance are not, strictly speaking, novels rather than romances. They do not play with some old superstition long outgrown, and they do not invent a new superstition to play with, but deal with things vital in every one's pulse. I am not saying that what may be called the fantastic romance—the romance that descends from Frankenstein rather than The Scarlet Letter—ought not to be. On the contrary, I should grieve to lose it, as I should grieve to lose the pantomime or the comic opera, or many other graceful things that amuse the passing hour, and help us to live agreeably in a world where men actually sin, suffer, and die. But it belongs to the decorative arts, and though it has a high place among them, it cannot be ranked with the works of the imagination—the works that represent and body forth human experience. Its ingenuity can always afford a refined pleasure, and it can often, at some risk to itself, convey a valuable truth.

Perhaps the whole region of historical romance might be reopened with advantage to readers and writers who cannot bear to be brought face to face with human nature, but require the haze of distance or a far perspective, in which all the disagreeable details shall be lost.

There is no good reason why these harmless people should not be amused, or their little preferences indulged.

But here, again, I have my modest doubts, some recent instances are so fatuous, as far as the portrayal of character goes, though I find them admirably contrived in some respects. When I have owned the excellence of the staging in every respect, and the conscience with which the carpenter (as the theatrical folks say) has done his work, I am at the end of my praises. The people affect me like persons of our generation made up for the parts; well trained, well costumed, but actors, and almost amateurs. They have the quality that makes the histrionics of amateurs endurable; they are ladies and gentlemen; the worst, the wickedest of them, is a lady or gentleman behind the scene.

Yet, no doubt it is well that there should be a reversion to the earlier types of thinking and feeling, to earlier ways of looking at human nature, and I will not altogether refuse the pleasure offered me by the poetic romancer or the historical romancer because I find my pleasure chiefly in Tolstoï and James and Gladós and Valdés and Thomas Hardy and Tourguéneff, and Balzac at his best.

The reversions or counter-currents in the general tendency of a time are very curious, and are worthy tolerant study. They are always to be found; perhaps they form the exception that establishes the rule; at least they distinguish it. They give us performances having an archaic charm by which, by-and-by, things captivate for reasons unconnected with their inherent beauty. They become quaint, and this is reason enough for liking them, for returning to them, and in art for trying to do them again. But I confess that I like better to go forward than to go backward, and it is saying very little to say that I value more such a novel as Mr. James's Tragic Muse than all the romantic attempts since Hawthorne. I call Mr. James a novelist because there is yet no name for the literary kind he has invented, and so none for the inventor. The fatuity of the story merely as a story is something that must early

impress the story-teller who does not live
in the stone age of fiction and criticism.
To spin a yarn for the yarn's sake, that
is an ideal worthy of a nineteenth-cen-
tury Englishman, doting in forgetfulness
of the English masters and grovelling in
ignorance of the Continental masters;
but wholly impossible to an American of
Mr. Henry James's modernity. To him it
must seem like the lies swapped between
men after the ladies have left the table
and they are sinking deeper and deeper
into their cups and growing dimmer and
dimmer behind their cigars. To such a
mind as his the story could never have
value except as a means; it could not
exist for him as an end; it could be used
only illustratively; it could be the frame,
not possibly the picture. But in the
mean time the kind of thing he wished
to do, and began to do, and has always
done, amid a stupid clamor, which still
lasts, that it was not a story, had to be
called a novel; and the wretched victim
of the novel habit (only a little less intel-
lectually degraded than the still more
miserable slave of the theatre habit), who

wished neither to perceive nor to reflect, but only to be acted upon by plot and incident, was lost in an endless trouble about it. Here was a thing called a novel, written with extraordinary charm; interesting by the vigor and vivacity with which phases and situations and persons were handled in it; inviting him to the intimacy of characters divined with creative insight; making him witness of motives and emotions and experiences of the finest import; and then suddenly requiring him to be man enough to cope with the question itself; not solving it for him by a marriage or a murder, and not spoon-victualling him with a moral minced small and then thinned with milk and water, and familiarly flavored with sentimentality or religiosity. I can imagine the sort of shame with which such a writer as Mr. James, so original and so clear-sighted, may sometimes have been tempted by the outcry of the nurslings of fable, to give them of the diet on which they had been pampered to imbecility; or to call together his characters for a sort of round-up in the last chapter.

XXI

IT is no doubt such work as Mr. James's that an English essayist (Mr. E. Hughes) has chiefly in mind, in a study of the differences of the English and American novel. He defines the English novel as working from within outwardly, and the American novel as working from without inwardly. The definition is very surprisingly accurate; and the critic's discovery of this fundamental difference is carried into particulars with a distinctness which is as unfailing as the courtesy he has in recognizing the present superiority of American work. He seems to think, however, that the English principle is the better, though why he should think so he does not make so clear. It appears a belated and rather voluntary effect of patriotism, disappointing in a philosopher of his degree; but it does not keep him from very explicit justice to the best characteristics of our fiction. " The American novelist is distinguished for the intellectual grip which he has of his characters. . . . He penetrates below the crust, and he recognizes no necessity of the crust to anticipate what is beneath. . . . He utterly discards heroics; he often even discards anything like a plot. . . . His story proper is often no more than a natural predicament. . . . It is no stage view we have of his characters, but one behind the scenes. . . . We are brought into contact with no strained virtues, illumined by strained lights upon strained heights of situation. . . . Whenever he appeals to the emotions it would seem to be with an appeal to the intellect too. . . . because he weaves his story of the finer, less self-evident though common threads of human nature, seldom calling into play the grosser and more powerful strain. . . . Everywhere in his pages we come across acquaintances undisguised. . . . The characters in an American novel are never unapproachable to the reader. . . . The

naturalness, with the every-day atmosphere which surrounds it, is one great
charm of the American novel. . . . It is
throughout examinative, discursory, even
more—quizzical. Its characters are undergoing, at the hands of the author,
calm, interested observation. . . . He is
never caught identifying himself with
them; he must preserve impartiality at
all costs . . . but . . . the touch of nature
is always felt, the feeling of kinship
always follows. . . . The strength of the
American novel is its optimistic faith.
. . . If out of this persistent hopefulness it
can evolve for men a new order of trust-
fulness, a tenet that between man and
man there should be less suspicion, more
confidence, since human nature sanctions
it, its mission will have been more than
an æsthetic, it will have been a moral
one."

Not all of this will be found true of
Mr. James, but all that relates to artistic
methods and characteristics will, and the
rest is true of American novels generally.
For the most part in their range and tendency they are admirable. I will not say

they are all good, or that any of them is wholly good; but I find in nearly every one of them a disposition to regard our life without the literary glasses so long thought desirable, and to see character, not as it is in other fiction, but as it abounds outside of all fiction. This disposition sometimes goes with poor enough performance, but in some of our novels it goes with performance that is excellent; and at any rate it is for the present more valuable than evenness of performance. It is what relates American fiction to the only living movement in imaginative literature, and distinguishes by a superior freshness and authenticity any group of American novels from a similarly accidental group of English novels, giving them the same good right to be as the like number of recent Russian novels, French novels, Spanish novels, Italian novels, Norwegian novels.

It is the difference of the American novelist's ideals from those of the English novelist that gives him his advantage, and seems to promise him the future. The love of the passionate and the heroic, as the Englishman has it, is such a crude and unwholesome thing, so deaf and blind to all the most delicate and important facts of art and life, so insensible to the subtle values in either that its presence or absence makes the whole difference, and enables one who is not obsessed by it to thank Heaven that he is not as that other man is.

There can be little question that many refinements of thought and spirit which every American is sensible of in the fiction of this continent, are necessarily lost upon our good kin beyond seas, whose thumb-fingered apprehension requires something gross and palpable for its assurance of reality. This is not their fault, and I am not sure that it is wholly their misfortune : they are made so as not to miss what they do not find, and they are simply content without those subtleties of life and character which it gives us so keen a pleasure to have noted in literature. If they perceive them at all it is as something vague and diaphanous, something that filmily wavers before their sense and teases them, much as the beings of an invisible world might mock one of our material frame by intimations of their presence. It is with reason, therefore, on the part of an Englishman, that Mr. Henley complains of our fiction as a shadow-land, though we find more and more in it the faithful report of our life, its motives and emotions, and all the comparatively etherealized passions and ideals that influence it.

In fact, the American who chooses to enjoy his birthright to the full, lives in a world wholly different from the Englishman's, and speaks (too often through his nose) another language : he breathes a rarefied and nimble air full of shining possibilities and radiant promises which the fog-and-soot-clogged lungs of those less-favored islanders struggle in vain to fill themselves with. But he ought to be modest in his advantage, and patient with the coughing and sputtering of his cousin who complains of finding himself in an exhausted receiver on plunging into one of our novels. To be quite just to the poor fellow, I have had some such experience as that myself in the atmosphere of some of our more attenuated romances.

Yet every now and then I read a book with perfect comfort and much exhilaration, whose scenes the average Englishman would gasp in. Nothing happens; that is, nobody murders or debauches anybody else; there is no arson or pillage of any sort; there is not a ghost, or a ravening beast, or a hair-breadth escape, or a shipwreck, or a monster of self-sacrifice, or a lady five thousand years old in the whole course of the story; " no promenade, no band of music, nossing!" as Mr. Du Maurier's Frenchman said of the meet for a fox-hunt. Yet it is all alive with the keenest interest for those who enjoy the study of individual traits and general conditions as they make themselves known to American experience.

These conditions have been so favorable hitherto (though they are becoming always less so) that they easily account for the optimistic faith of our novel which Mr. Hughes notices. It used to be one of the disadvantages of the practice of romance in America, which Hawthorne more or less whimsically lamented, that there were so few shadows and inequalities in our broad level of prosperity ; and it is one of the reflections suggested by Dostoïevsky's novel, The Crime and the Punishment, that whoever struck a note so profoundly tragic in American fiction would do a false and mistaken thing—as false and as mistaken in its way as dealing in American fiction with certain nudities which the Latin peoples seem to find edifying. Whatever their deserts, very few American novelists have been led out to be shot, or finally exiled to the rigors of a winter at Duluth ; and in a land where journeymen carpenters and plumbers strike for four dollars a day the sum of hunger and cold is comparatively small, and the wrong from class to class has been almost inappreciable, though all this is changing for the worse. Our novelists, therefore, concern themselves with the more smiling aspects of life, which are the more American, and seek the universal in the individual rather than the social interests. It is worth while, even at the risk of being called common-

place, to be true to our well-to-do actualities; the very passions themselves
seem to be softened and modified by
conditions which formerly at least could
not be said to wrong any one, to cramp
endeavor, or to cross lawful desire. Sin
and suffering and shame there must always be in the world, I suppose, but I believe that in this new world of ours it is
still mainly from one to another one, and
oftener still from one to one's self. We
have death too in America, and a great
deal of disagreeable and painful disease,
which the multiplicity of our patent medi-
cines does not seem to cure; but this is
tragedy that comes in the very nature of
things, and is not peculiarly American, as
the large, cheerful average of health and
success and happy life is. It will not do
to boast, but it is well to be true to the
facts, and to see that, apart from these
purely mortal troubles, the race here has
enjoyed conditions in which most of the
ills that have darkened its annals might
be averted by honest work and unselfish
behavior.

Fine artists we have among us, and

right-minded as far as they go; and we must not forget this at evil moments when it seems as if all the women had taken to writing hysterical improprieties, and some of the men were trying to be at least as hysterical in despair of being as improper. If we kept to the complexion of a certain school—which sadly needs a school - master—we might very well be despondent; but, after all, that school is not representative of our conditions or our intentions. Other traits are much more characteristic of our life and our fiction. In most American novels, vivid and graphic as the best of them are, the people are segregated if not sequestered, and the scene is sparsely populated. The effect may be in instinctive response to the vacancy of our social life, and I shall not make haste to blame it. There are few places, few occasions among us, in which a novelist can get a large number of polite people together, or at least keep them together. Unless he carries a snap-camera his picture of them has no probability; they affect one like the figures perfunctorily associated in such deadly

old engravings as that of "Washington
Irving and his Friends." Perhaps it is
for this reason that we excel in small
pieces with three or four figures, or in
studies of rustic communities, where there
is propinquity if not society. Our grasp
of more urbane life is feeble ; most attempts to assemble it in our pictures are
failures, possibly because it is too transitory, too intangible in its nature with us,
to be truthfully represented as really ex-
istent.

I am not sure that the Americans have
not brought the short story nearer perfection in the all-round sense than almost
any other people, and for reasons very
simple and near at hand. It might be
argued from the national hurry and impatience that it was a literary form peculiarly adapted to the American temperament, but I suspect that its extraordinary
development among us is owing much
more to more tangible facts. The success
of American magazines, which is nothing
less than prodigious, is only commensurate with their excellence. Their sort of
success is not only from the courage to

decide what ought to please, but from the knowledge of what does please ; and it is probable that, aside from the pictures, it is the short stories which please the readers of our best magazines. The serial novels they must have, of course ; but rather more of course they must have short stories, and by operation of the law of supply and demand, the short stories, abundant in quantity and excellent in quality, are forthcoming because they are wanted. By another operation of the same law, which political economists have more recently taken account of, the demand follows the supply, and short stories are sought for because there is a proven ability to furnish them, and people read them willingly because they are usually very good. The art of writing them is now so disciplined and diffused with us that there is no lack either for the magazines or for the newspaper "syndicates" which deal in them almost to the exclusion of the serials. In other countries the feuilleton of the journals is a novel continued from day to day, but with us the papers, whether daily or weekly, now more rarely print novels, whether they get them at first hand from the writers, as a great many do, or through the syndicates, which purvey a vast variety of literary wares, chiefly for the Sunday editions of the city journals. In the country papers the short story takes the place of the chapters of a serial which used to be given.

XXII

N interesting fact in regard to the different varieties of the short story among us is that the sketches and studies by the women seem faithfuler and more realistic than those of the men, in proportion to their number. Their tendency is more distinctly in that direction, and there is a solidity, an honest observation, in the work of such women as Mrs. Cooke, Miss Murfree, Miss Wilkins and Miss Jewett, which often leaves little to be desired. I should, upon the whole, be disposed to rank American short stories only below those of such Russian writers as I have read, and I should praise rather than blame their free use of our different local parlances, or "dialects," as people call them. I like this because I hope that our inherited English may be constantly freshened and revived from the

native sources which our literary decentralization will help to keep open, and I will own that as I turn over novels coming from Philadelphia, from New Mexico, from Boston, from Tennessee, from rural New England, from New York, every local flavor of diction gives me courage and pleasure. M. Alphonse Daudet, in a conversation which Mr. H. H. Boyesen has set down in a recently recorded interview with him, said, in speaking of Tourguéneff : " What a luxury it must be to have a great big untrodden barbaric language to wade into ! We poor fellows who work in the language of an old civilization, we may sit and chisel our little verbal felicities, only to find in the end that it is a borrowed jewel we are polishing. The crown jewels of our French tongue have passed through the hands of so many generations of monarchs that it seems like presumption on the part of any late-born pretender to attempt to wear them."

This grief is, of course, a little whimsical, yet it has a certain measure of reason in it, and the same regret has been more seriously expressed by the Italian poet Aleardi:

" Muse of an aged people, in the eve
   Of fading civilization, I was born.
   . . . . . . Oh, fortunate,
   My sisters, who in the heroic dawn
   Of races sung! To them did destiny give
   The virgin fire and chaste ingenuousness
   Of their land's speech; and, reverenced,
      their hands
   Ran over potent strings."

It will never do to allow that we are at such a desperate pass in English, but something of this divine despair we may feel too in thinking of "the spacious times of great Elizabeth," when the poets were trying the stops of the young language, and thrilling with the surprises of their own music. We may comfort ourselves, however, unless we prefer a luxury of grief by remembering that no language, is ever old on the lips of those who speak it, no matter how decrepit it drops from the pen. We have only to leave our studies, editorial and other, and go into the shops and fields to find the " spacious times " again ; and from the beginning Realism, before she had put on her capital letter, had divined this near-at-hand truth along with the rest. Mr. Lowell, almost the greatest and finest realist who ever wrought in verse, showed us that Elizabeth was still Queen where he heard Yankee farmers talk. One need not invite slang into the company of its betters, though perhaps slang has been dropping its " s " and becoming language ever since the world began, and is certainly sometimes delightful and forcible beyond the reach of the dictionary. I would not have any one go about for new words, but if one of them came aptly, not to reject its help. For our novelists to try to write Americanly, from any motive, would be a dismal error, but being born Americans, I would have the muse " Americanisms " whenever these serve their turn ; and when their characters speak, I should like to hear them speak true American, with all the varying Tennesseean, Philadelphian, Bostonian, and New York accents. If we bother ourselves to write what the critics imagine to be " English," we shall be priggish and artificial, and still more so if we make our Americans talk "English." There is also this serious disadvantage about " English," that if we wrote the best " English " in the world, probably the English themselves would not know it, or, if they did, certainly would not own it. It has always been supposed by grammarians and purists that a language can be kept as they find it; but languages, while they live, are perpetually changing. God apparently meant them for the common people—whom Lincoln believed God liked because he had made so many of them; and the common people will use them freely as they use other gifts of God. On their lips our continental English will differ more and more from the insular English, and I believe that this is not deplorable, but desirable.

In fine, I would have our American novelists be as American as they unconsciously can. Matthew Arnold complained that he found no "distinction" in our life, and I would gladly persuade all artists intending greatness in any kind among us that the recognition of the fact pointed out by Mr. Arnold ought to be a source of inspiration to them, and not discouragement. We have been now some hundred years building up a state on the affirmation of the essential equality of men in their rights and duties, and whether we have been right or been wrong the gods have taken us at our word, and have responded to us with a civilization in which there is no "distinction" perceptible to the eye that loves and values it. Such beauty and such grandeur as we have is common beauty, common grandeur, or the beauty and grandeur in which the quality of solidarity so prevails that neither distinguishes itself to the disadvantage of anything else. It seems to me that these conditions invite the artist to the study and the appreciation of the common, and to the portrayal in every art of those finer and higher aspects which unite rather than sever humanity, if he would thrive in our new order of things. The talent that is robust enough to front the every-day world and catch the charm of its work-worn, care-worn, brave, kindly face, need not fear the encounter, though it seems terrible to the sort nurtured in the superstition of the romantic, the bizarre, the heroic, the distinguished, as the things alone worthy of painting or carving or writing. The arts must become democratic, and then we shall have the expression of America in art; and the reproach which Mr. Arnold was half right in making us shall have no justice in it any longer; we shall be " distinguished."

XXIII

I N the mean time it has been said with a superficial justice that our fiction is narrow; though in the same sense I suppose the present English fiction is as narrow as our own; and most modern fiction is narrow in a certain sense. In Italy the best men are writing novels as brief and restricted in range as ours; in Spain the novels are intense and deep, and not spacious; the French school, with the exception of Zola, is narrow; the Norwegians are narrow; the Russians, except Tolstoï, are narrow, and the next greatest after him, Tourguéneff, is the narrowest great novelist, as to mere dimensions, that ever lived, dealing nearly always with small groups, isolated and analyzed in the most American fashion. In fact, the charge of narrowness accuses the

whole tendency of modern fiction as
much as the American school. But I
do not by any means allow that this narrowness is a defect, while denying that it
is a universal characteristic of our fiction ; it is rather, for the present, a virtue. Indeed, I should call the present
American work, North and South, thorough rather than narrow. In one sense
it is as broad as life, for each man is a
microcosm, and the writer who is able to
acquaint us intimately with half a dozen
people, or the conditions of a neighbor-
hood or a class, has done something
which cannot in any bad sense be called
narrow ; his breadth is vertical instead of
lateral, that is all ; and this depth is more
desirable than horizontal expansion in
a civilization like ours, where the differences are not of classes, but of types, and
not of types either so much as of characters. A new method was necessary in
dealing with the new conditions, and the
new method is world-wide, because the
whole world is more or less Americanized. Tolstoï is exceptionally voluminous among modern writers, even Rus-

sian writers; and it might be said that the forte of Tolstoï himself is not in his breadth sidewise, but in his breadth upward and downward. The Death of Ivan Illitch leaves as vast an impression on the reader's soul as any episode of War and Peace, which, indeed, can be recalled only in episodes, and not as a whole. I think that our writers may be safely counselled to continue their work in the modern way, because it is the best way yet known. If they make it true, it will be large, no matter what its superficies are; and it would be the greatest mistake to try to make it big. A big book is necessarily a group of episodes more or less loosely connected by a thread of narrative, and there seems no reason why this thread must always be supplied. Each episode may be quite distinct, or it may be one of a connected group; the final effect will be from the truth of each episode, not from the size of the group.

The whole field of human experience was never so nearly covered by imaginative literature in any age as in this; and American life especially is getting represented with unexampled fulness. It is true that no one writer, no one book, represents it, for that is not possible; our social and political decentralization forbids this, and may forever forbid it. But a great number of very good writers are instinctively striving to make each part of the country and each phase of our civilization known to all the other parts; and their work is not narrow in any feeble or vicious sense. The world was once very little, and it is now very large. Formerly, all science could be grasped by a single mind; but now the man who hopes to become great or useful in science must devote himself to a single department. It is so in everything—all arts, all trades; and the novelist is not superior to the universal rule against universality. He contributes his share to a thorough knowledge of groups of the human race under conditions which are full of inspiring novelty and interest. He works more fearlessly, frankly, and faithfully than the novelist ever worked before; his work, or much of it, may be destined never to be reprinted from the monthly magazines;

but if he turns to his book-shelf and regards the array of the British or other classics, he knows that they too are for the most part dead ; he knows that the planet itself is destined to freeze up and drop into the sun at last, with all its surviving literature upon it. The question is merely one of time. He consoles himself, therefore, if he is wise, and works on ; and we may all take some comfort from the thought that most things cannot be helped. Especially a movement in literature like that which the world is now witnessing cannot be helped ; and we could no more turn back and be of the literary fashions of any age before this than we could turn back and be of its social, economical, or political conditions.

If I were authorized to address any word directly to our novelists I should say, Do not trouble yourselves about standards or ideals ; but try to be faithful and natural : remember that there is no greatness, no beauty, which does not come from truth to your own knowledge of things ; and keep on working, even if your work is not long remembered.

At least three-fifths of the literature called classic, in all languages, no more lives than the poems and stories that perish monthly in our magazines. It is all printed and reprinted, generation after generation, century after century ; but it is not alive ; it is as dead as the people who wrote it and read it, and to whom it meant something, perhaps ; with whom it was a fashion, a caprice, a passing taste. A superstitious piety preserves it, and pretends that it has æsthetic qualities which can delight or edify ; but nobody really enjoys it, except as a reflection of the past moods and humors of the race, or a revelation of the author's character ; otherwise it is trash, and often very filthy trash, which the present trash generally is not.

XXIV

NE of the great newspapers
the other day invited the
prominent American au-
thors to speak their minds
upon a point in the theory
and practice of fiction which had already
vexed some of them. It was the question
of how much or how little the American
novel ought to deal with certain facts of
life which are not usually talked of before young people, and especially young
ladies. Of course the question was not
decided, and I forget just how far the
balance inclined in favor of a larger freedom in the matter. But it certainly inclined that way; one or two writers of
the sex which is somehow supposed to
have purity in its keeping (as if purity
were a thing that did not practically
concern the other sex, preoccupied with
serious affairs) gave it a rather vigorous

tilt to that side. In view of this fact it would not be the part of prudence to make an effort to dress the balance ; and indeed I do not know that I was going to make any such effort. But there are some things to say, around and about the subject, which I should like to have some one else say, and which I may myself possibly be safe in suggesting.

One of the first of these is the fact, generally lost sight of by those who censure the Anglo-Saxon novel for its prudishness, that it is really not such a prude after all; and that if it is sometimes apparently anxious to avoid those experiences of life not spoken of before young people, this may be an appearance only. Sometimes a novel which has this shuffling air, this effect of truckling to propriety, might defend itself, if it could speak for itself, by saying that such experiences happened not to come within its scheme, and that, so far from maiming or mutilating itself in ignoring them, it was all the more faithfully representative of the tone of modern life in dealing with love that was chaste, and with passion so honest that it could be openly spoken of before the tenderest society bud at dinner. It might say that the guilty intrigue, the betrayal, the extreme flirtation even, was the exceptional thing in life, and unless the scheme of the story necessarily involved it, that it would be bad art to lug it in, and as bad taste as to introduce such topics in a mixed company. It could say very justly that the novel in our civilization now always addresses a mixed company, and that the vast majority of the company are ladies, and that very many, if not most, of these ladies are young girls. If the novel were written for men and for married women alone, as in continental Europe, it might be altogether different. But the simple fact is that it is not written for them alone among us, and it is a question of writing, under cover of our universal acceptance, things for young girls to read which you would be put out-of-doors for saying to them, or of frankly giving notice of your intention, and so cutting yourself off from the pleasure—and it is a very high and sweet one—of appealing to these vivid, responsive intelligences, which are none the less brilliant and admirable because they are innocent.

One day a novelist who liked, after the manner of other men, to repine at his hard fate, complained to his friend, a critic, that he was tired of the restriction he had put upon himself in this regard; for it is a mistake, as can be readily shown, to suppose that others impose it. " See how free those French fellows are !" he rebelled. " Shall we always be shut up to our tradition of decency ?"

" Do you think it's much worse than being shut up to their tradition of indecency ?" said his friend.

Then that novelist began to reflect, and he remembered how sick the invariable motive of the French novel made him. He perceived finally that, convention for convention, ours was not only more tolerable, but on the whole was truer to life, not only to its complexion, but also to its texture. No one will pretend that there is not vicious love beneath the surface of our society ; if he did, the fetid explosions of the divorce trials would refute him ;

but if he pretended that it was in any just sense characteristic of our society, he could be still more easily refuted. Yet it exists, and it is unquestionably the material of tragedy, the stuff from which intense effects are wrought. The question, after owning this fact, is whether these intense effects are not rather cheap effects. I incline to think they are, and I will try to say why I think so, if I may do so without offence. The material itself, the mere mention of it, has an instant fascination; it arrests, it detains, till the last word is said, and while there is anything to be hinted. This is what makes a love intrigue of some sort all but essential to the popularity of any fiction. Without such an intrigue the intellectual equipment of the author must be of the highest, and then he will succeed only with the highest class of readers. But any author who will deal with a guilty love intrigue holds all readers in his hand, the highest with the lowest, as long as he hints the slightest hope of the smallest potential naughtiness. He need not at all be a great author; he may be a very shabby wretch, if he has but the courage or the trick of that sort of thing. The critics will call him "virile" and "passionate;" decent people will be ashamed to have been limed by him; but the low average will only ask another chance of flocking into his net. If he happens to be an able writer, his really fine and costly work will be unheeded, and the lure to the appetite will be chiefly remembered. There may be other qualities which make reputations for other men, but in his case they will count for nothing. He pays this penalty for his success in that kind; and every one pays some such penalty who deals with some such material. It attaches in like manner to the triumphs of the writers who now almost form a school among us, and who may be said to have established themselves in an easy popularity simply by the study of erotic shivers and fervors. They may find their account in the popularity, or they may not; there is no question of the popularity.

But I do not mean to imply that their case covers the whole ground. So far as it goes, though, it ought to stop the mouths of those who complain that fiction is enslaved to propriety among us. It appears that of a certain kind of impropriety it is free to give us all it will, and more. But this is not what serious men and women writing fiction mean when they rebel against the limitations of their art in our civilization. They have no desire to deal with nakedness, as painters and sculptors freely do in the worship of beauty; or with certain facts of life, as the stage does, in the service of sensation. But they ask why, when the conventions of the plastic and histrionic arts liberate their followers to the portrayal of almost any phase of the physical or of the emotional nature, an American novelist may not write a story on the lines of Anna Karenina or Madame Bovary. Sappho they put aside, and from Zola's work they avert their eyes. They do not condemn him or Daudet, necessarily, or accuse their motives; they leave them out of the question; they do not want to do that kind of thing. But they do sometimes wish to do another kind, to

touch one of the most serious and sorrow-
ful problems of life in the spirit of Tolstoï
and Flaubert, and they ask why they may
not. At one time, they remind us, the
Anglo-Saxon novelist did deal with such
problems—De Foe in his spirit, Richard-
son in his, Goldsmith in his. At what
moment did our fiction lose this privilege?
In what fatal hour did the Young Girl
arise and seal the lips of Fiction, with a
touch of her finger, to some of the most
vital interests of life?

Whether I wished to oppose them in
their aspiration for greater freedom, or
whether I wished to encourage them, I
should begin to answer them by saying that the Young Girl had never done
anything of the kind. The manners of
the novel have been improving with those
of its readers; that is all. Gentlemen
no longer swear or fall drunk under the
table, or abduct young ladies and shut
them up in lonely country-houses, or so
habitually set about the ruin of their
neighbors' wives, as they once did. Generally, people now call a spade an agri-
cultural implement; they have not grown

decent without having also grown a little
squeamish, but they have grown comparatively decent; there is no doubt about
that. They require of a novelist whom
they respect unquestionable proof of his
seriousness, if he proposes to deal with
certain phases of life; they require a sort
of scientific decorum. He can no longer
expect to be received on the ground of
entertainment only; he assumes a higher
function, something like that of a physician or a priest, and they expect him to
be bound by laws as sacred as those of
such professions; they hold him solemnly
pledged not to betray them or abuse their
confidence. If he will accept the conditions, they give him their confidence, and
he may then treat to his greater honor,
and not at all to his disadvantage, of such
experiences, such relations of men and
women as George Eliot treats in Adam
Bede, in Daniel Deronda, in Romola, in
almost all her books; such as Hawthorne
treats in the Scarlet Letter; such as Dickens treats in David Copperfield; such
as Thackeray treats in Pendennis, and
glances at in every one of his fictions; such

as most of the masters of English fiction
have at some time treated more or less
openly. It is quite false or quite mistaken
to suppose that our novels have left untouched these most important realities of
life. They have only not made them their
stock in trade ; they have kept a true perspective in regard to them ; they have
relegated them in their pictures of life to
the space and place they occupy in life itself, as we know it in England and America. They have kept a correct proportion, knowing perfectly well that unless
the novel is to be a map, with everything scrupulously laid down in it, a faithful record of life in far the greater extent
could be made to the exclusion of guilty
love and all its circumstances and conse-
quences.

I justify them in this view not only because I hate what is cheap and meretricious, and hold in peculiar loathing the
cant of the critics who require " passion "
as something in itself admirable and desirable in a novel, but because I prize
fidelity in the historian of feeling and
character. Most of these critics who de-

mand " passion " would seem to have no
conception of any passion but one. Yet
there are several other passions : the passion of grief, the passion of avarice, the
passion of pity, the passion of ambition,
the passion of hate, the passion of envy,
the passion of devotion, the passion of
friendship; and all these have a greater
part in the drama of life than the passion
of love, and infinitely greater than the
passion of guilty love. Wittingly or un-
wittingly, English fiction and American
fiction have recognized this truth, not
fully, not in the measure it merits, but in
greater degree than most other fiction.

XXV

WHO can deny that fiction would be incomparably stronger, incomparably truer, if once it could tear off the habit which enslaves it to the celebration chiefly of a single passion, in one phase or another, and could frankly dedicate itself to the service of all the passions, all the interests, all the facts? Every novelist who has thought about his art knows that it would, and I think that upon reflection he must doubt whether his sphere would be greatly enlarged if he were allowed to treat freely the darker aspects of the favorite passion. But, as I have shown, the privilege, the right to do this, is already perfectly recognized. This is proved again by the fact that serious criticism recognizes as master-works (I will not push the question of supremacy) the two great novels which above all others have moved the world by their study of guilty love. If by any chance, if by some prodigious miracle, any American should now arise to treat it on the level of Anna Karenina and Madame Bovary, he would be absolutely sure of success, and of fame and gratitude as great as those books have won for their authors.

But what editor of what American magazine would print such a story?

Certainly I do not think any one would; and here our novelist must again submit to conditions. If he wishes to publish such a story (supposing him to have once written it), he must publish it as a book. A book is something by itself, responsible for its character, which becomes quickly known, and it does not necessarily penetrate to every member of the household. The father or the mother may say to the child, "I would rather you wouldn't read that book;" if the child cannot be trusted, the book may be locked up. But with the magazine and its serial the affair is different. Between the editor of a reputable English or American magazine and

the families which receive it there is a
tacit agreement that he will print nothing
which a father may not read to his daugh-
ter, or safely leave her to read herself.
After all, it is a matter of business ; and
the insurgent novelist should consider the
situation with coolness and common-
sense. The editor did not create the
situation ; but it exists, and he could not
even attempt to change it without many
sorts of disaster. He respects it, therefore, with the good faith of an honest
man. Even when he is himself a novelist,
with ardor for his art and impatience of
the limitations put upon it, he interposes
his veto, as Thackeray did in the case of
Trollope when a contributor approaches
forbidden ground.

It does not avail to say that the daily
papers teem with facts far fouler and
deadlier than any which fiction could imagine. That is true, but it is true also
that the sex which reads the most novels
reads the fewest newspapers ; and, besides,
the reporter does not command the novelist's skill to fix impressions in a young
girl's mind or to suggest conjecture. The

magazine is a little despotic, a little arbitrary; but unquestionably its favor is essential to success, and its conditions are not such narrow ones. You cannot deal with Tolstoï's and Flaubert's subjects in the absolute artistic freedom of Tolstoï and Flaubert; since De Foe, that is unknown among us; but if you deal with them in the manner of George Eliot, of Thackeray, of Dickens, of society, you may deal with them even in the magazines. There is no other restriction upon you. All the horrors and miseries and tortures are open to you; your pages may drop blood; sometimes it may happen that the editor will even exact such strong material from you. But probably he will require nothing but the observance of the convention in question; and if you do not yourself prefer bloodshed he will leave you free to use all sweet and peaceable means of interesting his readers.

Believe me, it is no narrow field he throws open to you, with that little sign to keep off the grass up at one point only. Its vastness is still almost unexplored, and whole regions in it are un-

known to the fictionist. Dig anywhere,
and do but dig deep enough, and you
strike riches; or, if you are of the mind
to range, the gentler climes, the softer
temperatures, the serener skies, are all
free to you, and are so little visited that
the chance of novelty is greater among
them.

XXVI

HILE the Americans have greatly excelled in the short story generally, they have almost created a species of it in the Thanskgiving story. We have transplanted the Christmas story from England, while the Thanksgiving story is native to our air; but both are of Anglo - Saxon growth. Their difference is from a difference of environment; and the Christmas story when naturalized among us becomes almost identical in motive, incident, and treatment with the Thanksgiving story. If I were to generalize a distinction between them, I should say that the one dealt more with marvels and the other more with morals; and yet the critic should beware of speaking too confidently on this point. It is certain, however, that the Christmas season is meteorologically more favorable to the

effective return of persons long supposed
lost at sea, or from a prodigal life, or from
a darkened mind. The longer, denser,
and colder nights are better adapted to
the apparition of ghosts, and to all manner of signs and portents ; while they seem
to present a wider field for the active in
tervention of angels in behalf of orphans
and outcasts. The dreams of elderly
sleepers at this time are apt to be such
as will effect a lasting change in them
when they awake, turning them from the
hard, cruel, and grasping habits of a life-
time, and reconciling them to their sons,
daughters, and nephews, who have thwart-
ed them in marriage ; or softening them to
their meek, uncomplaining wives, whose
hearts they have trampled upon in their
reckless pursuit of wealth ; and generally
disposing them to a distribution of ham-
pers among the sick and poor, and to a
friendly reception of chubby gentlemen
with charity subscription papers. Ships
readily drive upon rocks in the early twi-
light, and offer exciting difficulties of sal-
vage ; and the heavy snows gather thickly
round the steps of wanderers who lie

down to die in them, preparatory to their discovery and rescue by immediate relatives. The midnight weather is also very suitable to encounter with murderers and burglars ; and the contrast of its freezing gloom with the light and cheer in-doors promotes the gayeties which merge, at all well-regulated country-houses, in love and marriage. In the region of pure character no moment could be so available for flinging off the mask of frivolity, or imbecility, or savagery, which one has worn for ten or twenty long years, say, for the purpose of foiling some villain, and surprising the reader, and helping the author out with his plot. Persons abroad in the Alps, or Apennines, or Pyrenees, or anywhere seeking shelter in the huts of shepherds or the dens of smugglers, find no time like it for lying in a feigned slumber, and listening to the whispered machinations of their suspicious-looking entertainers, and then suddenly starting up and fighting their way out; or else springing from the real sleep into which they have sunk exhausted, and finding it broad day and the good peasants whom they had so unjustly doubted, waiting breakfast for them. We need not point out the superior advantages of the Christmas season for anything one has a mind to do with the French Revolution, or the Arctic explorations, or the Indian Mutiny, or the horrors of Siberian exile; there is no time so good for the use of this material; and ghosts on shipboard are notoriously fond of Christmas Eve. In our own logging camps the man who has gone into the woods for the winter, after quarrelling with his wife, then hears her sad appealing voice, and is moved to good resolutions as at no other period of the year; and in the mining regions, first in California and later in Colorado, the hardened reprobate, dying in his boots, smells his mother's dough-nuts, and breathes his last in a soliloquized vision of the old home, and the little brother, or sister, or the old father coming to meet him from heaven; while his rude companions listen round him, and dry their eyes on the buts of their revolvers.

It has to be very grim, all that, to be

truly effective; and here, already, we have
a touch in the Americanized Christmas
story of the moralistic quality of the
American Thanksgiving story. This was
seldom written, at first, for the mere entertainment of the reader; it was meant
to entertain him, of course; but it was
meant to edify him, too, and to improve
him; and some such intention is still
present in it. I rather think that it deals
more probably with character to this end
than its English cousin, the Christmas
story, does. It is not so improbable that
a man should leave off being a drunkard
on Thanksgiving, as that he should leave
off being a curmudgeon on Christmas;
that he should conquer his appetite as
that he should instantly change his nature, by good resolutions. He would be
very likely, indeed, to break his resolutions in either case, but not so likely in
the one as in the other.

Generically, the Thanksgiving story is
cheerfuler in its drama and simpler in its
persons than the Christmas story. Rarely has it dealt with the supernatural,
either the apparition of ghosts or the in-

tervention of angels. The weather being
so much milder at the close of November
than it is a month later, very little can be
done with the elements; though on the
coast a north-easterly storm has been,
and can be, very usefully employed. The
Thanksgiving story is more restricted in
its range; the scene is still mostly in New
England, and the characters are of New
England extraction, who come home from
the West usually, or New York, for the
event of the little drama, whatever it
may be. It may be the reconciliation
of kinsfolk who have quarrelled; or the
union of lovers long estranged; or husbands and wives who have had hard
words and parted; or mothers who had
thought their sons dead in California and
find themselves agreeably disappointed
in their return; or fathers who for old
time's sake receive back their erring
and conveniently dying daughters. The
notes are not many which this simple
music sounds, but they have a Sabbath
tone, mostly, and win the listener to kind-
lier thoughts and better moods. The art
is at its highest in some strong sketch of

Mrs. Rose Terry Cooke's, or some perfectly satisfying study of Miss Jewett's,
or some graphic situation of Miss Wilkins's; and then it is a very fine art. But
mostly it is poor and rude enough, and
makes openly, shamelessly, sickeningly,
for the reader's emotions, as well as his
morals. It is inclined to be rather descriptive. The turkey, the pumpkin, the
cornfield, figure throughout; and the leaf-
less woods are blue and cold against the
evening sky behind the low hip-roofed,
old-fashioned homestead. The parlance
is usually the Yankee dialect and its western modifications.

The Thanksgiving story is mostly confined in scene to the country; it does not
seem possible to do much with it in town;
and it is a serious question whether with
its geographical and topical limitations it
can hold its own against the Christmas
story; and whether it would not be well
for authors to consider a combination
with its elder rival.

The two feasts are so near together in
point of time that they could be easily
covered by the sentiment of even a brief

narrative. Under the agglutinated style of A Thanksgiving-Christmas Story, fiction appropriate to both could be produced, and both could be employed naturally and probably in the transaction of its affairs and the development of its characters. The plot for such a story could easily be made to include a total-abstinence pledge and family reunion at Thanksgiving, and an apparition and spiritual regeneration over a bowl of punch at Christmas.

Not all Thanksgiving-Christmas stories need be of this pattern precisely; I wish to suggest merely one way of doing them. Perhaps when our writers really come to the work they will find sufficient inspiration in its novelty to turn to human life and observe how it is really affected on these holidays, and be tempted to present some of its actualities. This would be a great thing to do, and would come home to readers with surprise.

XXVII

IT would be interesting to know the far beginnings of holiday literature, and I commend the quest to the scientific spirit which now specializes research in every branch of history. In the mean time, without being too confident of the facts, I venture to suggest that it came in with the romantic movement about the beginning of this century, when mountains ceased to be horrid and became picturesque; when ruins of all sorts, but particularly abbeys and castles, became habitable to the most delicate constitutions; when the despised Gothick of Addison dropped its " k," and arose the chivalrous and religious Gothic of Scott; when ghosts were redeemed from the contempt into which they had fallen, and resumed their place in polite society; in fact, the politer the society, the welcomer the ghosts, and whatever else was out of the common. In that day the Annual flourished, and this artificial flower was probably the first literary blossom on the Christmas Tree which has since borne so much tinsel foliage and painted fruit. But the Annual was extremely Oriental; it was much preoccupied with Haidees and Gulnares and Zuleikas, with Hindas and Nourmahals, owing to the distinction which Byron and Moore had given such ladies; and when it began to concern itself with the actualities of British beauty, the daughters of Albion, though inscribed with the names of real countesses and duchesses, betrayed their descent from the well-known Eastern odalisques. It was possibly through an American that holiday literature became distinctively English in material, and Washington Irving, with his New World love of the past, may have given the impulse to the literary worship of Christmas which has since so widely established itself. A festival revived in popular interest by a New-Yorker to whom Dutch associations with New-year's had endeared the German ideal of Christmas, and whom the robust gayeties of the season in old - fashioned country-houses had charmed, would be one of those roundabout results which destiny likes, and "would at least be Early English." If we cannot claim with all the patriotic confidence we should like to feel that it was Irving who set Christmas in that light in which Dickens saw its æsthetic capabilities, it is perhaps because all origins are obscure. For anything that we positively know to the contrary, the Druidic rites from which English Christmas borrowed the inviting mistletoe, if not the decorative holly, may have been accompanied by the recitations of holiday triads. But it is certain that several plays of Shakespeare were produced, if not written, for the celebration of the holidays, and that then the black tide of Puritanism which swept over men's souls blotted out all such observance of Christmas with the festival itself. It came in again, by a natural reaction, with the returning Stuarts, and throughout the period of the Restoration it enjoyed a perfunctory favor. There is mention of it often enough in the eighteenth century essayists, in the Spectators and Idlers and Tatlers; but the World about the middle of the last century laments the neglect into which it had fallen. Irving seems to have been the first to observe its surviving rites lovingly, and Dickens divined its immense advantage as a literary occasion. He made it in some sort entirely his for a time, and there can be no question but it was he who again endeared it to the whole English-speaking world, and gave it a wider and deeper hold than it had ever had before upon the fancies and affections of our race.

The might of that great talent no one can gainsay, though in the light of the truer work which has since been done his literary principles seem almost as grotesque as his theories of political economy. In no one direction was his erring force more felt than in the creation of holiday literature as we have known it for the last half-century. Creation, of course, is the wrong word; it says too much; but in default of a better word, it may stand.

He did not make something out of nothing; the material was there before him; the mood and even the need of his time contributed immensely to his success, as the volition of the subject helps on the mesmerist; but it is within bounds to say that he was the chief agency in the development of holiday literature as we have known it, as he was the chief agency in universalizing the great Christian holiday as we now have it. Other agencies wrought with him and after him; but it was he who rescued Christmas from Puritan distrust, and humanized it and consecrated it to the hearts and homes of all.

Very rough magic, as it now seems, he used in working his miracle, but there is no doubt about his working it. One opens his Christmas stories in this later day—The Carol, The Chimes, The Haunted Man, The Cricket on the Hearth, and all the rest—and with "a heart high-sorrowful and cloyed," asks himself for the preternatural virtue that they once had. The pathos appears false and strained; the humor largely horse-play; the character theatrical; the joviality pumped;

the psychology commonplace; the sociology alone funny. It is a world of real clothes, earth, air, water, and the rest; the people often speak the language of life, but their motives are as disproportioned and improbable, and their passions and purposes as overcharged, as those of the worst of Balzac's people. Yet all these monstrosities, as they now appear, seem to have once had symmetry and verity; they moved the most cultivated intelligences of the time; they touched true hearts; they made everybody laugh and cry.

This was perhaps because the imagination, from having been fed mostly upon gross unrealities, always responds readily to fantastic appeals. There has been an amusing sort of awe of it, as if it were the channel of inspired thought, and were somehow sacred. The most preposterous inventions of its activity have been regarded in their time as the greatest feats of the human mind, and in its receptive form it has been nursed into an imbecility to which the truth is repugnant, and the fact that the beautiful resides nowhere else is inconceivable. It has been flattered out of all sufferance in its toyings with the mere elements of character, and its attempts to present these in combinations foreign to experience are still praised by the poorer sort of critics as masterpieces of creative work.

In the day of Dickens's early Christmas stories it was thought admirable for the author to take types of humanity which everybody knew, and to add to them from his imagination till they were as strange as beasts and birds talking. Now we begin to feel that human nature is quite enough, and that the best an author can do is to show it as it is. But in those stories of his Dickens said to his readers, Let us make believe so-and-so; and the result was a joint juggle, a child's-play, in which the wholesome allegiance to life was lost. Artistically, therefore, the scheme was false, and artistically, therefore, it must perish. It did not perish, however, before it had propagated itself in a whole school of unrealities so ghastly that one can hardly recall without a shudder those sentimentalities at second-hand to which holiday literature was abandoned long after the original conjurer had wearied of his performance.

Under his own eye and of conscious purpose a circle of imitators grew up in the fabrication of Christmas stories. They obviously formed themselves upon his sobered ideals; they collaborated with him, and it was often hard to know whether it was Dickens or Mr. Sala or Mr. Collins who was writing. The Christmas book had by that time lost its direct application to Christmas. It dealt with shipwrecks a good deal, and with perilous adventures of all kinds, and with unmerited suffering, and with ghosts and mysteries, because human nature, secure from storm and danger in a well-lighted room before a cheerful fire, likes to have these things imaged for it, and its long-puerilized fancy will bear an endless repetition of them. The wizards who wrought their spells with them contented themselves with the lasting efficacy of these simple means; and the apprentice - wizards and journeyman-wizards who have succeeded them practise the same arts at

the old stand ; but the ethical intention
which gave dignity to Dickens's Christmas stories of still earlier date has almost
wholly disappeared. It was a quality
which could not be worked so long as
the phantoms and hair-breadth escapes.
People always knew that character is not
changed by a dream in a series of tableaux ;
that a ghost cannot do much towards re-
forming an inordinately selfish person ;
that a life cannot be turned white, like a
head of hair, in a single night, by the most
allegorical apparition ; that want and sin
and shame cannot be cured by kettles
singing on the hob ; and gradually they
ceased to make believe that there was
virtue in these devices and appliances.
Yet the ethical intention was not fruit-
less, crude as it now appears. It was well
once a year, if not oftener, to remind men
by parable of the old, simple truths; to
teach them that forgiveness, and charity,
and the endeavor for life better and purer
than each has lived, are the principles
upon which alone the world holds together and gets forward. It was well for the
comfortable and the refined to be put in

mind of the savagery and suffering all round them, and to be taught, as Dickens was always teaching, that certain feelings which grace human nature, as tenderness for the sick and helpless, self-sacrifice and generosity, self-respect and manliness and womanliness, are the common heritage of the race, the direct gift of Heaven, shared equally by the rich and poor. It did not necessarily detract from the value of the lesson that, with the imperfect art of the time, he made his paupers and porters not only human, but superhuman, and too altogether virtuous; and it remained true that home life may be lovely under the lowliest roof, although he liked to paint it without a shadow on its beauty there. It is still a fact that the sick are very often saintly, although he put no peevishness into their patience with their ills. His ethical intention told for manhood and fraternity and tolerance, and when this intention disappeared from the better holiday literature, that literature was sensibly the poorer for the loss.

It never did disappear wholly from the writings of Dickens, whom it once vitally possessed, and if its action became more and more mechanical, still it always had its effect with the generation which hung charmed upon his lips, till the lips fell dumb and still forever. It imbued subordinate effort, and inspired his myriad imitators throughout the English - scribbling world, especially upon its remoter borders, so that all holiday fiction, which was once set to the tunes of The Carol and The Chimes, still grinds no other through the innumerable pipes of the humbler newspapers and magazines, though these airs are no longer heard in the politer literary centres.

This cannot go on forever, of course, but the Christmas whose use and beauty Dickens divined will remain, though Christmas literature is going the way of so much that was once admired, like the fine language, the beauties of style, and the ornate manners of the past, down through the ranks of the æsthetical poor, whom we have always with us, to the final rag-bag of oblivion.

It is still manufactured among us in the form of short stories; but the Christmas book, which now seems to be always a number of paste gems threaded upon a strand of tinsel, must be imported from England if we want it. With the constant and romantic public of the British islands it appears that spectres and imminent dangers still have favor enough to inspire their fabrication, while if I may judge from an absence of native phantasms and perils, the industry has no more encouragement among us than ship-building, though no prohibitive tariff has enhanced the cost of the raw materials, or interfered to paralyze the efforts of the American imagination.

XXVIII

BUT if the humanitarian impulse has mostly disappeared from Christmas fiction, I think it has never so generally characterized all fiction. One may refuse to recognize this impulse; one may deny that it is in any greater degree shaping life than ever before, but no one who has the current of literature under his eye can fail to note it there. People are thinking and feeling generously, if not living justly, in our time; it is a day of anxiety to be saved from the curse that is on selfishness, of eager question how others shall be helped, of bold denial that the conditions in which we would fain have rested are sacred or immutable. Especially in America, where the race has gained a height never reached before, the eminence enables more men than ever before to see how even here vast masses of men are sunk in misery that must grow every day more hopeless, or embroiled in a struggle for mere life that must end in enslaving and imbruting them.

Art, indeed, is beginning to find out that if it does not make friends with Need it must perish. It perceives that to take itself from the many and leave them no joy in their work, and to give itself to the few whom it can bring no joy in their idleness, is an error that kills. This has long been the burden of Ruskin's message: and if we can believe William Morris, the common people have heard him gladly, and have felt the truth of what he says. "They see the prophet in him rather than the fantastic rhetorician, as more superfine audiences do;" and the men and women who do the hard work of the world have learned from him and from Morris that they have a right to pleasure in their toil, and that when justice is done them they will have it. In all ages poetry has affirmed something of this sort, but it remained for ours to perceive it and express it somehow in every form of literature. But this is only one phase of the devotion of the best literature of our time to the service of humanity. No book written with a low or cynical motive could succeed now, no matter how brilliantly written; and the work done in the past to the glorification of mere passion and power, to the deification of self, appears monstrous and hideous. The romantic spirit worshipped genius, worshipped heroism, but at its best, in such a man as Victor Hugo, this spirit recognized the supreme claim of the lowest humanity. Its error was to idealize the victims of society, to paint them impossibly virtuous and beautiful; but truth, which has succeeded to the highest mission of romance, paints these victims as they are, and bids the world consider them not because they are beautiful and virtuous, but because they are ugly and vicious, cruel, filthy, and only not altogether loathsome because the divine can never wholly die out of the human. The truth does not find these victims among the poor alone, among the hungry, the houseless, the ragged; but it also finds

them among the rich, cursed with the aimlessness, the satiety, the despair of wealth,
wasting their lives in a fool's paradise of
shows and semblances, with nothing real
but the misery that comes of insincerity
and selfishness.

It is needless for me to say, either to the
many whom my opinions on this point incense or to the few who accept them, that
I do not think the fiction of our own time
even always equal to this work, or perhaps more than seldom so. But as I have
before expressed, to the still-reverberating
discontent of two continents, fiction is now
a finer art than it has ever been hitherto,
and more nearly meets the requirements
of the infallible standard. I have hopes
of real usefulness in it, because it is at
last building on the only sure foundation; but I am by no means certain that
it will be the ultimate literary form, or
will remain as important as we believe it
is destined to become. On the contrary,
it is quite imaginable that when the great
mass of readers, now sunk in the foolish
joys of mere fable, shall be lifted to an interest in the meaning of things through

the faithful portrayal of life in fiction, then fiction the most faithful may be superseded by a still more faithful form of contemporaneous history. I willingly leave the precise character of this form to the more robust imagination of readers whose minds have been nurtured upon romantic novels, and who really have an imagination worth speaking of, and confine myself, as usual, to the hither side of the regions of conjecture.

The art which in the mean time disdains the office of teacher is one of the last refuges of the aristocratic spirit which is disappearing from politics and society, and is now seeking to shelter itself in æsthetics. The pride of caste is becoming the pride of taste; but as before, it is averse to the mass of men; it consents to know them only in some conventionalized and artificial guise. It seeks to withdraw itself, to stand aloof; to be distinguished, and not to be identified. Democracy in literature is the reverse of all this. It wishes to know and to tell the truth, confident that consolation and delight are there; it does not care to paint the marvellous and impossible for the vulgar many, or to sentimentalize and falsify the actual for the vulgar few. Men are more like than unlike one another : let us make them know one another better, that they may be all humbled and strengthened with a sense of their fraternity. Neither arts, nor letters, nor sciences, except as they somehow, clearly or obscurely, tend to make the race better and kinder, are to be regarded as serious interests ; they are all lower than the rudest crafts that feed and house and clothe, for except they do this office they are idle ; and they cannot do this except from and through the truth.

THE

RESPONSIBILITIES

OF THE NOVELIST

THE RESPONSIBILITIES OF THE NOVELIST

It is not here a question of the "unarrived," the "unpublished"; these are the care-free irresponsibilities whose hours are halycon and whose endeavors have all the lure, all the recklessness of adventure. They are not recognized; they have made no standards for themselves, and if they play the *saltimbanque* and the charlatan nobody cares and nobody (except themselves) is affected.

But the writers in question are the successful ones who have made a public and to whom some ten, twenty or a hundred thousand people are pleased to listen. You may believe if you choose that the novelist, of all workers, is independent—that he can write what he pleases, and that certainly, certainly he should never "write down to his readers"—that he should never consult them at all.

On the contrary, I believe it can be proved that the successful novelist should be more than all others limited in the nature and character of his work, more than all others he should be careful of what he says; more than all others he should defer to his audience; more than all others—more even than the minister and the editor— he should feel "his public" and watch his every word, testing carefully his every utterance, weighing with the most relentless precision his every statement; in a word, possess a sense of his responsibilities.

For the novel is the great expression of modern life. Each form of art has had its turn at reflecting and expressing its contemporaneous thought. Time was when the world looked to the architects of the castles and great cathedrals to truly reflect and embody its ideals. And the architects—serious, earnest men— produced such "expressions of contemporaneous thought" as the Castle of Coucy and the Church of Notre Dame. Then with other times came other customs, and the painters had their day. The men of the Renaissance trusted Angelo and Da Vinci and Velasquez to speak for them, and trusted not in vain. Next came the age of drama. Shakespeare and Marlowe found the value of x for the life and the times in which they lived. Later on contemporary life had been so modified that neither painting, architecture nor drama was the best vehicle of expression, the day of the longer poems arrived, and Pope and Dryden spoke for their fellows.

Thus the sequence. Each age speaks with its own peculiar organ, and has left the Word for us moderns to read and understand. The Castle of Coucy and the Church of Notre Dame are the spoken words of the Middle Ages. The Renaissance speaks—and intelligibly—to us through the sibyls of the Sistine chapel and the Mona Lisa. "Macbeth" and "Tamerlane" *résumé* the whole spirit of the Elizabethan age, while the "Rape of the Lock" is a wireless message to us straight from the period of the Restoration.

To-day is the day of the novel. In no other day and by no other vehicle is contemporaneous life so adequately expressed; and the critics of the twenty-second century, reviewing our times, striving to reconstruct our civilization, will look not to the painters, not to the architects nor dramatists, but to the novelists to find our idiosyncrasy.

I think this is true. I think if the matter could in any way be statisticized, the figures would bear out the assumption. There is no doubt the novel will in time "go out" of popular favor as irrevocably as the long poem has gone and for the reason that it is no longer the right mode of expression.

It is interesting to speculate upon what will take its place. Certainly the coming civilization will revert to no former means of expressing its thought or its ideals. Possibly music will be the interpreter of the life of the twenty-first and twenty-second centuries. Possibly one may see a hint of this in the characterization of Wagner's operas as the "Music of the Future."

This, however, is parenthetical and beside the mark. Remains the fact that to-day is the day of the novel. By this one does not mean that the novel is merely popular. If the novel was not something more than a simple diversion, a means of whiling away a dull evening, a long railway journey, it would not, believe me, remain in favor another day.

If the novel, then, is popular, it is popular with a reason, a vital, inherent reason; that is to say, it is essential. Essential—to resume once more the proposition—because it expresses modern life better than architecture, better than painting, better than poetry, better than music. It is as necessary to the civilization of the twentieth century as the violin is necessary to Kubelik, as the piano is necessary to Paderewski, as the plane is necessary to the carpenter, the sledge to the blacksmith, the chisel to the mason. It is an instrument, a tool, a weapon, a vehicle. It is that thing which, in the hand of man, makes him civilized and no longer savage, because it gives him a power of durable, permanent expression. So much for the novel—the instrument.

Because it is so all-powerful to-day, the people turn to him who wields this instrument with every degree of confidence. They expect—and rightly—that results shall be commensurate with means. The unknown archer who grasps the bow of Ulysses may be expected by the multitude to send his shaft far and true. If he is not true nor strong he has no business with the bow. The people give heed to him only because he bears a great weapon. He himself knows before he shoots whether or no he is worthy.

It is all very well to jeer at the People and at the People's misunderstanding of the arts, but the fact is indisputable that no art that is not in the end understood by the People can live or ever did live a single generation. In the larger view, in the last analysis, the People pronounce the final judgment. The People, despised of the artist, hooted, caricatured and vilified, are, after all, and in the main, the real seekers after Truth. Who is it, after all, whose interest is liveliest in any given work of art? It is not now a question of *esthetic* interest—that is, the artist's, the amateur's, the *cognoscente's*. It is a question of *vital* interest. Say what you will, Maggie Tulliver—for instance—is far more a living being for Mrs. Jones across the street than she is for your sensitive, fastidious, keenly critical artist, litterateur, or critic. The People—Mrs. Jones and her neighbors—take the life history of these fictitious characters, these novels, to heart with a seriousness that the esthetic cult have no conception of. The cult consider them almost solely from their artistic sides. The People take them into their innermost lives. Nor do the People discriminate. Omnivorous readers as they are to-day, they make little distinction between Maggie Tulliver and the heroine of the last "popular novel." They do not stop to separate true from false; they do not care.

How necessary it becomes, then, for those who, by the simple art of writing, can invade the heart's heart of thousands, whose novels are received with such measureless earnestness—how necessary it becomes for those who wield such powers to use it rightfully.

Is it not expedient to act fairly? Is it not in Heaven's name essential that the People hear, not a lie, but the Truth?

If the novel were not one of the most important factors of modern life; if it were not the completest expression of our civilization; if its influence were not greater than all the pulpits, than all the newspapers between the oceans, it would not be so important that its message should be true.

But the novelist to-day is the one who reaches the greatest audience. Right or wrong, the People turn to him the moment he speaks, and what he says they believe.

For the Million, Life is a contracted affair, is bounded by the walls of the narrow channel of affairs in which their feet are set. They have no horizon. They look to-day as they never have looked before, as they never will look again, to the writer of fiction to give them an idea of life beyond their limits, and they believe him as they never have believed before and never will again.

This being so, is it not difficult to understand how certain of these successful writers of fiction—these favored ones into whose hands the gods have placed the great bow of Ulysses—can look so frivolously upon their craft? It is not necessary to specify. One speaks of those whose public is measured by "one hundred and fifty thousand copies sold." We know them, and because the gods have blessed us with wits beyond our deserving we know their work is false. But what of the "hundred and fifty thousand" who are not discerning and who receive this falseness as Truth, who believe this topsy-turvy picture of Life beyond their horizons is real and vital and sane?

There is no gauge to measure the extent of this malignant influence. Public opinion is made no one can say how, by infinitesimal accretions, by a multitude of minutest elements. Lying novels, surely, surely in this day and age of indiscriminate reading, contribute to this more than all other influences of present-day activity.

The Pulpit, the Press and the Novel—these indisputably are the great molders of public opinion and public morals to-day. But the Pulpit speaks but once a week; the Press is read with lightning haste and the morning news is waste-paper by noon. But the novel goes into the home to stay. It is read word for word; is talked about, discussed; its influence penetrates every chink and corner of the family.

Yet novelists are not found wanting who write for money. I do not think this is an unfounded accusation. I do not think it is asking too much of credulity. This would not matter if they wrote the Truth. But these gentlemen who are "in literature for their own pocket every time" have discovered that for the moment the People have confounded the Wrong with the Right, and prefer that which is a lie to that which is true. "Very well, then," say these gentlemen. "If they want a lie they shall have it"; and they give the People a lie in return for royalties.

The surprising thing about this is that you and I and all the rest of us do not consider this as disreputable—do not yet realize that the novelist has responsibilities. We condemn an editor who sells his editorial columns, and we revile the pulpit attainted of venality. But the venal novelist—he whose influence is greater than either the Press or Pulpit—*him* we greet with a wink and the tongue in the cheek.

This should not be so. Somewhere the protest should be raised, and those of us who see the practice of this fraud should bring home to ourselves the realization that the selling of one hundred and fifty thousand books is a serious business. The People have a right to the Truth as they have a right to life, liberty and the pursuit of happiness. It is *not* right that they be exploited and deceived with false views of life, false characters, false sentiment, false morality, false history, false philosophy, false emotions, false heroism, false notions of self-sacrifice, false views of religion, of duty, of conduct and of manners.

The man who can address an audience of one hundred and fifty thousand people who—unenlightened—*believe what he says,* has a heavy duty to perform, and tremendous responsibilities to shoulder; and he should address himself to his task not with the flippancy of a catch-penny juggler at the county fair, but with earnestness, with soberness, with a sense of his limitations, and with all the abiding sincerity that by the favor and mercy of the gods may be his.

THE TRUE REWARD OF THE NOVELIST

NOT that one quarrels with the historical novel as such; not that one does not enjoy good fiction wherever found, and in whatever class. It is the method of attack of the latter-day copyists that one deplores—their attitude, the willingness of so very, very many of them to take off the hat to Fashion, and then hold the same hat for Fashion to drop pennies in.

Ah, but the man must be above the work or the work is worthless, and the man better off at some other work than that of producing fiction. The eye never once should wander to the gallery, but be always with single purpose turned *inward* upon the work, testing it and retesting it that it rings true.

What one quarrels with is the perversion of a profession, the detestable trading upon another man's success. No one can find fault with those few good historical novels that started the fad. There was good workmanship in these, and honesty. But the copyists, the fakirs—they are not novelists at all, though they write novels that sell by the hundreds of thousands. They are business men. They find out—no, they allow *some one else* to find out— what the public wants, and they give it to the public cheap, and advertise it as a new soap is advertised. Well, they make money; and if that is their aim—if they are content to prostitute the good name of American literature for a sliding scale of royalties—let's have done with them. They have their reward. But the lamentable result will be that these copyists will in the end so prejudice the people against an admirable school of fiction—the school of Scott —that for years to come the tale of historic times will be discredited and many a great story remain unwritten, and many a man of actual worth and real power held back in the ranks for very shame of treading where so many fools have rushed in.

For the one idea of the fakir—the copyist—and of the public which for the moment listens to him, is Clothes, Clothes, Clothes, first, last, and always Clothes. Not Clothes only in the sense of doublet and gown, but Clothes of speech, Clothes of manner, Clothes of customs. Hear them expatiate over the fashion of wearing a cuff, over a trick of speech, over the architecture of a house, the archæology of armor and the like. It is all well enough in its way, but so easily dispensed with if there be flesh and blood underneath. Veronese put the people of his "Marriage at Cana" into the clothes of his contemporaries. Is the picture any less a masterpiece?

Do these Little People know that Scott's archæology was about one thousand years "out" in Ivanhoe, and that to make a parallel we must conceive of a writer describing Richelieu—say—in small clothes and a top hat? But is it not *Richelieu* we want, and *Ivanhoe*, not their clothes, their armor? And in spite of his errors Scott gave us a real Ivanhoe. He got beneath the clothes of an epoch and got the heart of it, and the spirit of it (different essentially and vitally from ours or from every other, the spirit of feudalism); and he put forth a masterpiece.

The Little People so very precise in the matter of buttons and "bacinets" do not so. Take the clothes from the people of their Romances and one finds only wooden manikins. Take the clothes from the epoch of which they pretend to treat and what is there beneath? It is only the familiar, well-worn, well-thumbed nineteenth or twentieth century after all. As well have written of Michigan Avenue, Chicago, as "La Rue de la Harpe," "The Great North Road" or the "Appian Way."

It is a masquerade, the novel of the copyists; and the people who applaud them—are they not the same who would hold persons in respect because of the finery of their bodies? A poor taste, a cheap one; the taste of serving-men, the literature of chambermaids.

To approach the same subject by a different radius: why must the historical novel of the copyist always be conceived of in the terms of Romance? Could not the formula of Realism be applied at least as well, not the Realism of mere externals (the copyists have that), but the Realism of motives and emotions? What would we not give for a picture of the fifteenth century as precise and perfect as one of Mr. James's novels? Even if that be impossible, the attempt, even though half-way successful, would be worth while, would be better than the wooden manikin in the tin-pot helmet and baggy hose. At least we should get somewhere, even if no further than Mr. Kingsley took us in "Hereward," or Mr. Blackmore in "Lorna Doone."

How about the business life and the student life, and the artisan life and the professional life, and above all, the home life of historic periods? Great Heavens! There was something else sometimes than the soldier life. There were not always cutting and thrusting, not always night-riding, escaping, venturing, posing.

Or suppose that cut-and-thrust must be the order of the day, where is the "man behind," and the heart in the man and the spirit in the heart and the essential vital, elemental, all-important true life within the spirit? We are all Anglo-Saxons enough to enjoy the sight of a fight, would go a block or so out of the way to see one, or be a dollar or so out of pocket. But let it not be these jointed manikins worked with a thread. At least let it be Mr. Robert Fitzsimmons or Mr. James Jeffries.

Clothes, paraphernalia, panoply, pomp and circumstance, and the copyist's public and the poor bedeviled, ink-corroded hack of an overdriven, underpaid reviewer on an inland paper speak of the "vivid coloring" and "the fine picture of a bygone age"—it is easy to be vivid with a pot of vermilion at the elbow. Any one can scare a young dog with a false face and a roaring voice, but to be vivid and use grays and browns, to scare the puppy with the lifted finger, that's something to the point.

The difficult thing is to get at the life immediately around you —the very life in which you move. No romance in it? No romance in *you*, poor fool. As much romance on Michigan Avenue as there is realism in King Arthur's court. It is as you choose to see it. The important thing to decide is, which formula is the best to help you grip the Real Life of this or any other age. Contemporaries always imagine that theirs is the prosaic age, and that chivalry and the picturesque died with their forebears. No doubt Merlin mourned for the old time of romance. Cervantes held that romance was dead. Yet most of the historical romances of the day are laid in Cervantes's time, or even after it.

Romance and Realism are constant qualities of every age, day and hour. They are here to-day. They existed in the time of Job. They will continue to exist till the end of time, not so much in things as in point of view of the people who see things.

The difficulty, then, is to get at the immediate life—immensely difficult, for you are not only close to the canvas, but are yourself part of the picture.

But the historic age is almost done to hand. Let almost any

one shut himself in his closet with a history and Violet LeDuc's "Dictionaire du Mobilier," and, given a few months' time, he can evolve a historical novel of the kind called popular. He need not know men—just clothes and lingo, the "what-ho-without-there" gabble. But if he only chose he could find romance and adventure in Wall Street or Bond Street. But romance there does not wear the gay clothes and the showy accoutrements, and to discover it— the real romance of it—means hard work and close study, not of books, but of people and actualities.

Not only this, but to know the life around you, you must live— if not *among* people, then *in* people. You must be something more than a novelist if you can, something more than just a writer. There must be that nameless sixth sense or sensibility in you that great musicians have in common with great inventors and great scientists; the thing that does not enter into the work, but that is back of it; the thing that would make of you a good *man* as well as a good novelist; the thing that differentiates the mere business man from the financier (for it is possessed of the financier and poet alike —so only they be big enough).

It is not genius, for genius is a lax, loose term, so flippantly used that its expressiveness is long since lost. It is more akin to sincerity. And there once more we halt upon the great word— sincerity, sincerity, and again sincerity. Let the writer attack his historical novel with sincerity and he can not then do wrong. He will see then the man beneath the clothes, and the heart beneath both, and he will be so amazed at the wonder of that sight that he will forget the clothes. His public will be small, perhaps, but he will have the better reward of the knowledge of a thing well done. Royalties on editions of hundreds of thousands will not pay him more to his satisfaction than that. To make money is not the province of a novelist. If he is the right sort, he has other responsibilities, heavy ones. He of all men can not think only of himself or for himself. And when the last page is written and the ink crusts on the pen-point and the hungry presses go clashing after another writer, the "new man" and the new fashion of the hour, he will think of the grim long grind of the years of his life that he has put behind him and of his work that he has built up volume by volume, sincere work, telling the truth as he saw it, independent of fashion and the gallery gods, holding to these with gripped hands and shut teeth—he will think of all this then, and he will be able to say: "I never truckled; I never took off the hat to Fashion and held it out for pennies. By God, I told them the truth. They liked it or they didn't like it. What had that to do with me? I told them the truth; I knew it for the truth then, and I know it for the truth now."

And that is his reward—the best that a man may know; the only one really worth the striving for.

THE NOVEL WITH A "PURPOSE"

AFTER years of indoctrination and expostulation on the part of the artists, the people who read appear at last to have grasped this one precept—"the novel must not preach," but "the purpose of the story must be subordinate to the story itself." It took a very long time for them to understand this, but once it became apparent they fastened upon it with a tenacity comparable only to the tenacity of the American schoolboy to the date "1492." "The novel must not preach," you hear them say.

As though it were possible to write a novel without a purpose, even if it is only the purpose to amuse. One is willing to admit that this savors a little of quibbling, for "purpose" and purpose to amuse are two different purposes. But every novel, even the most frivolous, must have some reason for the writing of it, and in that sense must have a "purpose."

Every novel must do one of three things—it must (1) tell something, (2) show something, or (3) prove something. Some novels do all three of these; some do only two; all must do at least one.

The ordinary novel merely tells something, elaborates a complication, devotes itself primarily to *things*. In this class comes the novel of adventure, such as "The Three Musketeers."

The second and better class of novel shows something, exposes the workings of a temperament, devotes itself primarily to the minds of human beings. In this class falls the novel of character, such as "Romola."

The third, and what we hold to be the best class, proves something, draws conclusions from a whole congeries of forces, social tendencies, race impulses, devotes itself not to a study of men but of man. In this class falls the novel with the purpose, such as "Les Miserables."

And the reason we decide upon this last as the highest form of the novel is because that, though setting a great purpose before it as its task, it nevertheless includes, and is forced to include, both the other classes. It must tell something, must narrate vigorous incidents and must show something, must penetrate deep into the motives and character of typemen, men who are composite pictures of a multitude of men. It must do this because of the nature of its subject, for it deals with elemental forces, motives that stir whole nations. These can not be handled.as abstractions in fiction. Fiction can find expression only in the concrete. The elemental forces, then, contribute to the novel with a purpose to provide it with vigorous action. In the novel, force can be expressed in no other way. The social tendencies must be expressed by means of analysis of the characters of the men and women who compose that society, and the two must be combined and manipulated to evolve the purpose—to find the value of x.

The production of such a novel is probably the most arduous task that the writer of fiction can undertake. Nowhere else is success more difficult; nowhere else is failure so easy. Unskilfully treated, the story may dwindle down and degenerate into mere special pleading, and the novelist become a polemicist, a pamphleteer, forgetting that, although his first consideration is to prove his case, his *means* must be living human beings, not statistics, and that his tools are not figures, but pictures from life as he sees it. The novel with a purpose *is,* one contends, a preaching novel. But it preaches by tellings things and showing things. Only, the author selects from the great storehouse of actual life the things to be told and the things to be shown which shall bear upon his problem, his purpose. The preaching, the moralizing, is the result not of direct appeal by the writer, but is made—should be made—to the reader by the very incidents of the story.

But here is presented a strange anomaly, a distinction as subtle as it is vital. Just now one has said that in the composition of the kind of novel under consideration the *purpose* is for the novelist the all-important thing, and yet it is impossible to deny that the *story,* as a mere story, is to the story-writer the one great object of attention. How reconcile then these two apparent contradictions?

For the novelist, the purpose of his novel, the problem he is to solve, is to his story what the keynote is to the sonata. Though the musician can not exaggerate the importance of the keynote, yet the thing that interests him is the sonata itself. The keynote simply co-ordinates the music, systematizes it, brings all the myriad little rebellious notes under a single harmonious code.

Thus, too, the purpose in the novel. It is important as an end and also as an ever-present guide. For the writer it is important only as a note to which his work must be attuned. The moment, however, that the writer becomes really and vitally interested in his purpose his novel fails.

Here is the strange anomaly. Let us suppose that Hardy, say, should be engaged upon a story which had for purpose to show the injustices under which the miners of Wales were suffering. It is conceivable that he could write a story that would make the blood boil with indignation. But he himself, if he is to remain an artist, if he is to write his novel successfully, will, as a novelist, care very little about the iniquitous labor system of the Welsh coal-mines. It will be to him as impersonal a thing as the key is to the composer of a sonata. As a man Hardy may or may not be vitally concerned in the Welsh coal-miner. That is quite unessential. But as a novelist, as an artist, his sufferings must be for him a matter of the mildest interest. They are important, for they constitute his keynote. They are *not* interesting for the reason that the working out of his *story*, its people, episodes, scenes, and pictures is for the moment the most interesting thing in all the world to him, exclusive of everything else. Do you think that Mrs. Stowe was more interested in the slave question than she was in the writing of "Uncle Tom's Cabin"? Her book, her manuscript, the page-to-page progress of the narrative. were more absorbing to her than all the Negroes that were ever whipped or sold. Had it not been so that great purpose-novel never would have succeeded.

Consider the reverse—"Fecondité," for instance. The purpose for which Zola wrote the book ran away with him. He really did care more for the depopulation of France than he did for his novel. Result—sermons on the fruitfulness of women, special pleading, a farrago of dry, dull incidents overburdened and collapsing under the weight of a theme that should have intruded only indirectly.

This is pre-eminently a selfish view of the question, but it is assuredly the only correct one. It must be remembered that the artist has a double personality: himself as a man, and himself as an artist. But, it will be urged, how account for the artist's sympathy in his fictitious characters, his emotion, the actual tears he sheds in telling of their griefs, their deaths, and the like?

The answer is obvious. As an artist his sensitiveness is quickened because they are characters in his novel It does not at all follow that the same artist would be moved to tears over the report of parallel catastrophes in real life. As an artist, there is every reason to suppose he would welcome the news with downright pleasure. It would be for him "good material." He would see a story in it, a good scene, a great character. Thus the artist. What he would do, how he would feel as a man is quite a different matter.

To conclude, let us consider one objection urged against the novel with a purpose by the plain people who read. For certain reasons, difficult to explain, the purpose novel always ends unhappily. It is usually a record of suffering, a relation of tragedy. And the plain people say, "Ah, we see so much suffering in the world, why put it into novels? We do not want it in novels."

One confesses to very little patience with this sort. "We see so much suffering in the world already." Do they? Is this really true? The people who buy novels are the well-to-do people. They belong to a class whose whole scheme of life is concerned solely with an aim to avoid the unpleasant. Suffering, the great catastrophes, the social throes, that annihilate whole communities, or that crush even isolated individuals—all these are as far removed from them as earthquakes and tidal-waves. Or, even if it were so, suppose that by some miracle these blind eyes were opened and the sufferings of the poor, the tragedies of the house around the corner, really were laid bare. If there is much pain in life, all the more reason that it should appear in a class of literature which, in its highest form, is a sincere transcription of life.

It is the complaint of the coward, this cry against the novel with a purpose, because it brings the tragedies and griefs of others to notice. Take this element from fiction, take from it the power and opportunity to prove that injustice, crime, and inequality do exist, and what is left? Just the amusing novels, the novels that entertain. The juggler in spangles, with his balancing pole and gilt ball, does this. You may consider the modern novel from this point of view. It may be a flippant paper-covered thing of swords and cloaks, to be carried on a railway journey and to be thrown out the window when read, together with the sucked oranges and peanut shells. Or it may be a great force, that works together with the pulpit and the universities for the good of the people, fearlessly proving that power is abused, that the strong grind the faces of the weak, that an evil tree is still growing in the midst of the garden, that undoing follows hard upon unrighteousness, that the course of Empire is not yet finished, and that the races of men have yet to work out their destiny in those great and terrible movements that crush and grind and rend asunder the pillars of the houses of the nations.

Fiction may keep pace with the Great March, but it will not be by dint of amusing the people. The Muse is a teacher, not a trickster. Her rightful place is with the leaders, but in the last analysis that place is to be attained and maintained not by cap-and-bells, but because of a serious and sincere interest, such as inspires the great teachers, the great divines, the great philosophers, a well-defined, well-seen, courageously sought-for purpose.

STORY-TELLERS *VS.* NOVELISTS

It is a thing accepted and indisputable that a story-teller is a novelist, but it has often occurred to one that the reverse is not always true and that the novelist is not of necessity a story-teller. The distinction is perhaps a delicate one, but for all that it seems to be decisive, and it is quite possible that with the distinction in mind a different judgment might be passed upon a very large part of present-day fiction. It would even be entertaining to apply the classification to the products of the standard authors.

The story-telling instinct seems to be a gift, whereas—we trend to the heretical—the art of composing novels—using the word in apposition to stories, long or short—may be an acquirement. The one is an endowment, the other an accomplishment. Accordingly, throughout the following paragraphs the expression, novelists of composition, for the time being will be used technically, and will be applied to those fiction-writers who have not the story-telling faculty.

It would not be fair to attempt a proof that the one is better or worse than the other. The difference is surely of kind and not of degree. One will only seek to establish the fact that certain eminent and brilliant novel-writers are quite bereft of a sense of fiction, that some of them have succeeded in spite of this deficiency, and that other novel-writers possessing this sense of fiction have succeeded *because* of it, and in spite of many drawbacks, such as lack of training and of education.

It is a proposition which one believes to be capable of demonstration that every child contains in himself the elements of every known profession, every occupation, every art, every industry. In the five-year-old you may see glimpses of the soldier, trader, farmer, painter, musician, builder, and so on to the end of the roster. Later, circumstances produce the atrophy of all these instincts but one, and from that one specialized comes the career. Thus every healthy-minded child—no matter if he develops in later years to be financier or boot-maker—is a story-teller. As soon as he begins to talk he tells stories. Witness the holocausts and carnage of the leaden platoons of the nursery table, the cataclysms of the Grand Trans-Continental Playroom and Front-Hall Railroad system. This, though, is not real story-telling. The toys practically tell the story for him and are no stimulant to the imagination. However, the child goes beyond the toys. He dramatizes every object of his surroundings. The books of the library shelves are files of soldiers, the rugs are isles in the seaway of the floor, the easy chair is a comfortable old gentleman holding out his arms, the sofa a private brig or a Baldwin locomotive, and the child creates of his surroundings an entire and complex work of fiction of which he is at one and the same time hero, author and public.

Within the heart of every mature human being, not a writer of fiction, there is the withered remains of a little story-teller who died very young. And the love of good fiction and the appreciation of a fine novel in the man of the world of riper years is—I like to think —a sort of memorial tribute which he pays to his little dead playmate of so very long ago, who died very quietly with his little broken tin locomotive in his hands on the cruel day when he woke to the realization that it had outlived its usefulness and its charm.

Even in the heart of some accepted and successful fiction-writer you shall find this little dead story-teller. These are the novelists of composition, whose sense of fiction, under stress of circumstances, has become so blunted that when they come at last to full maturity and to the power of using the faculty they can no longer command it. These are novelists rather of intellect than of spontaneous improvisation; and all the force of their splendid minds, every faculty other than the lost fiction faculty, must be brought into play to compensate for the lack. Some more than compensate for it, so prodigal in resource, so persistent in effort, so powerful in energy and in fertility of invention, that—as it were by main strength—they triumph over the other writer, the natural story-teller, from whose pen the book flows with almost no effort at all.

Of this sort—the novelists of intellect, in whom the born story-teller is extinct, the novelists of composition in a word—the great example, it would seem, is George Eliot. It was by taking thought that the author of "Romola" added to her stature. The result is superb, but achieved at what infinite pains, with what colossal labor—of head rather than of the heart! She did not *feel*, she *knew*, and to attain that knowledge what effort had to be expended! Even all her art can not exclude from her pages evidences of the labor, of the superhuman toil. And it was labor and toil for what? To get back, through years of sophistication, of solemn education, of worldly wisdom, back again to the point of view of the little lost child of the doll-house days.

But sometimes the little story-teller does not die, but lives on and grows with the man, increasing in favor with God, till at last he dominates the man himself, and the playroom of the old days simply widens its walls till it includes the street outside, and the street beyond and other streets, the whole city, the whole world, and the story-teller discovers a set of new toys to play with, and new objects of a measureless environment to dramatize about, and in exactly, *exactly* the same spirit in which he trundled his tin train through the halls and shouted boarding orders from the sofa he moves now through the world's playroom, "making up stories"; only now his heroes and his public are outside himself and he alone may play the author.

For him there is but little effort required. He has a *sense of fiction.* Every instant of his day he is dramatizing. The cable-car has for him a distinct personality. Every window in the residence quarters is an eye to the soul of the house behind. The very lamp-post on the corner, burning on through the night and through the storm, is a soldier, dutiful, vigilant in stress. A ship is Adventure; an engine a living brute; and the easy chair of his library is still the same comfortable and kindly old gentleman holding out his arms.

The men and women of his world are not apt to be—to him— so important in themselves as in relation to the whirl of things in which he chooses to involve them. They cause events, or else events happen to them, and by an unreasoned instinct the story-teller preserves the consistencies (just as the child would not have run the lines of the hall railway across the seaway of the floor between the rugs). Much thought is not necessary to him. Production is facile, a constant pleasure. The story runs from his pen almost of itself; it takes this shape or that, he knows not why; his people do this or that and by some blessed system of guesswork they are somehow always plausible and true to life. His work is haphazard, yet in the end and in the main tremendously probable. Devil-may-care, slipshod, melodramatic, but invincibly persuasive, he uses his heart, his senses, his emotions, every faculty but that of the intellect. He does not *know*; he *feels*.

Dumas was this, and "The Three Musketeers," different from

"Romola" in kind but not in degree, is just as superb as Eliot at her best. Only the Frenchman had a sense of fiction which the Englishwoman had not. Her novels are character studies, are portraits, are portrayals of emotions or pictures of certain times and certain events, are everything you choose, but they are not stories, and no stretch of the imagination, no liberalness of criticism can make them such. She succeeded by dint of effort where the Frenchman—merely wrote.

George Eliot compensated for the defect artificially and succeeded eminently and conclusively, but there are not found wanting cases—in modern literature—where "novelists of composition" have *not* compensated beyond a very justifiable doubt, and where, had they but rejoiced in a very small modicum of this dowry of the gods, their work would have been—to one's notion—infinitely improved.

As, for instance, Tolstoi; incontestably great though he be, all his unquestioned power has never yet won for him that same vivid sense of fiction enjoyed by so (comparatively) unimportant a writer as the author of "Sherlock Holmes." And of the two, judged strictly upon their merits as *story-tellers,* one claims for Mr. Doyle the securer if not the higher place, despite the magnificent genius of the novelist.

In the austere Russian—gloomy, sad, acquainted with grief— the child died irrevocably long, long ago; and no power however vast, no wisdom however profound, no effort however earnest, can turn one wheel on the little locomotive of battered tin or send it one inch along the old right-of-way between the nursery and the front room. One can not but feel that the great author of "Anna Karenina" realizes as much as his readers the limitations that the loss of this untainted childishness imposes. The power was all his, the wonderful intellectual grip, but not the fiction spirit—the child's knack and love of "making up stories." Given *that,* plus the force already his own, and what a book would have been there! The perfect novel! No doubt, clearer than all others, the great Russian sees the partial failure of his work, and no doubt keener and deeper than all others sees that, unless the child-vision and the child-pleasure be present to guide and to stimulate, the entrances of the kingdom must stay forever shut to those who would enter, storm they the gates never so mightily and beat they never so clamorously at the doors.

Whatever the end of fiction may be, whatever the reward and

recompense bestowed, whatever object is gained by good work, the end will not be gained, nor the reward won, nor the object attained by force alone—by strength of will or of mind. Without the auxiliary of the little playmate of the old days the great doors that stand at the end of the road will stay forever shut. Look once, however, with the child's eyes, or for once touch the mighty valves with the child's hand, and Heaven itself lies open with all its manifold wonders.

So that in the end, after all trial has been made and every expedient tested, the simplest way is the best and the humblest means the surest. A little child stands in the midst of the wise men and the learned, and their wisdom and their learning are set aside and they are taught that unless they become as one of these they shall in nowise enter into the Kingdom of Heaven.

THE NEED OF A LITERARY CONSCIENCE

PILATE saith unto them: "What is truth?" and it is of record that he received no answer—and for very obvious reasons. For is it not a fact, that he who asks that question must himself find the answer, and that not even one sent from Heaven can be of hope or help to him if he is not willing to go down into his own heart and into his own life to find it?

To sermonize, to elaborate a disquisition on nice distinctions of metaphysics is not appropriate here. But it is—so one believes—appropriate to consider a certain very large class of present-day novelists of the United States who seldom are stirred by that spirit of inquiry that for a moment disturbed the Roman, who do *not* ask what is truth, who do not in fact care to be truthful at all, and who—and this is the serious side of the business—are bringing the name of American literature perilously near to disrepute.

One does not quarrel for one instant with the fact that certain books of the writers in question have attained phenomenally large circulations. This is as it should be. There are very many people in the United States, and compared with such a figure as seventy million, a mere hundred thousand of books sold is no great matter.

But here—so it seems—is the point. He who can address a hundred thousand people is, no matter what his message may be, in an important position. It is a large audience, one hundred thousand, larger than any roofed building now standing could contain. Less than one-hundredth part of that number nominated Lincoln. Less than half of it won Waterloo.

And it must be remembered that for every one person who buys a book there are three who will read it and half a dozen who will read what some one else has written about it, so that the sphere of influence widens indefinitely, and the audience that the writer addresses approaches the half-million mark.

Well, and good; but if the audience is so vast, if the influence is so far-reaching, if the example set is so contagious, it becomes incumbent to ask, it becomes imperative to demand that the half-million shall be told the truth and not a lie.

And this thing called truth—"what is it?" says Pilate, and the average man conceives at once of an abstraction, a vague idea, a term borrowed from the metaphysicians, certainly nothing that has to do with practical, tangible, concrete work-a-day life.

Error! If truth is not an actual work-a-day thing, as concrete as the lamp-post on the corner, as practical as a cable-car, as real and homely and work-a-day and commonplace as a bootjack, then indeed are we of all men most miserable and our preaching vain.

And truth in fiction is just as real and just as important as truth anywhere else—as in Wall Street, for instance. A man who does not tell the truth there, and who puts the untruth upon paper over his signature, will be very promptly jailed. In the case of the Wall Street man the sum of money in question may be trivial—$100, $50. But the untruthful novelist who starts in motion something like half a million dollars invokes not fear nor yet reproach. If truth in the matter of the producing of novels is not an elusive, intangible abstraction, what, then, is it? Let us get at the hard nub of the business, something we can hold in the hand. It is the thing that is one's own, the discovery of a subject suitable for fictitious narration that has never yet been treated, and the conscientious study of that subject and the fair presentation of results. Not a difficult matter, it would appear, not an abstraction, not a philosophical kink. Newspaper reporters, who are not metaphysicians, unnamed, unrewarded, despised, even, and hooted and hounded, are doing this every day. They do it on a meagre salary, and they call the affair a "scoop." Is the standard of the novelist—he who is intrusted with the good name of his nation's literature—lower than that of a reporter?

"Ah, but it is so hard to be original," "ah, but it is so hard to discover anything new." Great Heavens! when a new life comes into the world for every tick of the watch in your pocket—a new life with all its complications, and with all the thousand and one other complications it sets in motion!

Hard to be original! when of all of those billion lives your own is as distinct, as individual, as "original," as though you were born out of season in the Paleozoic age and yours the first human face the sun ever shone upon.

Go out into the street and stand where the ways cross and hear the machinery of life work clashing in its grooves. Can the utmost resort of your ingenuity evolve a better story than any one of the millions that jog your elbow? Shut yourself in your closet and turn your eyes inward upon yourself—deep *into* yourself, down, down into the heart of you; and the tread of the feet upon the pavement is the systole and diastole of your own being—different only in degree. It is life; and it is that which you must have to make your book, your novel—life, not other people's novels.

Or look from your window. A whole Literature goes marching by, clamoring for a leader and a master hand to guide it. You have but to step from your doorway. And instead of this, instead of entering into the leadership that is yours by right divine, instead of this, you must toilfully, painfully endeavor to crawl into the armor of the chief of some other cause, the harness of the leader of some other progress.

But you will not fit into the panoply. You may never brace that buckler upon your arm, for by your very act you stand revealed as a littler man than he who should be chief—a littler man and a weaker; and the casque will fall so far over your face that it will only blind you, and the sword will trip you, and the lance, too ponderous, will falter in your grip, and all that life which surges and thunders behind you will in time know you to be the false leader, and as you stumble will trample you in its onrush, and leave you dead and forgotten upon the road.

And just as a misconception of the truth makes of this the simplest and homeliest of things, a vagary, an abstraction and a bugbear, so it is possible that a misconception of the Leader creates the picture of a great and dreadful figure wrapped in majesty, solemn and profound. So that perhaps for very lack of self-confidence, for very diffidence, one shrinks from lifting the sword of him and from enduing one's forehead with the casque that seems so ponderous.

In other causes no doubt the leader must be chosen from the wise and great. In science and finance one looks to him to be a strong man, a swift and a sure man. But the literature that to-day shouts all in vain for its chief needs no such a one as this. Here the battle is not to the strong nor yet the race to the swift. Here the leader is no vast, stern being, profound, solemn, knowing all things, but, on the contrary, is as humble as the lowliest that follow after him. So that it need not be hard to step into that place of eminence. Not by arrogance, nor by assumption, nor by the achievement of the world's wisdom, shall you be made worthy of the place of high command. But it will come to you, if it comes at all, because you shall have kept yourself young and humble and pure in heart, and so unspoiled and unwearied and unjaded that you shall find a joy in the mere rising of the sun, a wholesome, sane delight in the sound of the wind at night, a pleasure in the sight of the hills at evening, shall see God in a little child and a whole religion in a brooding bird.

A NEGLECTED EPIC

SUDDENLY we have found that there is no longer any Frontier. The westward-moving course of empire has at last crossed the Pacific Ocean. Civilization has circled the globe and has come back to its starting point, the vague and mysterious East.

The thing has not been accomplished peacefully. From the very first it has been an affair of wars—of invasions. Invasions of the East by the West, and of raids North and South—raids accomplished by flying columns that dashed out from both sides of the main army. Sometimes even the invaders have fought among themselves, as, for instance, the Trojan War, or the civil wars of Italy, England, and America; sometimes they have turned back on their tracks and, upon one pretext or another, reconquered the races behind them, as, for instance, Alexander's wars to the eastward, the Crusades, and Napoleon's Egyptian campaigns.

Retarded by all these obstacles, the march has been painfully slow. To move from Egypt to Greece took centuries of time. More centuries were consumed in the campaign that brought empire from Greece to Rome, and still more centuries passed before it crossed the Alps and invaded northern and western Europe.

But observe. Once across the Mississippi, the West—our Far West—was conquered in about forty years. In all the vast campaign from east to west here is the most signal victory, the swiftest, the completest, the most brilliant achievement—the wilderness subdued at a single stroke.

Now all these various fightings to the westward, these mysterious race-movements, migrations, wars and wanderings have produced their literature, distinctive, peculiar, excellent. And this literature we call epic. The Trojan War gave us the "Iliad," the "Odyssey," and the "Æneid"; the campaign of the Greeks in Asia Minor produced the "Anabasis"; a whole cycle of literature grew from the conquest of Europe after the fall of Rome—"The Song of Roland," "The Nibelungenlied," "The Romance of the Rose," "Beowulf," "Magnusson," "The Scotch Border Ballads," "The

Poem of the Cid," "The Heimskringla," "Orlando Furioso," "Jerusalem Delivered," and the like.

On this side of the Atlantic, in his clumsy, artificial way, but yet recognized as a producer of literature, Cooper has tried to chronicle the conquest of the eastern part of our country. Absurd he may be in his ideas of life and character, the art in him veneered over with charlatanism; yet the man was solemn enough and took his work seriously, and his work is literature.

Also a cycle of romance has grown up around the Civil War. The theme has had its poets to whom the public have been glad to listen. The subject is vast, noble; is, in a word, epic, just as the Trojan War and the Retreat of the Ten Thousand were epic.

But when at last one comes to look for the literature that sprang from and has grown up around the last great epic event in the history of civilization, the event which in spite of stupendous difficulties was consummated more swiftly, more completely, more satisfactorily than any like event since the westward migration began—I mean the conquering of the West, the subduing of the wilderness beyond the Mississippi—what has this produced in the way of literature? The dime novel! The dime novel and nothing else. The dime novel and nothing better.

The Trojan War left to posterity the character of Hector; the wars with the Saracens gave us Roland; the folklore of Iceland produced Grettir; the Scotch border poetry brought forth the Douglas; the Spanish epic the Cid. But the American epic, just as heroic, just as elemental, just as important and as picturesque, will fade into history, leaving behind no finer type, no nobler hero than Buffalo Bill.

The young Greeks sat on marble terraces overlooking the Ægean Sea and listened to the thunderous roll of Homer's hexameter. In the feudal castles the minstrel sang to the young boys of Roland. The farm folk of Iceland to this very day treasure up and read to their little ones hand-written copies of the Gretla Saga chronicling the deeds and death of Grettir the Strong. But the youth of the United States learn of their epic by paying a dollar to see the "Wild West Show."

The plain truth of the matter is that we have neglected our epic —the black shame of it be on us—and no contemporaneous poet or chronicler thought it worth his while to sing the song or tell the tale of the West because literature in the day when the West was being won was a cult indulged in by certain well-bred gentlemen in New England who looked eastward to the Old World, to the legends of England and Norway and Germany and Italy for their inspiration, and left the great, strong, honest, fearless, resolute deeds of their own countrymen to be defamed and defaced by the nameless hacks of the "yellow back" libraries.

One man—who wrote "How Santa Claus Came to Simpson's Bar"—one poet, one chronicler did, in fact, arise for the moment, who understood that wild, brave life and who for a time gave promise of bearing record of things seen.

One of the requirements of an epic—a true epic—is that its action must devolve upon some great national event. There was no lack of such in those fierce years after '49. Just that long and terrible journey from the Mississippi to the ocean is an epic in itself. Yet no serious attempt has ever been made by an American author to render into prose or verse this event in our history as "national" in scope, in origin and in results as the Revolution itself. The prairie schooner is as large a figure in the legends as the black ship that bore Ulysses homeward from Troy. The sea meant as much to the Argonauts of the fifties as it did to the Ten Thousand.

And the Alamo! There is a trumpet-call in the word; and only the look of it on the printed page is a flash of fire. But the very histories slight the deed, and to many an American, born under the same flag that the Mexican rifles shot to ribbons on that splendid day, the word is meaningless. Yet Thermopylæ was less glorious, and in comparison with that siege the investment of Troy was mere wanton riot. At the very least the Texans in that battered adobe church fought for the honor of their flag and the greater glory of their country, not for loot or the possession of the person of an adulteress. Young men are taught to consider the "Iliad," with its butcheries, its glorification of inordinate selfishness and vanity, as a classic. Achilles, murderer, egoist, ruffian, and liar, is a hero. But the name of Bowie, the name of the man who gave his life to his flag at the Alamo, is perpetuated only in the designation of a knife. Crockett is the hero only of a "funny story" about a sagacious coon; while Travis, the boy commander who did what Gordon with an empire back of him failed to do, is quietly and definitely ignored.

Because we have done nothing to get at the truth about the West; because our best writers have turned to the old-country folklore and legends for their inspiration; because "melancholy harlequins" strut in fringed leggings upon the street-corners, one hand held out for pennies, we have come to believe that our West, our epic, was an affair of Indians, road-agents, and desperadoes, and have taken no account of the brave men who stood for law and justice and liberty, and for those great ideas died by the hundreds, unknown and unsung—died that the West might be subdued, that the last stage of the march should be accomplished, that the Anglo-Saxon should fulfil his destiny and complete the cycle of the world.

The great figure of our neglected epic, the Hector of our ignored Iliad, is not, as the dime novels would have us believe, a lawbreaker, but a lawmaker; a fighter, it is true, as is always the case with epic figures, but a fighter for peace, a calm, grave, strong man who hated the lawbreaker as the hound hates the wolf.

He did not lounge in barrooms; he did not cheat at cards; he did not drink himself to maudlin fury; he did not "shoot at the drop of the hat." But he loved his horse, he loved his friend, he was kind to little children; he was always ready to side with the weak against the strong, with the poor against the rich. For hypocrisy and pretence, for shams and subterfuges, he had no mercy, no tolerance. He was too brave to lie and too strong to steal. The odds in that lawless day were ever against him; his enemies were many and his friends were few; but his face was always set bravely against evil, and fear was not in him even at the end. For such a man as this could die no quiet death in a land where law went no further than the statute books and life lay in the crook of my neighbor's forefinger.

He died in defence of an ideal, an epic hero, a legendary figure, formidable, sad. He died facing down injustice, dishonesty, and crime; died "in his boots"; and the same world that has glorified Achilles and forgotten Travis finds none too poor to do him reverence. No literature has sprung up around him—this great character native to America. He is of all the world-types the one distinctive to us—peculiar, particular and unique. He is dead and even his work is misinterpreted and misunderstood. His very memory will soon be gone, and the American epic, which, on the shelves of posterity, should have stood shoulder to shoulder with the "Heimskringla" and the "Tales of the Nibelungen" and the "Song of Roland," will never be written.

THE FRONTIER GONE AT LAST

UNTIL the day when the first United States marine landed in China we had always imagined that out yonder somewhere in the West was the borderland where civilization disintegrated and merged into the untamed. Our skirmish-line was there, our posts that scouted and scrimmaged with the wilderness, a thousand miles in advance of the steady march of civilization.

And the Frontier has become so much an integral part of our conception of things that it will be long before we shall all understand that it is gone. We liked the Frontier; it was romance the place of the poetry of the Great March, the firing-line where there was action and fighting, and where men held each other's lives in the crook of the forefinger. Those who had gone out came back with tremendous tales, and those that stayed behind made up other and even more tremendous tales.

When we—we Anglo-Saxons—busked ourselves for the first stage of the march, we began from that little historic reach of ground in the midst of the Friesland swamps, and we set our faces Westward, feeling no doubt the push of the Slav behind us. Then the Frontier was Britain and the sober peacefulness of land where are the ordered, cultivated English farmyards of to-day was the Wild West of the Frisians of that century; and for the little children of the Frisian peat cottages Hengist was the Apache Kid and Horsa Deadwood Dick—freebooters, law-defiers, slayers of men, epic heroes, blood brothers, if you please, of Boone and Bowie.

Then for centuries we halted and the van closed up with the firing-line, and we filled all England and all Europe with our clamor because for a while we seemed to have gone as far Westward as it was possible; and the checked energy of the race reacted upon itself. rebounded as it were, and back we went to the Eastward again —crusading, girding at the Mahommedan, conquering his cities, breaking into his fortresses with mangonel, siege-engine and catapult—just as the boy shut indoors finds his scope circumscribed and fills the whole place with the racket of his activity.

But always, if you will recall it, we had a curious feeling that we had not reached the ultimate West even yet, and there was still a Frontier. Always that strange sixth sense turned our heads toward the sunset; and all through the Middle Ages we were peeking and prying into the Western horizon, trying to reach it, to run it down, and the queer tales about Vineland and that storm-driven Viking's ship would not down.

And then at last a naked savage on the shores of a little island in what is now our West Indies, looking Eastward one morning, saw the caravels, and on that day the Frontier was rediscovered, and promptly a hundred thousand of the more hardy rushed to the skirmish-line and went at the wilderness as only the Anglo-Saxon can.

And then the skirmish-line decided that it would declare itself independent of the main army behind and form an advance column of its own, a separate army corps; and no sooner was this done than again the scouts went forward, went Westward, pushing the Frontier ahead of them, scrimmaging with the wilderness, blazing the way. At last they forced the Frontier over the Sierra Nevada down to the edge of the Pacific. And here it would have been supposed that the Great March would have halted again as it did before the Atlantic, that here at last the Frontier ended.

But on the first of May, 1898, a gun was fired in the Bay of Manila, still further Westward, and in response the skirmish-line crossed the Pacific, still pushing the Frontier before it. Then came a cry for help from Legation Street in Peking, and as the first boat bearing its contingent of American marines took ground on the Asian shore, the Frontier—at last after so many centuries, after so many marches, after so much fighting, so much spilled blood, so much spent treasure—dwindled down and vanished; for the Anglo-Saxon in his course of empire had circled the globe and brought the new civilization to the old civilization, and reached the starting-point of history, the place from which the migrations began. So soon as the marines landed there was no longer any West, and the equation of the horizon, the problem of the centuries for the Anglo-Saxon, was solved.

So, lament it though we may, the Frontier is gone, an idiosyncrasy that has been with us for thousands of years, the one peculiar picturesqueness of our life, is no more. We may keep alive for many years the idea of a Wild West, but the hired cowboys and paid rough riders of Mr. William Cody are more like "the real thing" than can be found to-day in Arizona, New Mexico, or Idaho. Only the imitation cowboys, the college-bred fellows who "go out on a ranch," carry the revolver or wear the concho. The Frontier has become conscious of itself, acts the part for the Eastern visitor; and this self-consciousness is a sign, surer than all others, of the decadence of a type, the passing of an epoch. The Apache Kid and Deadwood Dick have gone to join Hengist and Horsa and the heroes of the Magnusson Saga.

But observe. What happened in the Middle Ages when for a while we could find no Western Frontier? The race impulse was irresistible. March we must, conquer we must, and checked in the Westward course of empire, we turned Eastward and expended the resistless energy that by blood was ours in conquering the Old World behind us.

To-day we are the same race, with the same impulse, the same power and, because there is no longer a Frontier to absorb our overplus of energy, because there is no longer a wilderness to conquer and because we still must march, still must conquer, we remember the old days when our ancestors before us found the outlet for their activity checked and, rebounding, turned their faces Eastward, and went down to invade the Old World. So we. No sooner have we found that our path to the Westward has ended than, reacting Eastward, we are at the Old World again, marching against it, invading it, devoting our overplus of energy to its subjugation.

But though we are the same race, with the same impulses, the same blood-instincts as the old Frisian marsh people, we are now come into a changed time and the great word of our century is no longer War, but Trade.

Or, if you choose, it is only a different word for the same race characteristic. The desire for conquest—say what you will—was as big in the breast of the most fervid of the Crusaders as it is this very day in the most peacefully disposed of American manufacturers. Had the Lion-Hearted Richard lived to-day he would have become a "leading representative of the Amalgamated Steel Companies," and doubt not for one moment that he would have underbid his Manchester rivals in the matter of bridge girders. Had Mr. Andrew Carnegie been alive at the time of the preachings of Peter the Hermit he would have raised a company of *gens d'armes* sooner than all of his brothers-in-arms, would have equipped his men better and more effectively, would have been first on the ground before Jerusalem, would have built the most ingenious siege-engine and have hurled the first cask of Greek fire over the walls

Competition and conquest are words easily interchangeable, and the whole spirit of our present commercial crusade to the Eastward betrays itself in the fact that we can not speak of it but in terms borrowed from the glossary of the warrior. It is a commercial "invasion," a trade "war," a "threatened attack" on the part of America; business is "captured," opportunities are "seized," certain industries are "killed," certain former monopolies are "wrested away." Seven hundred years ago a certain Count Baldwin, a great leader in the attack of the Anglo-Saxon Crusaders upon the Old World, built himself a siege-engine which would help him enter the beleaguered city of Jerusalem. Jerusalem is beleaguered again today, and the hosts of the Anglo-Saxon commercial crusaders are knocking at the gates. And now a company named for another Baldwin—and, for all we know, a descendant of the Count—leaders of the invaders of the Old World, advance upon the city, and, to help in the assault, build an engine—only now the engine is no longer called a *mangonel*, but a locomotive.

The difference is hardly of kind and scarcely of degree. It is a mere matter of names, and the ghost of Saladin watching the present engagement might easily fancy the old days back again.

So perhaps we have not lost the Frontier, after all. A new phrase, reversing that of Berkeley's, is appropriate to the effect that "Eastward the course of commerce takes its way," and we must look for the lost battle-line not toward the sunset, but toward the East. And so rapid has been the retrograde movement that we must go far to find it, that scattered firing-line, where the little skirmishes are heralding the approach of the Great March. We must already go further afield than England. The main body, even to the reserves, are intrenched there long since, and even continental Europe is to the rear of the skirmishers.

Along about Suez we begin to catch up with them where they are deepening the great canal, and we can assure ourselves that we are fairly abreast of the most distant line of scouts only when we come to Khiva, to Samarcand, to Bokhara, and the Trans-Baikal country.

Just now one hears much of the "American commercial invasion of England." But adjust the field-glasses and look beyond Britain and search for the blaze that the scouts have left on the telegraph poles and mile-posts of Hungary, Turkey, Turkey in Asia, Persia,

Baluchistan, India, and Siam. You'll find the blaze distinct and the road, though rough hewn, is easy to follow. Prophecy and presumption be far from us, but it would be against all precedent that the Grand March should rest forever upon its arms and its laurels along the Thames, the Mersey, and the Clyde, while its pioneers and frontiersmen are making roads for it to the Eastward.

Is it too huge a conception, too inordinate an idea, to say that the American conquest of England is but an incident of the Greater Invasion, an affair of outposts preparatory to the real manœuvre that shall embrace Europe, Asia, the whole of the Old World? Why not? And the blaze is ahead of us, and every now and then from far off there in the countries that are under the rising sun we catch the faint sounds of the skirmishing of our outposts. One of two things invariably happens under such circumstances as these: either the outposts fall back upon the main body or the main body moves up to the support of its outposts. One does not think that the outposts will fall back.

And so goes the great movement, Westward, then Eastward, forward and then back. The motion of the natural forces, the elemental energies, somehow appear to be thus alternative—action first, then reaction. The tides ebb and flow again, the seasons have their slow vibrations, touching extremes at periodic intervals. Not impossibly, in the larger view, is the analogy applicable to the movements of the races. First Westward with the great migrations, now Eastward with the course of commerce, moving in a colossal arc measured only by the hemispheres, as though upon the equator a giant dial hand oscillated, in gradual divisions through the centuries, now marking off the Westward progress, now traveling proportionately to the reaction toward the East.

Races must follow their destiny blindly, but is it not possible that we can find in this great destiny of ours something a little better than mere battle and conquest, something a little more generous than mere trading and underbidding? Inevitably with constant change of environment comes the larger view, the more tolerant spirit, and every race movement, from the first step beyond the Friesland swamp to the adjustment of the first American theodolite on the Himalayan watershed, is an unconscious lesson in patriotism. Just now we can not get beyond the self-laudatory mood, but is it not possible to hope that, as the progress develops, a new patriotism, one that shall include all peoples, may prevail? The past would indicate that this is a goal toward which we trend.

In the end let us take the larger view, ignoring the Frieslanders, the Anglo-Saxons, the Americans. Let us look at the peoples as people and observe how inevitably as they answer the great Westward impulse the true patriotism develops. If we can see that it is so with all of them we can assume that it must be so with us, and may know that mere victory in battle as we march Westward, or mere supremacy in trade as we react to the East, is not after all the great achievement of the races, but patriotism. Not our present day selfish conception of the word, but a new patriotism, whose meaning is now the secret of the coming centuries.

Consider then the beginnings of patriotism. At the very first, the seed of the future nation was the regard of family; the ties of common birth held men together, and the first feeling of patriotism was the love of family. But the family grows, develops by lateral branches, expands and becomes the clan. Patriotism is the devotion to the clan, and the clansmen will fight and die for its supremacy.

Then comes the time when the clans, tired of the roving life of herders, halt a moment and settle down in a chosen spot; the tent, becoming permanent, evolves the dwelling-house, and the encampment of the clan becomes at last a city. Patriotism now is civic pride; the clan absorbed into a multitude of clans is forgotten; men speak of themselves as Athenians, not as Greeks, as Romans, not as Italians. It is the age of cities.

The city extends its adjoining grazing fields; they include outlying towns, other cities, and finally the State comes into being. Patriotism no longer confines itself to the walls of the city, but is enlarged to encompass the entire province. Men are Hanoverians or Wurtemburgers, not Germans; Scots or Welsh, not English; are even Carolinians or Alabamans rather than Americans.

But the States are federated, pronounced boundaries fade, State makes common cause with State, and at last the nation is born. Patriotism at once is a national affair, a far larger, broader, truer sentiment than that first huddling about the hearthstone of the family. The word "brother" may be applied to men unseen and unknown, and a countryman is one of many millions.

We have reached this stage at the present, but if all signs are true, if all precedent may be followed, if all augury may be relied on and the tree grow as we see the twig is bent, the progress will not stop here.

By war to the Westward the family fought its way upward to the dignity of the nation; by reaction Eastward the nation may in patriotic effect merge with other nations, and others and still others, peacefully, the bitterness of trade competition may be lost, the business of the nations seen as a friendly *quid pro quo,* give and take arrangement, guided by a generous reciprocity. Every century the boundaries are widening, patriotism widens with the expansion, and our countrymen are those of different race, even different nations.

Will it not go on, this epic of civilization, this destiny of the races, until at last and at the ultimate end of all we who now arrogantly boast ourselves as Americans, supreme in conquest, whether of battleship or of bridge-building, may realize that the true patriotism is the brotherhood of man and know that the whole world is our nation and simple humanity our countrymen?

THE GREAT AMERICAN NOVELIST

Of all the overworked phrases of overworked book reviewers, the phrase, the "Great American Novelist," is beyond doubt worn the thinnest from much handling—or mishandling. Continually the little literary middlemen who come between the producers and the consumers of fiction are mouthing the words with a great flourish of adjectives, scare-heading them in Sunday supplements or placarding them on posters, crying out, "Lo, he is here!" or "lo, there!" But the heathen rage and the people imagine a vain thing. The G. A. N. is either as extinct as the dodo or as far in the future as the practical aeroplane. He certainly is not discoverable at the present.

The moment a new writer of fiction begins to make himself felt he is gibbeted upon this elevation—upon this *false,* insecure elevation, for the underpinning is of the flimsiest, and at any moment is liable to collapse under the victim's feet and leave him hanging in midair by head and hands, a fixture and a mockery.

And who is to settle the title upon the aspirant in the last issue? Who is to determine what constitutes the G. A. N.? Your candidate may suit *you,* but your neighbor may have a very different standard to which he must conform. It all depends upon what you mean by *Great,* what you mean by *American.* Shakespeare has been called great and so has Mr. Stephen Phillips. Oliver Wendell Holmes was *American,* and so is Bret Harte. Who is to say?

And many good people who deplore the decay of American letters are accustomed to refer to the absence of a G. A. N. as though there were a Great English Novelist or a Great French Novelist. But do these two people exist? Ask any dozen of your friends to mention the Great English Novelist, and out of the dozen you will get at least a half-dozen different names. It will be Dickens or Scott or Thackeray or Brontë or Eliot or Stevenson, and the same with the Frenchman. And it seems to me that if a novelist were great enough to be universally acknowledged to be the Great one of his country, he would cease to belong to any particular geographical area and would become a heritage of the whole world; as, for instance, Tolstoi; when one thinks of him it is—is it not?—as a novelist first and as a Russian afterward.

But if one wishes to split hairs, one might admit that while the Great American Novelist is yet to be born, the possibility of *A*—note the indefinite article—*A* Great American Novel is not too remote for discussion. But such a novel will be sectional. The United States is a Union, but not a unit, and the life of one part is very, very different from the life in another. It is as yet impossible to construct a novel which will represent all the various characteristics of the different sections. It is only possible to make a picture of a single locality. What is true of the South is not true of the North. The West is different, and the Pacific Coast is a community by itself.

Many of our very best writers are working on this theory. Bret Harte made a study of the West as he saw it, and Mr. Howells has done the same for the East. Cable has worked the field of the Far South, and Eggleston has gone deep into the life of the Middle West.

But consider a suggestion. It is an argument on the other side, and to be fair one must present it. It is a good argument, and if based on fact is encouraging in the hope that the *Great* man may yet appear. It has been said that "what is true—vitally and inherently true—for any one man is true for all men." Accordingly, then, what is vitally true of the Westerner is true of the Bostonian —yes, and of the creole. So that if Mr. Cable, say, should only go *deep enough* into the hearts and lives of his creoles, he would at last strike the universal substratum and find the elemental thing that is common to the creole and to the Puritan alike—yes, and to the Cowboy and Hoosier and Greaser and Buckeye and Jay Hawker, and that, once getting hold of *that,* he could produce the Great American Novel that should be a picture of the entire nation.

Now, that is a very ingenious argument and sounds very plausible. But it won't do, and for this reason: If an American novelist should go so deep into the lives of the people of any one community that he would find the thing that is common to another class of people a thousand miles away, he would have gone *too* deep to be exclusively American. He would not only be American, but English as well. He would have sounded the world-note; he would be a writer not national, but international, and his countrymen would be all humanity, not the citizens of any one nation. He himself would be a heritage of the whole world, a second Tolstoi, which brings us back to the very place from which we started.

And the conclusion of the whole matter? That fiction is very good or very bad—there is no middle ground; that writers of fiction in their points of view are either limited to a circumscribed area or see humanity as a tremendous conglomerate whole; that it must be either Mary Wilkins or George Eliot, Edward Eggleston or William Shakespeare; that the others do not weigh very much in the balance of the world's judgment; and that the Great American Novel is not extinct like the dodo, but mythical like the hippogriff, and that the thing to be looked for is not the Great American Novelist, but the Great Novelist who shall also be an American.

NEW YORK AS A LITERARY CENTRE

It has been given to the present writer to know a great many of what one may call The Unarrived in literary work, and of course to be one himself of that "innumerable caravan," and speaking authoritatively and of certain knowledge, the statement may be made that of all the ambitions of the Great Unpublished, the one that is strongest, the most abiding, is the ambition to get to New York. For these, New York is the "point de depart," the pedestal, the niche, the indispensable vantage ground; as one of the unpublished used to put it: "It is a place that I can stand on and holler."

This man lived in a second-class town west of the Mississippi, and one never could persuade him that he might holler from his own, his native heath, and yet be heard. He said it would be "the voice of one crying in the wilderness." New York was the place for him. Once land him in New York and all would be gas and gaiters.

There are so many thousands like this young man of mine that a word in this connection seems appropriate; and the object of this present writing is to protest against this blind and unreasoned hegira, and to urge the point that, tradition precedent to the contrary notwithstanding, New York is not a literary centre.

I am perfectly well aware that this statement savors of heresy, but at the same time I think it can be defended. As for instance:

Time was when Boston claimed the distinction that one now denies to New York. But one asserts that Boston made her claims good. In those days the reactionary movement of populations from the cities toward the country had not set in. A constant residence winter and summer in the country was not dreamed of by those who had the leisure and the money to afford it. As much as possible the New England writers crowded to Boston, or to Cambridge, which is practically the same thing, and took root in the place. There was their local habitation; there they lived, and thence they spread their influence. Remember that at the height of the development of the New England school there were practically no other writers of so great importance the length and breadth of the land. This huddling about a common point made it possible to visit all the homes of nearly all of the most eminent American literati in a single day. The younger men, the aspirants, the Unpublished, however, thrown into such society, could not fail to be tremendously impressed, and, banded together as these great ones were, their influence counted enormously. It was no unusual sight to see half a dozen of these at the same dinner table. They all knew each other intimately, these Bostonians, and their word was *Lex,* and the neophites came from all corners of the compass to hear them speak, and Boston did in good earnest become the Hub, the centre of Literary thought and work in the United States.

But no such conditions obtain in New York to-day. During the last ten years two very important things have happened that bear upon this question. First has come the impulse toward a country life—a continued winter and summer residence in the country. Authors more than any other class of workers can afford this, since their profession can be carried anywhere. They need no city offices They are not forced to be in touch with the actual business life of Broadway. Secondly, since the days of the Bostonian supremacy a tremendous wave of literary production has swept over the United States. New England has ceased to be the only place where books are written. Poems are now indited in Dakota, novels composed in Wyoming, essays written in Utah, and criticisms flourish in Kansas. A thousand and one Little Centres have sprung up. Literary groups are formed everywhere, in Buffalo, in San Francisco, in Indianapolis and Chicago.

All this detracts from the preponderance of any one city, such as New York, as Literary dictator. You shall find but a very small and meagre minority of the Greater Men of Letters who have their homes in Manhattan. Most of them prefer to live in the places whereof they treat in their books, in New Orleans, in Indiana, in Kentucky, or Virginia, or California, or Kansas, or Illinois. If they come to New York at all it is only temporarily, to place their newest book or to arrange with publishers for future work.

The result of this is as is claimed. New York is not a literary centre. The publishing houses are there, the magazines, all the distributing machinery; but not the writers. They do not live there. They do not care to come there. They regard the place simply as a distributing point for their wares.

Literary centres produce literary men. Paris, London, and

Boston all have their long lists of native-born writers—men who were born in these cities and whose work was identified with them. But New York can claim but ridiculously few of the men of larger calibre as her own. James Whitcomb Riley is from Indiana. Joel Chandler Harris is a Southerner. Howells came from Boston, Cable from New Orleans, Hamlin Garland from the West, Bret Harte from California, Mark Twain from the Middle West. Harold Frederic and Henry James found England more congenial than the greatest cities of their native land. Even among the younger generation there are but few who can be considered as New Yorkers. Although Richard Harding Davis wrote accurately and delightfully of New York people, he was not born in New York, did not receive his first impetus from New York influences, and does not now live in New York. Nor is his best work upon themes or subjects in any way related to New York.

In view of all these facts it is difficult to see what the Great Unpublished have to gain by a New York residence. Indeed, it is much easier to see how very much they have to lose.

The writing of fiction has many drawbacks, but one of its blessed compensations is the fact that of all the arts it is the most independent—independent of time, of manner, and of place. Wherever there is a table and quiet, there the novel may be written. "Ah, but the publishing houses are in New York!" What has that to do with it? Do not for a moment suppose that your novel will be considered more carefully because you submit it in person. It is not as though you were on the lookout for odd jobs which, because of a personal acquaintance with editors and publishers, might be put in your way. The article, the story, the essay, poem or novel is just as good, just as available, just as salable whether it comes from Washington Territory or Washington Square.

Not only this, but one believes that actual residence in New York is hostile and inimical to good work. The place, admittedly, teems with literary clubs, circles, associations, organizations of pseudo-literati, who foregather at specified times to "read papers" and "discuss questions." It is almost impossible for the young writer who comes for a first time to the city to avoid entangling himself with them; and of the influences that tend to stultify ambition, warp original talent, and definably and irretrievably stamp out the last spark of productive ability one knows of none more effective than the literary clubs.

You will never find the best men at these gatherings. You will never hear the best work read in this company, you will never evolve any original, personal, definite ideas or ideals under such influence. The discussions of the literary clubs are made up of puerile arguments that have done duty for years in the college text-books. Their work—the papers quoted and stories read aloud—is commonplace and conventional to the deadliest degree, while their "originality"—the ideas that they claim are their very own—is nothing but a distortion and dislocation of preconceived notions, mere bizarre effects of the grotesque and the improbable. "Ah, but the spur of competition." Competition is admirable in trade—it is even desirable in certain arts. It has no place in a literary career. It is not as though two or more writers were working on the same story, each striving to better the others. That would, indeed, be true competition. But in New York, where the young writer—any writer—may see a dozen instances in a week of what he knows is inferior work succeeding where he fails, competition is robbed of all stimulating effect and, if one is not very careful, leaves only the taste of ashes in the mouth and rancor and discontent in the heart.

With other men's novels the novelist has little to do. What this writer is doing, what that one is saying, what books this publishing house is handling, how many copies of so-and-so's book are selling—all this fuss and feathers of "New York as a literary centre" should be for him so many distractions. It is all very well to say, "Let us keep in touch with the best thought in our line of work." "Let us be in the movement." The best thought is not in New York; and even if it were, the best thought of other men is not so good for you as your own thought, dug out of your own vitals by your own unaided efforts, be it never so inadequate.

You do not have to go to New York for that. Your own ideas, your own work will flourish best if left alone untrammeled and uninfluenced. And believe this to be true, that wherever there is a table, a sheet of paper and a pot of ink, there is a Literary Centre if you will. You will find none better the world over.

THE AMERICAN PUBLIC AND "POPULAR" FICTION

THE American people judged by Old World standards—even sometimes according to native American standards—have always been considered a practical people, a material people.

We have been told and have also told ourselves that we are hard-headed, that we rejoiced in facts and not in fancies, and as an effect of this characteristic were not given to books. We were not literary, we assumed, were not fond of reading. We, who were subjugating a continent, who were inventing machinery and building railroads, left it to the older and more leisurely nations—to France and to England—to read books.

On the face of it this would seem a safe assumption. As a matter of fact, the American people are the greatest readers in the world. That is to say, that, count for count, there are more books read in the United States in one year than in any other country of the globe in the same space of time.

Nowhere do the circulations attain such magnitude as they do with us. A little while ago—ten years ago—the charge that we did not read was probably true. But there must exist some mysterious fundamental connection between this recent sudden expansion of things American—geographic, commercial, and otherwise—and the demand for books. Imperialism, Trade Expansion, the New Prosperity and the Half Million Circulation all came into existence at about the same time.

Merely the fact of great prosperity does not account for the wider reading. Prosperous periods, good prices, easy credit and a mobile currency have occurred often before without producing the demand for books. Something more than prosperity has suddenly swept across the continent and evaded the spirit of the times. Something very like an awakening, something very like a renaissance and the 70,000,000 have all at once awakened to the fact that there are books to be read. As with all things sudden, there is noticeable with this awakening a lack of discrimination, the 70,000,000 are so eager for books that, *faute de mieux*, anything printed will pass current for literature. It is a great animal, this American public and having starved for so long, it is ready, once aroused, to devour anything. And the great presses of the country are for the most part merely sublimated sausage machines that go dashing along in a mess of paper and printer's ink turning out the meat for the monster.

There are not found wanting many who deplore this and who blackguard the great brute for his appetite. Softly, softly. If the Megatherium had been obliged to swallow wind for sustenance for several hundred years, it would be unkind to abuse him because he eats the first lot of spoiled hay or overripe twigs that is thrust under the snout of him. Patience and shuffle the cards. Once his belly filled, and the pachyderm will turn to the new-mown grass and fruit trees in preference to the hay and twigs.

So the studios and the Browning classes need not altogether revile the great American public. Better bad books than no books; better half a loaf of hard bread than *no* frosted wedding-cake. The American people, unlike the English, unlike the French and other Europeans, have not been educated and refined and endoctrinated for 2,000 years, and when you remember what they have done in *one hundred* years, tamed an entire continent, liberated a race, produced a Lincoln, invented the telegraph, spanned the plains—when you remember all this, do not spurn the 70,000,000 because they do not understand Henry James, but be glad that they even care for "The Duchess" and "Ouida." The wonder of it is not that they do not read or appreciate the best, but that they have set apart any time at all in the struggle of civilizing the wilderness and forging steel rivets to so much as pick up any kind or description of a book.

Consider the other nations, France for instance—the very sanctum of Art, the home and birthplace of literature. Compare the rural districts of France with the rural districts of the United States, and in the comparison allow, if you like, for all the centuries of quiet, uninterrupted growth, the wilderness tamed, life domesticated, reduced to routine, that modern France enjoys. Do you suppose for one moment that a bourgeois family of—say—Tours is on the same level in the matter of its reading as the household of a contractor's family in—for example—Martinez, California, or Cheyenne, Wyoming?

I tell you there is no comparison whatever. The West may be

wild even yet, may be what Boston would call uncultured, but it *reads*. There are people in Cheyenne and Martinez who can express an opinion—and a more intelligent opinion, mark you—on Maeterlinck and Bourget, better than the same class of readers in Belgium and France. And quite as likely as not the same class of people in the very native countries of the two writers named have never so much as heard of these writers.

This, admittedly, is the exception, but if our exceptional Martinez and Cheyenne people are so far advanced in literary criticism, we may reasonably expect that the rank and file below them are proportionately well on. Maeterlinck and Bourget are closed books to those rank-and-file readers yet. But again I say, this is not the point. The point is, that they are readers at all. Let them—in the name of future American literature—read their Duchesses and Ouidas and Edna Lyalls and Albert Rosses. What are their prototypes in France, Germany, and Russia reading? They simply are not reading at all, and as often as not it is not because of the lack of taste, but because of the lack of sheer downright ability, because they do not know how to read.

A very great man once said that "books never have done harm," and under this sign let us conquer. There is hardly a better to be found. Instead, then, of deploring the vast circulation of mediocre novels, let us take the larger view and find in the fact not a weakness, but a veritable strength. The more one reads—it is a curious consolatory fact—the more one is apt to discriminate. The ten-year-old who reads "Old Sleuth" to-day, in a little while will find Scott more to his liking. Just now the 70,000,000 is ten years old. But it is started right. Patience. Books have never done harm, and in the end let us be certain that the day will come when the real masterpiece, the real literature, will also be selling in its "five hundredth thousand."

CHILD STORIES FOR ADULTS

There was a time, none too remote at this date of writing, when juvenile and adult fiction were two separate and distinct classifications. Boys read stories for boys and girls stories for girls, and the adults contented themselves with the wise lucubrations of their equals in years. But the last few years have changed all that—have changed everything in American literature, in fact.

Some far-distant day, when the critics and *litterateurs* of the twenty-second and twenty-third centuries shall be writing of our day and age, they will find a name for the sudden and stupendous demand for reading matter that has penetrated to all classes and corners since 1890. A great deal could be said upon this sudden demand in itself, and I think it can be proved to be the first effects of a genuine awakening—a second Renaissance. But the subject would demand an article by itself, and in the meanwhile we may use the term awakening as a self-evident fact and consider not so much the cause as the effects.

One of the effects, as has been already suggested, is the change in classifications. Old forms and formulas are being rapidly broken up, one school and style merging into others, till now what was once amusement for the children has become entertaining for the elders. And vice versa. The abruptness of the awakening has disjointed and inverted all the old fabric. "Robinson Crusoe," written for adults, is now exclusively a "juvenile," while "Treasure Island," written for boys, has been snapped up by the parents.

Simultaneously with this topsy-turvy business, and I am sure in some way connected with it, comes the craze for stories about very young children for adult reading. A boy's story must now be all about the doings of men, fighters preferably, man-slayers, terrible fellows full of blood and fury, stamping on their quarter-decks or counting doubloons by torchlight on unnamed beaches. Meanwhile the boy's father with a solemn interest is following the fortunes of some terrible infant of the kindergarten, or the vagaries of a ten-year-old of a country town, or the teacup tragedy of "The

Very Little Girl," or "The Indiscretion of Pinky Trevethan," or "The Chastening of Skinny McCleave," etc., etc.

It is interesting to try to account for this. It may either be a fad or a phase. It is almost too soon to tell, but in either case the matter is worth considering.

Roughly speaking, the Child's Stories for Adults fall into three classes. First there is "The Strange Child Story." This is a very old favorite, and was pretty well installed long before the more recent developments. In "The Strange Child Story" the bid for the reader's pity and sympathy fairly clamored from between the lines. Always and persistently The Strange Child was misunderstood. He had "indefinable longings" that were ridiculed, budding talents that were nipped, heartaches—terrible, tear-compelling heartaches—that were ignored; and he lived in an atmosphere of gloom, hostility and loneliness that would have maddened an eremite.

But as his kind declined in popular estimate the country boy, the ten-year-old—who always went in swimmin' and lost his tow—appeared in the magazines. There is no sentiment about him. Never a tear need be shed over the vicarious atonements of Pinky Trevethan or Skinny McCleave.

It is part of the game to pretend that the Pinkys and Skinnys and Peelys and Mickeys are different indivdiuals. Error. They are merely different names of the boy that perenially and persistently remains the same. Do you know who he is? He is the average American business man before he grew up. That accounts for his popularity. The average business man had clean forgotten all about those early phases of primitive growth, and it amuses him immensely to find out that the scribe has been making a study of him and bringing to light the forgotten things that are so tremendously familiar when presented to the consideration. It is not fiction nor yet literature in the straightest sense of the word, this rehabilitation of Skinny McCleave. It has a value vaguely scientific, the same value that a specimen, a fossil insect, has when brought to the attention of the savant. It is the study of an extinct species, a report upon the American boy of thirty years ago.

Then lastly—the latest development—there is the cataclysm of the kindergarten. the checked apron drama, the pigtail passion, the epic of the broken slate-pencil. This needs a delicacy of touch that only a woman can supply, and as a matter of fact it is for the most part women who sign the stories. The interest in these is not so personal and retrospective as in the Skinny McCleave circle, for the kindergarten is too recent to be part of the childhood memories of the present generation of adult magazine readers. It is more informative, a presentation of conditions hitherto but vaguely known, and at the same time it is an attempt to get at and into the heart and head of a little child.

And in this last analysis it would seem as if here existed the barrier insurmountable. It is much to be doubted if ever a genius will arise so thoughtful, so sensitive, that he will penetrate into more than the merest outside integument of a child's heart. Certain phases have been guessed at with beautiful intuition, certain rare insights have been attained with exquisite nicety, but somehow even the most sympathetic reader must feel that the insight is as rare as the interest is misguided.

Immanuel Kant conceived of and, in the consummate power of his intellect, executed the "Critique of Pure Reason"; Darwin had taken the adult male and female human and tracked down their every emotion, impulse, quality and sentiment. The intellectual powers and heart-beats of a Napoleon or a Shakespeare have been reduced to mere commonplace corner gossip, but after thousands of years of civilization, with the subject ever before us, its workings as near to us as air itself, the mind of a little child is as much a closed book, as much an enigma, as much a blank space upon the charts of our intellectual progress as at the very first.

Volumes have been written about the child, and stories for and of the child, and very learned men have lectured and other very eminent and noble men have taught, and it has all been going on for nineteen hundred and two years. And yet, notwithstanding all this, there lurks a mystery deep down within the eye of the five-year-old, a mystery that neither you nor I may know. You may see and understand what he actually does, but the thinking part of him is a second hidden nature that belongs to him and to other children, not to adults, not even to his mother. Once the older person invades the sphere of influence of this real undernature of the child and it congeals at once. It thaws and thrives only in the company of other children, and at the best we older ones may see it from a distance and from the outside. Between us and them it would appear that a great gulf is bridged; there is no knowing the child as he really is, and until the real child can be known the stories about him and the fiction and literature about him can at best be only a substitute for the real knowledge that probably never shall be ours.

NEWSPAPER CRITICISMS AND AMERICAN FICTION

THE limitations of space impose a restricted title, and one hastens to qualify the substantive "criticisms" by the adjective "average." Even "average" is not quite specialized enough; "vast majority" is more to the sense, and the proposition expanded to its fullest thus stands, "How is the vast majority of newspaper criticisms made, and how does it affect American Fiction?" And it may not be inappropriate at the outset to observe that one has adventured both hazards—criticism (of the "vast majority" kind) and also Fiction. One has criticised and has been criticised. Possibly then it may be permitted to speak a little authoritatively; not as the Scribes. Has it not astonished you how many of those things called by the new author "favorable reviews" may attach themselves— barnacles upon a lifeless hulk—to a novel that you know, that you know every one must, must know, is irretrievably bad? "On the whole, Mr. ——'s story is a capital bit of vigorous writing that we joyfully recommend"—"A thrilling story palpitating with life," "One of the very best novels that has appeared in a long time," and the ever-new, ever-dutiful, ever-ready encomium, "Not a dull page in the book" (as if by the furthest stretch of conceivable human genius a book could be written that did not have a dull page; as if dull pages were not an absolute necessity). All these you may see strung after the announcement of publication of the novel; no matter, I repeat, how outrageously bad the novel may be. Now, there is an explanation of this matter, and it is to be found not in the sincere admiration of little reviewers who lack the ingenuity to invent new phrases, but in the following fact: it is easier to write favorable than unfavorable reviews. It must be borne in mind that very few newspapers (comparatively) employ regularly paid book-reviewers whose business it is to criticise novels—and nothing else. Most book-reviewing is done as an odd job by sub-editors, assistants, and special writers in the intervals between their regular work. They come to the task with a brain already jaded, an interest so low as to be almost negligible, and with—as often as not—a mind besieged by a thousand other cares, responsibilities, and projects.

The chief has said something like this (placing upon the scribe's table a column of novels easily four feet high, sent in for review) :

"Say, B——, these things have been stacking up like the devil lately, and I don't want 'em kicking 'round the office any longer. Get through with them as quick as you can, and remember that in an hour there's such and such to be done."

I tell you I have seen it happen like this a hundred times. And the scribe "must" read and "review" between twenty and thirty books in an hour's time. One way of doing it is to search in the pages of the book for the "publisher's notice," a printed slip that has a favorable review—that is what it amounts to—all ready-made. The scribe merely turns this in with a word altered here and there. How he reviews the books that have not this publisher's notice Heaven only knows. He is not to blame, as they must be done in an hour. Twenty books in sixty minutes—three minutes to each book. Now, it is impossible to criticise a book adversely after a minute and a half of reading (we will allow a minute and a half for writing the review). In order to write unfavorably it is necessary to know what one is writing about. But it is astonishing how much commendatory palaver already exists that can be applied to any kind or condition of novel. Is it a novel of adventure (the reviewer may know if it be such by the ship on the cover design—it will be appropriate to use these terms: "Vibrant with energy," or "Full of fine fighting," or "The reader is carried with breathless interst from page to page of this exciting romance." Is it a novel of rural life? These may be made use of: "Replete with quaint humor," "A faithful picture of an interesting phase of American life," etc., etc. Is it a story of the West (you can guess that from the chapter headings), it will be proper to say, "A strong and vital portraying of the wild life of the trail and frontier."

And so one might run through the entire list. The books must be reviewed, the easiest way is the quickest, and the quickest way is to write in a mild and meaningless phraseology, innocuous, "favorable." In this fashion is made the greater mass of American criticism. As to effects: It has of course no effect upon the novel's circulation. Only one person is at all apt to take these reviews, this hack-work, seriously.

Only one person, I observed, is at all apt to take these reviews seriously—this way lies the harm—the new writer, the young fellow with his first book, who may not know the ways of reviewers; the author, who collects these notices and pastes them in a scrap-book. He is perilously prone to believe what the hacks say, to believe that there is "no dull page in the story," that his novel is "one of the notable contributions to recent fiction," and cherishing this belief he is fated to a wrench and a heartache when, six months after publication day, the semi-annual account of copies sold is rendered. There is unfortunately no palaver in the writing of this— no mild-mannered phraseology; and the author is made to see suddenly that "this exciting romance" which the reviewers have said the readers "would follow with a breathless interest till the end is reached and then wish for more," has circulated among—possibly —five hundred of the breathless.

Thus, then, the vast majority of criticisms. It is not all, however, and it is only fair to say that there are exceptions—great papers which devote whole supplements to the consideration of literary matters and whose reviewers are deliberate, thoughtful fellows, who do not read more than one book a week, who sign their opinions and who have themselves a name, a reputation, to make or keep. These must have an effect. But even the most conspicuous among them can not influence very widely. They may help, so one believes, a good book which is already becoming popular. No one of them can "make" a book by a "favorable review," as they could a little while ago in France. No number of them could do it, here in America. There are too many other reviewers. No one man, nor aggregation of men, can monopolize the requisite authority. And then with us the spirit of independent thinking and judgment is no doubt too prevalent.

NOVELISTS TO ORDER—WHILE YOU WAIT

NOT at all absurd, "Novelists to order—while you wait," provided you order the right sort, and are willing to wait long enough. In other words, it is quite possible to make a novelist, and a good one, too, if the thing is undertaken in the right spirit, just as it is possible to make a painter, or an actor, or a business man.

I am prepared to hear the old objections raised to this: "Ah, it must be born in you"; "no amount of training can 'make' an artist"; "poets are born and not made," etc., etc. But I am also willing to contend that a very large percentage of this talk is sheer nonsense, and that what the world calls "genius" is, as often as not, the results of average ability specialized and developed. The original "spark" in the child-mind, that later on "kindles the world into flame with its light," I do believe could be proved to be the same for the artist, the actor, the novelist, the inventor, even the financier and "magnate." It is only made to burn in different lamps. Nor does any one believe that this "spark" is any mysterious, supernatural gift, some marvelous, angelic "genius," God-given, Heaven-given, etc., etc., etc., but just plain, forthright, rectangular, everyday common-sense, nothing more extraordinary or God-given than sanity. If it were true that Genius is the gift of the gods, it would also be true that hard work in cultivating it would be superfluous. As well be without genius if some plodder, some dullard, can by such work equal the best you can do—you with your God-given faculties.

Is it not much more reasonable—more noble, for the matter of that—to admit at once that all faculties, all intellects, are God-given, the only difference being that some are specialized to one end, some to another, some not specialized at all. We call Rostand and Mr. Carnegie geniuses, but most of us would be unwilling to admit that the genius of the American financier differed in kind from the genius of the French dramatist. However, one believes that this is open to debate. As for my part, I suspect that, given a difference in environment and training, Rostand would have consolidated the American steel companies and Carnegie have written "L'Aiglon." But one dares to go a little further—a great deal further—and claims that the young Carnegie and the young Rostand were no more than intelligent, matter-of-fact boys, in no wise different from the common house variety, grammer school product. They have been trained differently, that is all.

Given the ordinary intelligent ten-year-old, and, all things being equal, you can make anything you like out of him—a minister of the gospel or a green-goods man, an electrical engineer or a romantic poet, or—return to our muttons—a novelist. If a failure is the result, blame the method of training, not the quantity or quality of the ten-year-old's intellect. Don't say, if he is a failure as a fine novelist, that he lacks genius for writing, and would have been a fine business man. Make no mistake, if he did not have enough "genius" for novel-writing he would certainly have not had enough for business.

"Why, then," you will ask, "is it so impossible for some men, the majority of them, to write fine novels, or fine poems, or paint fine pictures? Why is it that this faculty seems to be reserved for the chosen few, the more refined, cultured, etc.? Why is it, in a word, that, for every artist (using the word to include writers, painters, actors, etc.) that appears there are thousands of business men, commercial "geniuses"?

The reason seems to lie in this: and it is again a question of training. From the very first the average intelligent American boy is trained not with a view toward an artistic career, but with a view to entering a business life. If the specialization of his faculties along artistic lines ever occurs at all it begins only when the boy is past the formative period. In other words, most people who eventually become artists are educated for the first eighteen or twenty years of their life along entirely unartistic lines. Biographies of artists are notoriously full of just such instances. The boy who is to become a business man finds, the moment he goes to school, a whole vast machinery of training made ready for his use, and not only is it a matter of education for him, but the whole scheme of modern civilization works in his behalf. No one ever heard of obstacles thrown in the way of the boy who announces for himself a money-making career; while for the artist, as is said, education, environment, the trend of civilization are not merely indifferent, but openly hostile and inimical. One hears only of those men who surmount—and at what cost to their artistic powers—

those obstacles. How many thousands are there who succumb unrecorded!

So that it has not often been tried—the experiment of making a novelist while you wait—*i. e.*, taking a ten-year-old of average intelligence and training him to be a novelist. Suppose all this modern, this gigantic perfected machinery—all this resistless trend of a commercial civilization were set in motion in favor of the little aspirant for honors in artistic fields, who is to say with such a training he would not in the end be a successful artist, painter, poet, musician, or novelist? Training, not "genius," would make him.

Then, too, another point. The artistic training should begin much, much earlier than the commercial training—instead of, as at present, so much later.

Nowadays, as a rule, the artist's training begins, as was said, after a fourth of his life, the very best, the most important, has been lived. You can take a boy of eighteen and make a business man of him in ten years. But at eighteen the faculties that make a good artist are very apt to be atrophied, hardened, unworkable. Even the ten-year-old is almost too old to begin on. The first ten years of childhood are the imaginative years, the creative years, the observant years, the years of a fresh interest in life. The child "imagines" terrors or delights, ghosts or fairies, creates a world out of his toys, and observes to an extent that adults have no idea of. ("Give me," a detective once told me, "a child's description of a man that is wanted. It beats an adult's every single time.") And imagination, creation, observation, and an unblunted interest in life are exactly the faculties most needed by novelists.

At eighteen there comes sophistication—or a pretended sophistication, which is deadlier. Other men's books take the place of imagination for the young man; creation in him is satisfied by dramas, horse-races, and amusements. The newspapers are his observation, and oh, how he assumes to be above any pleasure in simple, vigorous life!

So that at eighteen it is, as a rule, too late to make a fine novelist out of him. He may start out in that career, but he will not go far —so far as he would in business. But if he were taken in hand as soon as he could write in words of three syllables, and instead of being crammed with commercial arithmetic (How many marbles did A have? If a man buys a piece of goods at 12½ cents and sells it for 15 cents, etc., etc.)—

If he had been taken in hand when his imagination was alive, his creative power vigorous, his observation lynxlike, and his interest keen, and trained with a view toward the production of original fiction, who is to say how far he would have gone?

One does not claim that the artist is above the business man. Far from it. Only, when you have choked the powers of imagination and observation, and killed off the creative ability, and deadened the interest in life, don't call it lack of genius.

Nor when some man of a different race than ours, living in a more congenial civilization, whose training from his youth up has been adapted to a future artistic profession, succeeds in painting the great picture, composing the great prelude, writing the great novel, don't say he was born a "genius," but rather admit that he was made "to order" by a system whose promoters knew how to wait.

THE "NATURE" REVIVAL IN LITERATURE

IT has been a decade of fads, and "the people have imagined a vain thing," as they have done from the time of Solomon and as no doubt they will till the day of the New Jerusalem. And in no other line of activity has the instability and changeableness of the taste of the public been so marked as in that of literature. Such an over-turning of old gods and such a setting up of new ones, such an image-breaking, shrine-smashing, relic-ripping carnival I doubt has ever been witnessed in all the history of writing. It has been a sort of literary Declaration of Independence. For half a century certain great names, from Irving down to Holmes, were veritable *Abra-cadabras*—impeccable, sanctified. Then all at once the *fin-de-siècle* irreverence seemed to invade all sorts and conditions simultaneously, and the sombre, sober idols were shouldered off into the dark niches, and not a man of us that did not trundle forth his own little tin-god-on-wheels, kowtowing and making obeisance, and going before with cymbals and a great noise, proclaiming a New Great One; now it was the great Colonial Image, now the Great Romantic Image, now the Great Minor-German Kingdom Image.

There are a great many very eminent and very wise critics who frown upon and deplore the reaction. But it is a question if, after all, the movement will not prove—ultimately—beneficial. Con-vention, blind adherence to established forms, inertia, is the dry rot of a national literature. Better the American public should read bad books than no books, and that same public is reading now as never before. It is a veritable upheaval, a breaking-up of all the old grounds. Better this than supineness; better this than immo-bility. Once the ground turned over a bit, harrowed and loosened, and the place is made ready for the good seed.

Some of this, one chooses to believe, has already been implanted. In all the parade of the new little tin-gods some may be discovered that are not tin, but sterling. Of all the fads, the most legitimate, the most abiding, the most inherent—so it would appear—is the "Nature" revival. Indeed, it is not fair to call it a fad at all. For it is a return to the primitive, sane life of the country, and the natural thing by its very character can not be artificial, can not be a "fad." The writers who have followed where Mr. Thompson Seton blazed the way are so numerous and so well known that it is almost superfluous in this place to catalogue or criticise them. But it is significant of the strength of this movement that such an outdoor book as "Bob, Son of Battle," was unsuccessful in England, and only attained its merited popularity when published here in America. We claimed the "good gray dog" as our own from the very first, recognizing that the dog has no nationality, being indeed a citizen of the whole world. The flowers in "Elizabeth's German Garden"—also world citizens—we promptly transplanted to our own soil. Mr. Mowbray, with his mingling of fact and fiction, made his country home for the benefit—I have no doubt—of hundreds who have actually worked out the idea suggested in his pages. The butterfly books, the garden books, the flower books, expensive as they are, have been in as much demand as some very popular novels. Mr. Dugmore astonished and delighted a surprisingly large public with his marvelous life-photographs of birds, while even President Roosevelt himself deemed Mr. Wallihan's "Photographs of Big Game" of so much importance and value that he wrote the introductory notice to that excellent volume.

It is hardly possible to pick up a magazine now that does not contain the story of some animal hero. Time was when we relegated this sort to the juvenile periodicals. But now we can not get too much of it. Wolves, rabbits, hounds, foxes, the birds, even the reptilia, all are dramatized, all figure in their little rôles. Tobo and the Sand-hill Stag parade upon the same pages as Mr. Christy's *débutantes* and Mr. Smedley's business men, and, if you please, have their love affairs and business in precisely the same spirit. All this can not but be significant, and, let us be assured, significant of good. The New England school for too long dominated the entire range of American fiction—limiting it, specializing it, polishing, refining and embellishing it, narrowing it down to a veritable cult, a thing to be safeguarded by the elect, the few, the aristocracy. It is small wonder that the reaction came when and as it did; small wonder that the wearied public, roused at length, smashed its idols with such vehemence; small wonder that, declaring its independence and finding itself suddenly untrammeled and unguided, it flew off *mobbishly* toward false gods, good only because they were new.

All this is small wonder. The great wonder is this return to nature, this unerring groping backward toward the fundamentals, in order to take a renewed grip upon life. If you care to see a proof of how vital it is, how valuable, look into some of the magazines of the seventies and eighties. It is astonishing to consider that we ever found an interest in them. The effect is like entering a darkened room. And not only the magazines, but the entire literature of the years before the nineties is shadowed and oppressed with the bugbear of "literature." Outdoor life was a thing apart from our reading. Even the tales and serials whose *mise en scène* was in the country had no breath of the country in them. The "literature" in them suffocated the life, and the humans with their everlasting consciences, their heated and artificial activities, filled all the horizon, admitting the larks and the robins only as accessories; considering the foxes, the deer and the rabbits only as creatures to be killed, to be pursued, to be exterminated. But Mr. Seton and his school, and the Mowbrays, and the Ollivants, the Dugmores and the Wallihans opened a door, opened a window, and mere literature has had to give place to life. The sun has come in and the great winds, and the smell of the baking alkali on the Arizona deserts, and the reek of the tar-weed on the Colorado slopes; and nature has ceased to exist as a classification of science, has ceased to be *mis*-understood as an aggregate of botany, zoölogy, geology and the like, and has become a thing intimate and familiar and rejuvenating.

There is no doubt that the estate of American letters is experiencing a renaissance. Formality, the old idols, the demi-gorgons and autocrats no longer hold an absolute authority. A multitude of false gods are clamoring for recognition, shouldering one another about to make room for their altars, soliciting incense as if it were patronage. No doubt these "draw many after them," but the "nature revival" has brought the galvanizing, vital element into this tumult of little inkling sham divinities and has shown that life is better than "literature," even if the "literature" be of human beings and the life be that of a faithful dog.

Vitality is the thing, after all. Dress the human puppet never so gayly, bedeck it never so brilliantly, pipe before it never so cunningly, and, fashioned in the image of God though it be, just so long as it is a puppet and not a person, just so long the great heart of the people will turn from it, in weariness and disgust, to find its interest in the fidelity of the sheep-dog of the North o' England, the intelligence of a prairie wolf of Colorado, or the death-fight of a bull moose in the timberlands of Ontario.

THE MECHANICS OF FICTION

WE approach a delicate subject. And if the manner of approach is too serious it will be very like the forty thousand men of the King of France who marched terribly and with banners to the top of the hill with the meagre achievement of simply getting there. Of all the arts, as one has previously observed, that of novel-writing is the least mechanical. Perhaps, after all, rightly so; still it is hard to escape some formality, some forms. There must always be chapter divisions; also a beginning and an end, which implies a middle; continuity, which implies movement, which in turn implies a greater speed or less, an accelerated, retarded or broken action; and before the scoffer is well aware he is admitting a multitude of set forms. No one who sets a thing in motion but keeps an eye and a hand upon its speed. No one who constructs but keeps watch upon the building, strengthening here, lightening there, here at the foundations cautious and conservative, there at the cornice fantastic and daring. In all human occupations, trades, arts or business, science, morals or religion, there exists, 'way at the bottom, a homogeneity and a certain family likeness, so that, quite possibly after all, the discussion of the importance of the mechanics of fiction may be something more than mere speculative sophistry.

A novel addresses itself primarily to a reader, and it has been so indisputably established that the reader's time and effort of attention must be economized that the fact need not be mentioned in this place—it would not economize the reader's time nor effort of attention.

Remains then the means to be considered, or, in other words, How best to tell your story.

It depends naturally upon the nature of the story. The formula which would apply to one would not be appropriate for another. That is very true, but at the same time it is hard to get away from that thing in any novel which is let us call the pivotal event All good novels have one. It is the peg upon which the fabric of the thing hangs, the nucleus around which the shifting drifts and currents must—suddenly—coagulate, the sudden releasing of the brake to permit for one instant the entire machinery to labor, full steam, ahead. Up to that point the action must lead; from it, it must decline.

But—and here one holds at least one mechanical problem—the approach, the leading up to this pivotal event, must be infinitely slower than the decline. For the reader's interest in the story centres around it, and once it is disposed of attention is apt to dwindle very rapidly—and thus back we go again to the economy proposition.

It is the slow approach, however, that tells. The unskilled, impatient of the tedium of meticulous elaboration, will rush at it in a furious gallop of short chapters and hurried episodes, so that he may come the sooner to the purple prose declamation and drama that he is sure he can handle with such tremendous effect.

Not so the masters. Watch them during the first third—say—of their novels. Nothing happens—or at least so you fancy. People come and go, plans are described, localities, neighborhoods; an incident crops up just for a second for which you can see no reason, a note sounds that is puzzlingly inappropriate. The novel continues. There seems to be no progress; again that perplexing note, but a little less perplexing. By now we are well into the story. There are no more new people, but the old ones come back again and again, and yet again; you remember them now after they are off the stage; you are more intimate with the two main characters. Then comes a series of petty incidents in which these two are prominent. The action still lags, but little by little you are getting more and more acquainted with these principal actors. Then perhaps comes the first acceleration of movement. The approach begins—ever so little—to rise, and that same note which seemed at first so out of tune sounds again and this time drops into place in the progression, beautifully harmonious, correlating the whole gamut. By now all the people are "on"; by now all the groundwork is prepared. You know the localities so well that you could find your way about among them in the dark; hero and heroine are intimate acquaintances.

Now the action begins to increase in speed. The complication suddenly tightens; all along the line there runs a sudden alert. An episode far back there in the first chapter, an episode with its appropriate group of characters, is brought forward and, coming suddenly to the front, collides with the main line of development and sends it off upon an untirely unlooked-for tangent. Another episode of the second chapter—let us suppose—all at once makes common cause with a more recent incident, and the two produce a wholly unlooked-for counter-influence which swerves the main theme in still another direction, and all this time the action is speeding faster and faster, the complication tightening and straining to the breaking point, and then at last a "motif" that has been in preparation ever since the first paragraph of the first chapter of the novel suddenly comes to a head, and in a twinkling the complication is solved with all the violence of an explosion, and the catastrophe, the climax, the pivotal event fairly leaps from the pages with a rush of action that leaves you stunned, breathless and overwhelmed with the sheer power of its presentation. And there is a master-work of fiction.

Reading, as the uninitiated do, without an eye to the mechanics, without a consciousness of the wires and wheels and cogs and springs of the affair, it seems inexplicable that these great scenes of fiction—short as they are—some of them less than a thousand words in length—should produce so tremendous an effect by such few words, such simple language; and that sorely overtaxed word, "genius," is made to do duty as the explanation. But the genius is rare that in one thousand simple words, taken by themselves, could achieve the effect—for instance—of the fight aboard "The Flying Scud" in Stevenson's "Wrecker." Taken by itself, the scene is hardly important except from the point of view of style and felicity of expression. It is the context of the story that makes it so tremendous, and because Osbourne and Stevenson prepared for that very scene from the novel's initial chapter.

And it seems as if there in a phrase one could resume the whole system of fiction mechanics—preparations of effect.

The unskilled will invariably attempt to atone for lack of such painstaking preparation for their "Grand Scenes" by hysteria, and by exclamation in presenting the catastrophe. They declaim, they shout stamp, shake their fists and flood the page with sonorous adjectives, call upon heaven and upon God. They summon to their aid every broken-down device to rouse the flaccid interest of the reader, and conclusively, irretrievably and ignominiously fail. It is too late for heroic effort then, and the reader, uninterested in the character, unfamiliar with the *locale*, unattracted by any charm of "atmosphere," lays down the book unperturbed and forgets it before dinner.

Where is the fault? Is it not in defective machinery? The

analogies are multitudinous. The liner with hastily constructed boilers will flounder when she comes to essay the storm; and no stoking however vigorous, no oiling however eager, if delayed till then, will avail to aid her to ride through successfully. It is not the time to strengthen a wall when the hurricane threatens; prop and stay will not brace it then. Then the thing that tells is the plodding, slow, patient, brick-by-brick work, that only half shows down there at the foot half-hidden in the grass, obscure, unnoted. No genius is necessary for this sort of work, only great patience and a willingness to plod, for the time being.

No one is expected to strike off the whole novel in one continued fine frenzy of inspiration. As well expect the stone-mason to plant his wall in a single day. Nor is it possible to lay down any rule of thumb, any hard-and-fast schedule in the matter of novel-writing. But no work is so ephemeral, so delicate, so—in a word—artistic that it can not be improved by systematizing.

There is at least one indisputably good manner in which the unskilled may order his work—besides the one of preparation already mentioned. He may consider each chapter as a unit, distinct, separate, having a definite beginning, rise, height and end, the action continuous, containing no break in time, the locality unchanged throughout—no shifting of the scene to another environment. Each chapter thus treated is a little work in itself, and the great story of the whole novel is told thus as it were in a series of pictures, the author supplying information as to what has intervened between the end of one chapter and the beginning of the next by suggestion or by actual *résumé*. As often as not the reader himself can fill up the gap by the context.

This may be over-artificial, and it is conceivable that there are times when it is necessary to throw artificiality to the winds. But it is the method that many of the greatest fiction writers have employed, and even a defective system is—at any rate, in fiction—better than none.

FICTION WRITING AS A BUSINESS

THE exaggerated and exalted ideas of the unenlightened upon this subject are, I have found, beyond all reason and beyond all belief. The superstition that with the publication of the first book comes fame and affluence is as firmly rooted as that other delusion which asks us to suppose that "a picture in the Paris Salon" is the certificate of success, ultimate, final, definite.

One knows, of course, that very naturally the "Eben Holden" and "David Harum" and "Richard Carvel" fellows made fortunes, and that these are out of the discussion; but also one chooses to assume that the average, honest, middle-class author supports himself and even a family by the sale of his novels—lives on his royalties.

Royalties! Why in the name of heaven were they called that, those microscopic sums that too, too often are less royal than beggarly? It has a fine sound—royalty. It fills the mouth. It can be said with an air—royalty. But there are plenty of these same royalties that will not pay the typewriter's bill.

Take an average case. No, that will not do, either, for the average published novel—I say it with my right hand raised—is irretrievably, hopelessly and conclusively, a financial failure.

Take, then, an unusually lucky instance, literally a novel whose success is extraordinary, a novel which has sold 2,500 copies. I repeat that this is an extraordinary success. Not one book out of fifteen will do as well. But let us consider it. The author has worked upon it for—at the very least—three months. It is published. Twenty-five hundred copies are sold. Then the sale stops. And by the word stop one means cessation in the completest sense of the word. There are people—I know plenty of them—who suppose that when a book is spoken of as having stopped selling, a generality is intended, that merely a falling off of the initial demand has occurred. Error. When a book—a novel—stops selling, it stops with the definiteness of an engine when the fire goes out. It stops with a suddenness that is appalling, and thereafter not a copy, not one single, solitary copy is sold. And do not for an instant suppose that ever after the interest may be revived. A dead book can no more be resuscitated than a dead dog.

But to go back. The 2,500 have been sold. The extraordinary, the marvelous has been achieved. What does the author get out of it? A royalty of ten per cent. Two hundred and fifty dollars for three months' hard work. Roughly less than $20 a week, a little more than $2.50 a day. An expert carpenter will easily make twice that, and the carpenter has infinitely the best of it in that he can keep the work up year in and year out, where the novelist must wait for a new idea, and the novel writer must then jockey and manœuvre for publication. Two novels a year is about as much as the writer can turn out and yet keep a marketable standard. Even admitting that both the novels sell 2,500 copies, there is only $500 of profit. In the same time the carpenter has made his $1,800, nearly four times as much. One may well ask the question: Is fiction writing a money-making profession?

The astonishing thing about the affair is that a novel may make a veritable stir, almost a sensation, and yet fail to sell very largely.

There is so-and-so's book. Everywhere you go you hear about it. Your friends have read it. It is in demand at the libraries. You don't pick up a paper that does not contain a review of the story in question. It is in the "Books of the Month" column. It is even, even—the pinnacle of achievement—in that shining roster, the list of best sellers of the week.

Why, of course, the author is growing rich! Ah, at last he has arrived! No doubt he will build a country house out of his royalties. Lucky fellow; one envies him.

Catch him unawares and what is he doing? As like as not writing unsigned book reviews at five dollars a week in order to pay his board bill—and glad of the chance.

It seems incredible. But one must remember this: That for every one person who buys a book there will be six who will talk about it. And the half-thousand odd reviewers who are writing of the book do not buy it, but receive "editorial" copies from the publishers, upon which no royalty is paid.

I know it for an undisputed fact that a certain novel which has ever been called the best American novel of the nineteenth century, and which upon publication was talked about, written about and even preached about, from the Atlantic to the Pacific, took ten years in which to attain the sale of 10,000 copies. Even so famous, so brilliant an author as Harold Frederic did not at first sell conspicuously. "That Lawton Girl," "The Copperhead," "Seth's Brother's Wife," masterpieces though they are, never made money for the writer. Each sold about 2,000 copies. Not until "Theron Ware" was published did Mr. Frederic reap his reward.

Even so great a name as that of George Meredith is not a "sesame," and only within the last few years has the author of "Evan Harrington" made more than five or six hundred dollars out of any one of his world-famous books.

But of course there is another side. For one thing, the author is put to no expense in the composing of his novel. (It is not always necessary to typewrite the manuscript.) The carpenter must invest much money in tools; must have a shop. Shop rent and tools repaired or replaced cut into his $1,800 of profit. Or take it in the fine arts. The painter must have a studio, canvases, models, brushes, a whole equipment; the architect must have his draughting room, the musician his instrument. But so far as initial expense is concerned, a half-dollar will buy every conceivable necessary tool the novelist may demand. He needs no office, shop or studio; models are not required. The libraries of the city offer him a quiet working place if the home is out of the question. Nor, as one has so often urged, is any expensive training necessary before his money-earning capacity is attained. The architect must buy instruction for many years. The painter must study in expensive studios, the musician must learn in costly conservatories, the singer must be taught by high-priced maestros. Furthermore, it is often necessary for the aspirant to travel great distances to reach the cities where his education is to be furthered; almost invariably a trip to and a residence in Europe is indispensable. It is a great undertaking and an expensive one to prepare for the professions named, and it takes years of time—years during which the aspirant is absolutely non-productive.

But the would-be novel writer may determine between breakfast and dinner to essay the plunge, buy (for a few cents) ink and paper between dinner and supper, and have the novel under way before bedtime.

How much of an outlay of money does his first marketable novel represent? Practically nothing. On the other hand, let us ask the same question of, say, the painter. How much money has he had to spend before he was able to paint his first marketable picture? To reach a total sum he must foot up the expenses of at least five years of instruction and study, the cost of living during that time, the cost of materials, perhaps even the price of a trip to Paris. Easily the sum may reach $5,000. Fifty cents' worth of ink and paper do not loom large beside this figure.

Then there are other ways in which the fiction writer may earn money—by fiction. The novelist may look down upon the mere writer of short stories, or may even look down upon himself in the same capacity, but as a rule the writer of short stories is the man who has the money. It is much easier to sell the average short story than the average novel. Infinitely easier. And the short story of the usual length will fetch $100. One thousand people—think of it—one thousand people must buy copies of your novel before it will earn so much for you. It takes three months to complete the novel—the novel that earns the $250. But with ingenuity the writer should be able to turn out six short stories in the same time, and if he has luck in placing them there is $600 earned—more than twice the sum made by the novel. So that the novelist may eke out the alarming brevity of his semi-annual statements by writing and selling "short stuff."

Then—so far as the novel is concerned—there is one compensation, one source of revenue which the writer enjoys, and which is, as a rule, closed to all others. Once the carpenter sells his piece of work it is sold for good and all. The painter has but one chance to make money from the sale of his picture. The architect receives payment for his design and there is the end. But the novelist—and one speaks now of the American—may sell the same work over many times. Of course, if the novel is a failure it is a failure, and no more is said. But suppose it is a salable, readable, brisk bit of narrative, with a swift action and rapid movement. Properly managed, this, under favorable conditions, might be its life history: First it is serialized either in the Sunday press or, less probably, in a weekly or monthly. Then it is made up into book form and sent over the course a second time. The original publisher sells sheets to a Toronto or Montreal house and a Canadian edition reaps a like harvest. It is not at all unlikely that a special cheap cloth edition may be bought and launched by some large retailer either of New York or Chicago. Then comes the paper edition—with small royalties, it is true, but based upon an enormous number of copies, for the usual paper edition is an affair of tens of thousands. Next the novel crosses the Atlantic and a small sale in England helps to swell the net returns, which again are added to—possibly—by the "colonial edition" which the English firm issues. Last of all comes the Tauchnitz edition, and with this (bar the improbable issuing of later special editions) the exploitation ceases. Eight separate times the same commodity has been sold, no one of the sales militating against the success of the other seven, the author getting his fair slice every time. Can any other trade, profession or art (excepting only the dramatist, which is, after all, a sister art) show the like? Even (speaking of the dramatist) there may be a ninth reincarnation of the same story and the creatures of the writer's pages stalk forth upon the boards in cloak and buskin.

And there are the indirect ways in which he may earn money. Some of his ilk there are who lecture. Nor are there found wanting those who read from their own works. Some write editorials or special articles in the magazines and newspapers with literary departments. But few of them have "princely" incomes.

THE "VOLUNTEER MANUSCRIPT"

At a conservative estimate there are 70,000,000 people in the United States. At a liberal estimate 100,000 of these have lost the use of both arms; remain then 69,900,000 who write novels. Indeed, many are called, but few—oh, what a scanty, skimped handful that few represent—are chosen!

The work of choosing these few, or rather of rejecting these many, devolves upon the manuscript readers for the baker's dozen of important New York publishing houses, and a strange work it is, and strange are the contributions that pass under their inspection.

As one not unfamiliar with the work of "reading," the present writer may offer a little seasonable advice.

1. First have your manuscript typewritten. The number of manuscripts is too great and the time too short to expect the reader to decipher script; and, besides, ideas presented or scenes described in type are infinitely more persuasive, more plausible than those set down in script. A good story typewritten will appear to better advantage; a poor one similarly treated seems less poverty-stricken.

2. Do not, by any manner of means, announce in a prefatory note that you "lay no claim to literary excellence," with the intention thereby of ingratiating yourself with regard to the "reader," winning him over by a parade of modesty. Invariably the statement is prejudicial, producing an effect exactly contrary to the one desired. It will make the mildest of "readers" angry. If you have no claims upon literary excellence, why in Heaven's name are you bothering him to read your work?

3. Inclose a forwarding address in case of rejection. This, seemingly, is superfluous advice. But it is astonishing how many manuscripts come in innocent even of the author's name, with never a scrap nor clew as to their proper destination.

4. Don't ask for criticism. The reader is not a critic. He passes only upon the availability of the manuscript for the uses of the publisher who employs him. And a manuscript of para-

mount literary quality may be rejected for any number of reasons, none of which have anything to do with its literary worth—or accepted for causes equally outside the domain of letters. Criticism is one thing, professional "reading" quite another.

5. Don't bother about "inclosing stamps for return." The manuscript will go back to you by c. o. d. express.

6. Don't submit a part of a manuscript. It is hard enough sometimes to judge the story as a whole, and no matter how discouraging the initial chapter may be the publisher will always ask to see the remaining portions before deciding.

7. Don't write to the publisher beforehand asking him if he will consider your manuscript. If it is a novel he will invariably express his willingness to consider it. How can he tell whether he wants it or not until he, through his "reader," has seen it?

8. Don't expect to get an answer much before a month. Especially if your story has merit, it must pass through many hands and be considered by many persons before judgment is rendered. The better it is the longer you will wait before getting a report.

9. Don't in Heaven's name, inclose commendatory letters written by your friends, favorable reviews by your pastor or by the president of the local college. The story will speak for itself more distinctly than any of your acquaintances.

10. Don't say you will revise or shorten to suit the tastes or judgment of the publisher. At best that's a servile humility that in itself is a confession of weakness and that will make you no friends at court.

11. Don't forward a letter of introduction, no matter from how near a friend of the publisher. The publisher will only turn the MS. over to his "readers," and with them the letter from a stranger carries no weight.

12. Don't write a Colonial novel.

13. Don't write a Down East novel.

14. Don't write a "Prisoner of Zenda" novel.

15. Don't write a novel.

16. Try to keep your friends from writing novels.

And of all the rules, one is almost tempted to declare that the last two are the most important. For to any one genuinely interested in finding "good stuff" in the ruck and run of volunteer manuscripts, nothing is more discouraging, nothing more apparently hopeless of ultimate success, than the consistent and uniform trashiness of the day's batch of submitted embryonic novels.

Infinitely better for their author had they never been written; infinitely better for him had he employed his labor—at the very least it is labor of three months—upon the trade or profession to which he was bred. It is very hard work to write a good novel, but it is much harder to write a bad one. Its very infelicity is a snare to the pen, its very clumsiness a constant demand for laborious boosting and propping.

And consider another and further word of advice—number 17, if you please. Don't go away with that popular idea that your manuscript will not be considered, or if really and undeniably good will be heedlessly rejected. Bad manuscripts are not read from cover to cover. The reader has not the right to waste his employer's time in such unremunerative diligence. Often a page or two will betray the hopelessness of the subsequent chapters, and no one will demand of the "reader" a perusal of a work that he knows will be declined in the end.

Nor was there ever a sincere and earnest effort that went unappreciated in a publisher's place of business. I have seen an entire office turned upside down by a "reader" who believed he had discovered among the batch of voluminous MS. something "really good, you know," and who almost forced a reading of the offering in question upon every member of the firm from the senior partner down to the assistant salesman.

As a rule, all manuscripts follow the same routine. From the clerk who receives them at the hands of the expressman they go to the recorder, who notes the title, address, and date of arrival, and also, after turning them over to the junior reader, the fact of the transfer. The junior reader's report upon the manuscript is turned in to one of the members of the firm, whose decision is final. The manuscript itself goes up to the senior reader, who also reports upon it to the firm member. If both reports are unfavorable, this latter directs the manuscript to be returned with or without a personal letter, as he deems proper. If both the readers' reports are favorable, or even if one is sufficiently laudatory, he calls for the manuscript and reads it himself. If he disagrees with the readers' reports, the manuscript is declined. If not, he passes the manuscript on to one of the partners of the house, who also reads it. The two "talk it over," and out of the conference comes the ultimate decision in the matter.

Sometimes the circulation manager and head salesman are consulted to decide whether or not—putting all questions of the book's literary merits aside—the "thing will sell." And doubt not for a moment that their counsel carries weight.

Another feature of the business which it is very well to remember is that all publishers can not be held responsible for the loss of or damage to unsolicited manuscripts. If you submit the MS. of a novel you do it at your own risk, and the carelessness of an office-boy may lose for you the work of many months—years, even; work that you could never do over again. You could demand legally no reparation. The publishers are not responsible. Only in a case where a letter signed by one of the "heads" has been sent to the author requesting that the manuscript be forwarded does the situation become complicated. But in the case of an unknown writer the monetary value of his work in a court of law would be extremely difficult to place, and even if an award of damages could be extorted it would hardly more than pay the typewriter's bill.

But the loss of manuscript may be of serious import to the publisher for all that. That reputation for negligence in the matter of handling unsolicited matter fastens upon a firm with amazing rapidity. Bothersome as the number of volunteer manuscripts are, they do—to a certain extent—gauge the importance of a given concern. And as they arrive in constantly increasing quantities, the house may know that it is growing in favor and in reputation: and so a marked falling off reverses the situation. Writers will be naturally averse to submitting manuscripts to offices which are known to be careless. And I know of at least one instance where the loss of a couple of manuscripts within a month produced a marked effect upon the influx of the volunteers. Somehow the news of the loss always gets out, and spreads by some mysterious means till it is heard of from strangely remote quarters. The author will, of course, tell his friends of the calamity, and will make more ado over the matter than if his story was accepted. Of course, this particular story is the one great masterpiece of his career; the crass stupidity of the proud and haughty publisher has ruined his chance of success, and the warning: "Don't send your stuff to that firm. It will be lost!" is passed on all along the line. So that repeated instances of the negligence may in the end embarrass the publisher, and the real masterpiece, the first novel of a New Man, goes to a rival.

I have in mind one case where a manuscript was lost under peculiarly distressing circumstances. The "reader," who had his office in the editorial rooms of a certain important house of New York, was on a certain day called to the reception room to interview one of the host of writers who came daily to submit their offerings in person.

In this case the reader confronted a little gentleman in the transition period of genteel decay. He was a Frenchman. His mustache, tight, trim, and waxed, was white. The frock coat was buttoned only at the waist; a silk handkerchief puffed from the pocket, and a dried carnation, lamentably faded, that had done duty for many days, enlivened with a feeble effort the worn silk lapel.

But the innate French effervescence, debonair, *insouciant,* was not gone yet. The little gentleman presented a card. Of course the name boasted that humblest of titles—baron. The Baron, it appeared, propitiated destiny by "Instruction in French, German, and Italian," but now instruction was no longer propitious. With a deprecating giggle this was explained; the Baron did not wish to make the "reader" feel bad—to embarrass him.

"I will probably starve very soon," he observed, still with the modifying little giggle, and, of course, the inevitable shrug, "unless—my faith—something turns up."

It was to be turned up, evidently, by means of an attenuated manuscript which he presented. He had written—during the intervals of instruction—a series of articles on the character of Americans as seen by a Frenchman, and these had been published by a newspaper of the town in which he instructed—an absolutely obscure town, lost and forgotten, away up among the New Hampshire hills.

The articles, he insinuated, might be made into a book—a book that might be interesting to the great American public. And, with a *naiveté* that was absolutely staggering, he assumed without question that the firm would publish his book—that it was really an important contribution to American literature.

He would admit that he had not been paid very liberally by the country paper for the articles as they appeared. He was not Emile Zola. If he was he might have sold his articles at fifteen or twenty dollars each.

He said just that. Think of it! The poor little Instructor-Baron Zola! Fifteen dollars! Well!

He left the articles—neatly cut out and pasted in a copy-book —with the "reader," and gave as his address a dreadfully obscure hotel.

The "reader" could not make up his mouth to tell him, even before looking over the first paragraph of the first article, that as a book the commercial value of the offering was absolutely, irrevocably, and hopelessly nil, and so the little manuscript went into the mill—and in two days was lost.

I suppose that never in the history of that particular firm was the search for a missing manuscript prosecuted with half the energy or ardor that ensued upon the discovery of this particular loss. From the desk-files of the senior partner to the shipping-slips of the packer's assistant the hunt proceeded—and all in vain.

Meanwhile the day approached on which the Baron was to come for his answer and at last it arrived, and promptly at the appointed hour the poor little card with the hyphenated titled name written carefully and with beautiful flourishes in diluted ink was handed in.

Do you know what the publisher did? He wrote the absurd, pompous name across the order line of a check and signed his own name underneath, and the check was for an amount that would make even unpropitious Destiny take off his hat and bow politely.

And I tell you that my little Instructor-Baron, with eminent good-humor, but with the grand manner of a *Maréchal du royaume* waved it aside. Turenne could have been no more magnificent. (They do order these matters better in France.) His whole concern—hunger-pinched as he may easily have been at the very moment—his whole concern was to put the embarrassed publisher at his ease, to make this difficulty less difficult.

He assured him that his articles were written *comme-ci comme-ca,* for his own amusement, that he could not think of accepting, etc.

And I like to remember that this whole affair, just as if it had been prepared in advance for a popular magazine whose editor insisted upon "happy endings," did end well, and the publisher, who at the moment was involved in the intricacies of a vast correspondence with a Parisian publishing house, found a small position as translator in one of his sub-departments for the little Instructor-Baron who had the great good fortune to suffer the loss of a manuscript—in the right place.

And now the card—engraved, if you please—bears proudly the Baron's name, supported by the inscription, "Official Translator and Director of Foreign Correspondence to the Firm of —— & Co., Publishers."

RETAIL BOOKSELLER: LITERARY DICTATOR

Of all the various and different kinds and characters of people who are concerned in the writing and making of a novel, including the author, the publisher, the critic, the salesman, the advertisement writer, the drummer—of all this "array of talent," as the billboards put it, which one has the most influence in the success of the book? Who, of all these, can, if he chooses, help or hurt the sales the most?—assuming for the moment that sales are the index of success, the kind of success that at the instant we are interested in.

Each one of these people has his followers and champions. There are not found wanting those who say the publisher is the all-in-all. And again it is said that a critic of authority can make a book by a good review or ruin it by an unfavorable one. The salesman, others will tell you—he who is closest allied to the money transaction—can exert the all-powerful influence. Or again, surely in this day of exploitation and publicity the man who concocts great "ads" is the important one.

The author is next included. He can do no more than write the book, and as good books have failed and bad ones have succeeded—always considering failure and success in their most sordid meanings—the mere writing need not figure. But the fact remains that there are cases where publishers have exerted every device to start a book and still have known it to remain upon their hands; that critics have raved to heaven or damned to hell, and the novel has fallen or flown in spite and not because of them; that salesmen have cajoled and schemed, and yet have returned with unfilled orders, and that advertisements that have clamored so loudly that even they who ran must have read, and yet the novel in question remained inert, immovable, a failure, a "plug."

All these, then, have been tried and at times have been found wanting. There yet remains one exponent of the business of distributing fiction who has not been considered. He, one claims, can do more than any or all of the gentlemen just mentioned to launch or strand a novel.

Now let it be understood that by no possible manner of means does one consider him infallible. Again and again have his best efforts come to nothing. This, however, is what is claimed: he has more influence on success or failure than any of the others. And who is he?

The retailer. One can almost affirm that he is a determining factor in American fiction; that, in a limited sense, with him, his is the future. Author, critic, analyst and essayist may hug to themselves a delusive phantom of hope that they are the molders of public opinion, they and they alone. That may be, sometimes. But consider the toiling and spinning retailer. What does the failure or success of the novel mean to the critic? Nothing more than a minute and indefinite increase or decrease of prestige. The publisher who has many books upon his list may recoup himself on one failure by a compensating success. The salesman's pay goes on just the same whether his order slips are full or blank; likewise the stipend of the writer of "ads." The author has no more to lose—materially—than the price of ink and paper. But to the retail bookseller a success means money made; failure, money lost. If he can dispose of an order of fifty books he is ahead by calculable, definite, concrete profits. If he can not dispose of the fifty his loss is equally calculable, equally definite, equally concrete. Naturally, being a business man, he is a cautious man. He will not order a book which he deems unsalable, but he will lay in a stock of one that promises returns. Through him the book is distributed to the public. If he has a book in stock, the public gets it. If he does not have it, the public goes without. The verdict of the public is the essential to popularity or unpopularity, and the public can only pass verdict upon what it has read. The connection seems clear and the proposition proved that the retail bookseller is an almost paramount influence in American literature.

It is interesting to see what follows from this and to note how the retailer in the end can effectually throttle the sham novelist who has fooled the public once. Were it not for the retailer, the sham novelist would get an indefinite number of chances for his life; but so long as the small book-dealer lives and acts, just so long will bad work—and one means by this wholly bad, admittedly bad, hopelessly bad work—fail to trick the reading public twice. Observe now the working of it. Let us take a typical case. A story by an unknown writer is published. By strenuous exploitation the publishers start a vogue. The book begins to sell. The retailer, observing the campaign of publicity managed by the publishers, stocks up with the volume; surely when the publishers are backing the thing so strong it will be a safe venture; surely the demand will be great. It does prove a safe venture; the demand is great; the retailer disposes of fifty, then of a second order of one hundred, then of two hundred, then of five hundred. The book is now in the hands of the public. It is read and found sadly, sadly wanting. It is not a good story; it is trivial; it is insincere. Far and wide the story is condemned.

Meanwhile the unknown writer, now become famous, is writing a second novel. It is finished, issued, and the salesman who travels for the publishers begins to place his orders. The retailer, remembering the success of this author's past venture, readily places a large order. Two hundred is not, in his opinion, an overstock. So it goes all over the country. Returns are made to the author, and he sees that some fifty thousand have been sold. Encouraging, is it not? Yes, fifty thousand have been sold—by the publisher to the retailer; but here is the point—not by the retailer to the public. Of the two hundred our dealer took from the publisher's traveling salesman, one hundred and ninety yet remain upon his counters. The public, fooled once, on the first over-praised, over-exploited book, refuse to be taken in a second time. Who is the loser now? Not the author, who draws royalties on copies sold to the tradesman—the retailer; not the publisher, who makes his profit out of the same transaction; but the retailer, who is loaded down with an unsalable article.

Meanwhile our author writes his third novel. So far as he can see, his second book is as great a popular success as his first. His semi-annual statements are there to show it—there it is in black and white; figures can't lie. The third novel is finished and launched. At the end of the first six months after publication day the author gets his publisher's statement of sales. Instead of the expected 10,000 copies sold, behold the figure is a bare 1,500. At the end of the second six months the statement shows about 250. The book has failed. Why? Because the retailer refuses to order it. He has said to the soliciting salesman, "Why should I, in Heaven's name, take a third book by this man when I have yet one hundred and ninety copies of his second novel yet to sell?"

It is hard for the salesman to controvert that argument. He may argue that the third book is a masterpiece, and—mark this—it may in fact be a veritable, actual masterpiece, a wonderful contribution to the world's literature; it is all of no effect. There stands the block of unsold books, 190 strong, and all the eloquence in the world will not argue them off the counter. After this our author's publisher will have none of his books. Even if he writes a fourth and submits it, the publisher incontinently declines it. This author is no longer a "business proposition."

There can not but be an element of satisfaction in all this, and a source of comfort to those who take the welfare of their country's literature seriously to heart. The sham novelist who is in literature (what shall we say?) "for his own pocket every time" sooner or later meets the wave of reaction that he can not stem nor turn and under which he and his sham are conclusively, definitely, and irrevocably buried. Observe how it works out all down the line. He fools himself all of the time, he fools the publisher three times, he fools the retail dealer twice, and he fools the Great American Public just exactly once.

AN AMERICAN SCHOOL OF FICTION?

IT seems to me that it is a proposition not difficult of demonstration that the United States of America has never been able to boast of a school of fiction distinctively its own. And this is all the more singular when one considers that in all other activities Americans are peculiarly independent in thought and in deed, and have acquired abroad a reputation—even a notoriety—for being original.

In the mechanical arts, in the industries, in politics, in business methods, in diplomacy, in shipbuilding, in war, even in dentistry, if you please—even in the matter of riding race-horses—Americans have evolved their own methods, quite different from European methods.

Hardy and adventurous enough upon all other lines, disdainful of conventions, contemptuous of ancient custom, we yet lag behind in the arts—slow to venture from the path blazed long ago by Old World masters.

It is pre-eminently so in the fine arts. No sooner does an American resolve upon a career of painting, sculpture, or architecture than straight he departs for Paris, the Beaux Arts and the Julien atelier; and, his education finished, returns to propagate French ideas, French methods; and our best paintings to-day are more French than American; French in conception, in composition, in technique and treatment.

I suppose that the nearest we ever came to an organized school of native-born Americans, writing about American things from an American point of view, was in the days of Lowell, Longfellow, Holmes, Whittier, and the rest of that illustrious company. But observe: How is this group spoken of and known to literature? Not as the American school, but as the New England school. Even the appellation "New" England as differentiated from "old" England is significant. And New England is not America.

Hawthorne, it will be urged, is a great name among American

writers of fiction. Not peculiarly American, however. Not so distinctively and unequivocally as to lay claim to a vigorous original Americanism. "The Scarlet Letter" is not an American story, but rather a story of an English colony on North American soil. "The Marble Faun" is frankly and unreservedly foreign. Even the other novels were pictures of a very limited and circumscribed life—the life of New England again.

Cooper, you will say, was certainly American in attitude and choice of subject; none more so. None less, none less American. As a novelist he is saturated with the romance of the contemporary English story-tellers. It is true that his background is American. But his heroes and heroines talk like the characters out of Bulwer in their most vehement moods, while his Indians stalk through all the melodramatic tableaux of Byron, and declaim in the periods of the border noblemen in the pages of Walter Scott.

Poe we may leave out of classification; he shone in every branch of literature but that of novel-writing. Bret Harte was a writer of short stories and—oh, the pity of it, the folly of it!—abandoned the field with hardly more than a mere surface-scratching.

There can be no doubt that had Mr. Henry James remained in America he would have been our very best writer. If he has been able to seize the character and characteristics so forcibly of a people like the English, foreign to him, different, unfamiliar, what might he not have done in the very midst of his own countrymen, into whose company he was born, reared and educated? All the finish of style, the marvelous felicity of expression would still have been his, and at the same time, by the very nature of the life he lived and wrote about, the concrete, the vigorous, the simple direct action would have become a part of his work, instead of the present ultimate vagueness and indecision that so mars and retards it.

Of all the larger names remain only those of Mr. Howells and Mr. Clemens. But as the novelists, as such, are under consideration, even Mark Twain may be left out of the discussion. American to the core, posterity will yet know him not as a novel-writer, but as a humorist. Mr. Howells alone is left, then, after the elimination is complete. Of all producers of American fiction he has had the broadest vision, at once a New Englander and a New Yorker, an Easterner and—in the Eastern sense—a Westerner. But one swallow does not make a summer, nor does one writer constitute a "school." Mr. Howells has had no successors. Instead, just as we had with "Lapham" and "The Modern Instance" laid the foundation of fine, hardy literature, that promised to be our very, very own, we commence to build upon it a whole confused congeries of borrowed, faked, pilfered romanticisms, building a crumbling gothic into a masonry of honest brownstone, or foisting colonial porticos upon façades of Montpelier granite, and I can not allow this occasion to pass without protest against what I am sure every serious-minded reader must consider a lamentable discrowning.

Of the latter-day fiction writers Miss Wilkins had more than all others convinced her public of her sincerity. Her field was her own; the place was ceded to her. No other novelist could invade her domain and escape the censure that attaches to imitation. Her public was loyal to her because it believed in her, and it was a foregone conclusion that she would be loyal to it.

More than this: A writer who occupies so eminent a place as Miss Wilkins, who has become so important, who has exerted and still can exert so strong an influence, cannot escape the responsibilities of her position. She can not belong wholly to herself, can not be wholly independent. She owes a duty to the literature of her native country.

Yet in spite of all this, and in spite of the fact that those who believe in the future of our nation's letters look to such established reputations as hers to keep the faith, to protest, though it is only by their attitude, silently and with dignity, against corruptions, degradations; in spite of all this, and in the heyday of her power, Miss Wilkins chooses to succumb to the momentary, transitory set of the tide, and, forsaking her own particular work, puts forth, one of a hundred others, a "colonial romance." It is a discrowning. It can be considered as no less. A deliberate capitulation to the clamor of the multitude. Possibly the novelist was sincere, but it is perilously improbable that she would have written her "Colonial Romance" had not "colonial romances" been the fashion. On the face of it Miss Wilkins has laid herself open to a suspicion of disingenuousness that every honest critic can only deplore. Even with all the sincerity in the world she had not the right to imperil the faith of her public, to undermine its confidence in her. She was one of the leaders. It is as if a captain, during action, had deserted to the enemy.

It could not have been even for the baser consideration of money. With her success assured in advance Miss Wilkins can be above such influences. Nor of fame. Surely no great distinction centres upon writers of "colonial romances" of late. Only the author herself may know her motives, but we who looked to her to keep the standard firm—and high—have now to regret the misfortune of a leader lost, a cause weakened.

However, it is a question after all if a "school," understood in the European sense of the word, is possible for America just yet. France has had its schools of naturalism and romance, Russia its schools of realism, England its schools of psychologists. But France, Russia, and England now, after so many centuries of growth, may be considered as units. Certain tendencies influence each one over its whole geographical extent at the same time. Its peoples have been welded together to a certain homogeneousness. It is under such conditions that "schools" of fiction, of philosophy, of science and the like arise.

But the United States are not yet, in the European sense, united. We have existed as a nation hardly more than a generation and during that time our peoples have increased largely by emigration. From all over the globe different races have been pouring in upon us. The North has been settled under one system, the South under another, the Middle West under another, the East under another. South Central and Far West under still others. There is no homogeneousness among us as yet.

The Westerner thinks along different lines from the Easterner and arrives at different conclusions. What is true of California is false of New York. Mr. Cable's picture of life is a far different thing than that of Mr. Howells.

The school of fiction American in thought, in purpose, and in standard. But no such thing is possible to-day for American writers. Mr. Hamlin Garland could not merge his personality nor pool his ideals with Edith Wharton. Their conceptions of art are as different as the conditions of life they study in their books.

The school of fiction American in thought, in purpose, and in treatment will come in time, inevitably. Meanwhile the best we can expect of the leaders is to remain steadfast, to keep unequivocally to the metes and bounds of the vineyards of their labors; no trespassing, no borrowing, no filching of the grapes of another man's vines. The cultivation of one's own vine is quite sufficient for all energy. We want these vines to grow—in time—to take root deep in American soil so that by and by the fruit shall be all of our own growing.

We do not want—distinctly and vehemently we do not want—the vine-grower to leave his own grapes to rot while he flies off to the gathering of—what? The sodden lees of an ancient crushing.

NOVELISTS OF THE FUTURE

It seems to me that a great deal could be said on this subject—a great deal that has not been said before. There are so many novelists these latter days, so many whose works show that they have had no training, and it does seem that so long as the fiction writers of the United States go fumbling and stumbling along in this undisciplined fashion, governed by no rule, observing no formula, setting for themselves no equation to solve, that just so long shall we be far from the desirable thing—an American school of fiction. Just now (let us say that it is a pity) we have no school at all. We acknowledge no master, and we are playing at truant, incorrigible, unmanageable, sailing paper boats in the creek behind the schoolhouse, or fishing with bent pins in the pools and shallows of popular favor. That some catch goldfish there is no great matter, and is no excuse for the truancy. We are not there for the goldfish, if you please, but to remain in the school at work till we have been summoned to stand up in our places and tell the master what we have learned.

There's where we should be, and if we do not observe the rules and conform to some degree of order, we should be rapped on the knuckles or soundly clumped on the head, and by vigorous discipline taught to know that formulas (a—b; a+b) are important things for us to observe, and that each and all of us should address ourselves with all diligence to finding the value of x in our problems.

It is the class in the Production of Original Fiction which of all the school contains the most truants. Indeed, its members believe that schooling for them is unnecessary. Not so with the other classes. Not one single member of any single one of them who does not believe that he must study first if he would produce afterward. Observe, there on the lower benches, the assiduous little would-be carpenters and stone-masons; how carefully they con their tables of measurement, their squares and compasses. "Ah, the toilers," you say, "the grubby manual fellows—of course they must learn their trade!"

Very well, then. Consider—higher up the class, on the very front row of benches—the Fine Arts row, the little painters and architects and musicians and actors of the future. See how painfully they study, and study and study. The little stone-mason will graduate in a few months; but for these others of the Fine Arts classes there is no such thing as graduation. For them there shall never be a diploma, signed and sealed, giving them the right to call themselves perfected at their work. All their lives they shall be students. In the vacations—maybe—they write, or build, or sing, or act, but soon again they are back to the benches, studying, studying always; working as never carpenter or stone-mason worked. Now and then they get a little medal, a bit of gold and enamel, a bow of ribbon, that is all; the stone-mason would disdain it, would seek it for the value of the metal in it. The Fine Arts people treasure it as the veteran treasures his cross.

And these little medals you—the truants, the bad boys of the paper boats and the goldfish—you want them, too; you claim them and clamor for them. You who declare that no study is necessary for you; you who are not content with your catch of goldfish, you must have the bits of ribbon and enamel, too. Have you deserved them? Have you worked for them? Have you found the value of x in your equation? Have you solved the parenthesis of your problem? Have you ever done the problem at all? Have you even glanced or guessed at the equation? The shame of it be upon you! Come in from the goldfish and go to work, or stay altogether at the fishing and admit that you are not deserving of the medal which the master gives as a reward of merit.

"But there are no books that we can study," you contest. "The architect and the musician, the painter and the actor—all of these have books ready to hand; they can learn from codified, systematized knowledge. For the novelist, where is there a cut-and-dried science that he can learn that will help him?"

And that is a good contention. No, there are no such books. Of all the arts, the art of fiction has no handbook. By no man's teaching can we learn the knack of putting a novel together in the best way. No one has ever risen to say, "Here is how the plan should be; thus and so should run the outline."

We admit the fact, but neither does that excuse the goldfishing and the paper-boat business. Some day the handbook may be compiled—it is quite possible—but meanwhile, and, *faute de mieux*, there is that which you may study better than all handbooks.

Observe, now. Observe, for instance, the little painter scholars. On the fly-leaves of their schoolbooks they are making pictures—of what? Remember it, remember it and remember it—of the people around them. So is the actor, so the musician—all of the occupants of the Fine Arts bench. They are studying one another quite as much as their books—even more—and they will tell you that it is the most important course in the curriculum.

You—the truant little would-be novelist—you can do this, quite as easily as they, and for you it is all the more important, for you must make up for the intimate knowledge of your fellows what you are forced to lack in the ignorance of forms. But you can not get this knowledge out there behind the schoolhouse—hooking gold-fish. Come in at the tap of the bell and, though you have no books, make pictures on your slate, pictures of the Fine Arts bench struggling all their lives for the foolish little medals, pictures of the grubby little boys in the stone-mason's corner, jeering the art classes for their empty toiling. The more you make these pictures, the better you shall do them. That is the kind of studying you can do, and from the study of your fellows you shall learn more than from the study of all the text-books that ever will be written.

But to do this you must learn to sit very quiet, and be very watchful, and so train your eyes and ears that every sound and every sight shall be significant to you and shall supply all the deficiency made by the absence of text-books.

This, then, to drop a very protracted allegory, seems to be the proper training of the novelist: The achieving less of an aggressive faculty of research than of an attitude of mind—a receptivity, an acute sensitiveness. And this can be acquired.

But it can not be acquired by shutting one's self in one's closet, by a withdrawal from the world, and that, so it would appear, is just the mistake so many would-be fiction writers allow themselves. They would make the art of the novelist an aristocracy, a thing exclusive, to be guarded from contact with the vulgar, humdrum, bread-and-butter business of life, to be kept unspotted from the world, considering it the result of inspirations, of exaltations, of subtleties and—above all things—of refinement, a sort of velvet jacket affair, a studio hocus-pocus, a thing loved of women and of æsthetes.

What a folly! Of all the arts it is the most virile; of all the arts it will not, will not, will not flourish indoors. Dependent solely upon fidelity to life for existence, it must be practiced in the very heart's heart of life, on the street corner, in the market-place, not in the studios. God enlighten us! It is not an affair of women and æsthetes, and the Muse of American fiction is no chaste, delicate, superfine mademoiselle of delicate poses and "elegant" attitudinizings, but a robust, red-armed *bonne femme,* who rough-shoulders her way among men and among affairs, who finds a healthy pleasure in the jostlings of the mob and a hearty delight in the honest, rough-and-tumble, Anglo-Saxon give-and-take knockabout that for us means life. Choose her, instead of the sallow, pale-faced statue-creature, with the foolish tablets and foolish, upturned eyes, and she will lead you as brave a march as ever drum tapped to. Stay at her elbow and obey her as she tells you to open your eyes and ears and heart, and as you go she will show things wonderful beyond wonder in this great, new, blessed country of ours, will show you a life untouched, untried, full of new blood and promise and vigor.

She is a Child of the People, this Muse of our Fiction of the future, and the wind of a new country, a new heaven and a new earth is in her face and has blown her hair from out the fillets that the Old World muse has bound across her brow, so that it is all in disarray. The tan of the sun is on her cheeks, and the dust of the highway is thick upon her buskin, and the elbowing of many men has torn the robe of her, and her hands are hard with the grip of many things. She is hail-fellow-well-met with every one she meets, unashamed to know the clown and unashamed to face the king, a hardy, vigorous girl, with an arm as strong as a man's and a heart as sensitive as a child's.

Believe me, she will lead you far from the studios and the æsthetes, the velvet jackets and the uncut hair, far from the sexless creatures who cultivate their little art of writing as the fancier cultivates his orchid. Tramping along, then, with a stride that will tax your best paces, she will lead you—if you are humble with her and honest with her—straight into a World of Working Men, crude of speech, swift of action, strong of passion, straight to the heart of a new life, on the borders of a new time, and there and there only will you learn to know the stuff of which must come the American fiction of the future.

A PLEA FOR ROMANTIC FICTION

LET us at the start make a distinction. Observe that one speaks of romanticism and not sentimentalism. One claims that the latter is as distinct from the former as is that other form of art which is called Realism. Romance has been often put upon and overburdened by being forced to bear the onus of abuse that by right should fall to sentiment; but the two should be kept very distinct, for a very high and illustrious place will be claimed for romance, while sentiment will be handed down the scullery stairs.

Many people to-day are composing mere sentimentalism, and calling it and causing it to be called romance; so with those who are too busy to think much upon these subjects, but who none the less love honest literature, Romance, too, has fallen into disrepute. Consider now the cut-and-thrust stories. They are all labeled Romances, and it is very easy to get the impression that Romance must be an affair of cloaks and daggers, or moonlight and golden hair. But this is not so at all. The true Romance is a more serious business than this. It is not merely a conjurer's trick-box full of flimsy quackeries, tinsel and claptraps, meant only to amuse, and relying upon deception to do even that. Is it not something better than this? Can we not see in it an instrument, keen, finely tempered, flawless—an instrument with which we may go straight through the clothes and tissues and wrappings of flesh down deep into the red, living heart of things?

Is all this too subtle, too merely speculative and intrinsic, too *precieuse* and nice and "literary"? Devoutly one hopes the contrary. So much is made of so-called Romanticism in present-day fiction that the subject seems worthy of discussion, and a protest against the misuse of a really noble and honest formula of literature appears to be timely—misuse, that is, in the sense of limited use. Let us suppose for the moment that a romance can be made out of a cut-and-thrust business. Good Heavens, are there no other things that are romantic, even in this—falsely, falsely called—humdrum world of to-day? Why should it be that so soon as the novelist addresses himself—seriously—to the consideration of contemporary life he must abandon Romance and take up the harsh, loveless, colorless, blunt tool called Realism?

Now, let us understand at once what is meant by Romance and what by Realism. Romance, I take it, is the kind of fiction that takes cognizance of variations from the type of normal life. Realism is the kind of fiction that confines itself to the type of normal life. According to this definition, then, Romance may even treat of the sordid, the unlovely—as, for instance, the novels of M. Zola. (Zola has been dubbed a Realist, but he is, on the contrary, the very head of the Romanticists.) Also, Realism, used as it sometimes is as a term of reproach, need not be in the remotest sense or degree offensive, but on the other hand respectable as a church and proper as a deacon—as, for instance, the novels of Mr. Howells.

The reason why one claims so much for Romance, and quarrels so pointedly with Realism, is that Realism stultifies itself. It notes only the surface of things. For it, Beauty is not even skin deep, but only a geometrical plane, without dimensions and depth, a mere outside. Realism is very excellent so far as it goes, but it goes no further than the Realist himself can actually see, or actually hear. Realism is minute; it is the drama of a broken teacup, the tragedy of a walk down the block, the excitement of an afternoon call, the adventure of an invitation to dinner. It is the visit to my neighbor's house, a formal visit, from which I may draw no conclusions. I see my neighbor and his friends—very, oh, such very! probable people—and that is all. Realism bows upon the doormat and goes away and says to me, as we link arms on the sidewalk: "That is life." And I say it is not. It is not, as you would very well see if you took Romance with you to call upon your neighbor.

Lately you have been taking Romance a weary journey across the water—ages and the flood of years—and haling her into the fuzzy, musty, worm-eaten, moth-riddled, rust-corroded "Grandes Salles" of the Middle Ages and the Renaissance, and she has found the drama of a bygone age for you there. But would you take her across the street to your neighbor's front parlor (with the bisque fisher-boy on the mantel and the photograph of Niagara Falls on glass hanging in the front window); would you introduce her there? Not you. Would you take a walk with her on Fifth Avenue, or Beacon Street, or Michigan Avenue? No, indeed. Would you choose her for a companion of a morning spent in Wall Street, or an afternoon in the Waldorf-Astoria? You just guess you would not.

She would be out of place, you say—inappropriate. She might be awkward in my neighbor's front parlor, and knock over the little bisque fisher-boy. Well, she might. If she did, you might find underneath the base of the statuette, hidden away, tucked away—what? God knows. But something that would be a complete revelation of my neighbor's secretest life.

So you think Romance would stop in the front parlor and discuss medicated flannels and mineral waters with the ladies! Not for more than five minutes. She would be off upstairs with you, prying, peeping, peering into the closets of the bedroom, into the nursery, into the sitting-room; yes, and into that little iron box screwed to the lower shelf of the closet in the library; and into those compartments and pigeon-holes of the *secretaire* in the study. She would find a heartache (maybe) between the pillows of the mistress's bed, and a memory carefully secreted in the master's deed-box. She would come upon a great hope amid the books and papers of the study-table of the young man's room, and—perhaps— who knows?—an affair, or, great Heavens, an intrigue, in the scented ribbons and gloves and hairpins of the young lady's bureau. And she would pick here a little and there a little, making up a bag of hopes and fears and a package of joys and sorrows—great ones, mind you—and then come down to the front door, and, stepping out into the street, hand you the bags and package and say to you— "That is Life!"

Romance does very well in the castles of the Middle Ages and the Renaissance chateaux, and she has the *entrée* there and is very well received. That is all well and good. But let us protest against limiting her to such places and such times. You will find her, I grant you, in the chatelaine's chamber and the dungeon of the man-at-arms; but, if you choose to look for her, you will find her equally at home in the brownstone house on the corner and in the office building downtown. And this very day, in this very hour, she is sitting among the rags and wretchedness, the dirt and despair of the tenements of the East Side of New York.

"What?" I hear you say, "look for Romance—the lady of the silken robes and golden crown, our beautiful, chaste maiden of soft voice and gentle eyes—look for her among the vicious ruffians, male and female, of Allen Street and Mulberry Bend?" I tell you she is there, and to your shame be it said you will not know her in those surroundings. You, the aristocrats, who demand the fine linen and the purple in your fiction; you, the sensitive, the delicate, who will associate with your Romance only so long as she wears a silken gown. You will not follow her to the slums, for you believe that Romance should only amuse and entertain you, singing you sweet songs and touching the harp of silver strings with rosy-tipped fingers. If haply she should call to you from the squalor of a dive, or the awful degradation of a disorderly house, crying: "Look! listen! This, too, is life. These, too, are my children! Look at them, know them and, knowing, help!" Should she call thus you would stop your ears; you would avert your eyes and you would answer, "Come from there, Romance. Your place is not there!" And you would make of her a harlequin, a tumbler, a sword-dancer, when, as a matter of fact, she should be by right divine a teacher sent from God.

She will not often wear the robe of silk, the golden crown, the jeweled shoon; will not always sweep the silver harp. An iron note is hers if so she choose, and coarse garments, and stained hands; and, meeting her thus, it is for you to know her as she passes—know her for the same young queen of the blue mantle and lilies. She can teach you if you will be humble to learn—teach you by showing. God help you if at last you take from Romance her mission of teaching; if you do not believe that she has a purpose—a nobler purpose and a mightier than mere amusement, mere entertainment. Let Realism do the entertainment with its meticulous presentation of teacups, rag carpets, wall-paper and haircloth sofas, stopping with these, going no deeper than it sees, choosing the ordinary, the untroubled, the commonplace.

But to Romance belongs the wide world for range, and the unplumbed depths of the human heart, and the mystery of sex, and the problems of life, and the black, unsearched penetralia of the soul of man. You, the indolent, must not always be amused. What matter the silken clothes, what matter the prince's houses? Romance, too, is a teacher, and if—throwing aside the purple—she wears the camel's-hair and feeds upon the locusts, it is to cry aloud unto the people, "Prepare ye the way of the Lord; make straight his path."

A PROBLEM IN FICTION

So many people—writers more especially—claim stridently and with a deal of gesturing that because a thing has happened it is therefore true. They have written a story, let us say, and they bring it to you to criticise. You lay your finger upon a certain passage and say "Not true to life." The author turns on you and then annihilates you—in his own mind—with the words, "But it actually happened." Of course, then, it must be true. On the contrary, it is accurate only.

For the assumption is, that truth is a higher power of accuracy —that the true thing includes the accurate; and, assuming this, the authors of novels—that are not successful—suppose that if they are accurate, if they tell the thing just as they saw it, that they are truthful. It is not difficult to show that a man may be as accurate as the spectroscope and yet lie like a Chinese diplomat. As, for instance: Let us suppose you have never seen a sheep, never heard of sheep, don't know sheep from shavings. It devolves upon me to enlighten your ignorance. I go out into the field and select from the flock a black sheep, bring it before you, and, with the animal there under our eyes, describe it in detail, faithfully, omitting nothing, falsifying nothing, exaggerating nothing. I am painfully accurate. But you go away with the untrue conviction that all sheep are black! I have been accurate, but I have not been true.

So it is with very, very many novels, written with all earnestness and seriousness. Every incident has happened in real life, and because it is picturesque, because it is romantic, because, in a word, it is like some other novel, it is seized upon at once, and serves as the nucleus of a tale. Then, because this tale fails of success, because it fails to impress, the author blames the public, not himself. He thinks he has gone to life for his material, and so must be original, new, and true. It is not so. Life itself is not always true; strange as it may seem, you may be able to say that life is not always true to life—from the point of view of the artist. It happened once that it was my unfortunate duty to tell a certain man of the violent death of his only brother, whom he had left well and happy but an hour before. This is how he took it: He threw up both hands and staggered back, precisely as they do in melodrama, exclaiming all in a breath: "Oh, my God! This is terrible! What will mother say?" You may say what you please, this man was not true to life. From the point of view of the teller of tales he was theatrical, false, untrue, and though the incident was an actual fact and though the emotion was real, it had no value as "material," and no fiction writer in his senses would have thought of using it in his story.

Naturally enough it will be asked what, then, is the standard. How shall the writer guide himself in the treatment of a pivotal, critical scene, or how shall the reader judge whether or no he is true? Perhaps, after all, the word "seem," and not the word "true," is the most important. Of course no good novelist, no good artist, can represent life as it actually is. Nobody can, for nobody knows. Who is to say what life actually is? It seems easy—easy for us who have it and live in it and see it and hear it and feel it every millionth part of every second of the time. I say that life is actually this or that, and you say it is something else, and number three says "Lo! here," and number four says "Lo! there." Not even science is going to help you; no two photographs, even, will convey just the same impression of the same actuality; and here we are dealing not with science, but with art, that instantly involves the personality of the artist and all that that means. Even the same artist will not see the same thing twice exactly alike. His personality is one thing to-day and another thing to-morrow—is one thing before dinner and another thing after it. How, then, to determine what life actually is?

The point is just this. In the fine arts we do not care one little bit about what life actually is, but what it looks like to an interesting, impressionable man, and if he tells history or paints his picture so that the majority of intelligent people will say, "Yes, that must have been just about what would have happened under these circumstances," he is true. His accuracy cuts no figure at all. He need not be accurate if he does not choose to be. If he sees fit to be inaccurate in order to make his point—so only his point be the conveying of a truthful impression—that is his affair. We have nothing to do with that. Consider the study of a French cuirassier by Detaille; where the sunlight strikes the brown coat of the horse, you will see, if you look close, a mere smear of blue—light blue. This is inaccurate. The horse is not blue, nor has he any blue spots.

Stand at the proper distance and the blue smear resolves itself in the glossy reflection of the sun, and the effect is true.

And in fiction: Take the fine scene in "Ivanhoe," where Rebecca, looking from the window, describes the assault upon the outer walls of the castle to the wounded knight lying on the floor in the room behind her. If you stop and think, you will see that Rebecca never could have found such elaborate language under the stress of so great excitement—those cleverly managed little climaxes in each phrase, building up to the great climax of the paragraph, all the play of rhetoric, all the nice chain and adjustment of adjectives; she could not possibly have done it. Neither you nor I, nor any of us, with all the thought and time and labor at our command, could have ever written the passage. But is it not admirably true— true as the truth itself? It is not accurate: it is grossly, ludicrously inaccurate; but the fire and leap and vigor of it; there is where the truth is. Scott wanted you to get an impression of that assault on the barbican, and you do get it. You can hear those axes on the outer gate as plainly as Rebecca could; you can see the ladders go up, can hear them splinter, can see and feel and know all the rush and trample and smashing of that fine fight, with the Fetterlock Knight always to the fore, as no merely accurate description—accurate to five points of decimals—could ever present it.

So that one must remember the distinction, and claim no more for accuracy than it deserves—and that's but little. Anybody can be accurate—the man with the foot-rule is that. Accuracy is the attainment of small minds, the achievement of the commonplace, a mere machine-made thing that comes with niggardly research and ciphering and mensuration and the multiplication table, good in its place, so only the place is very small. In fiction it can under certain circumstances be dispensed with altogether. It is not a thing to be striven for. To be true is the all-important business, and, once attaining that, "all other things shall be added unto you." Paint the horse pea-green if it suits your purpose; fill the mouth of Rebecca with gasconades and rodomontades interminable: these things do not matter. It is truth that matters, and the point is whether the daubs of pea-green will look like horseflesh and the mouth-filling words create the impression of actual battle.

WHY WOMEN SHOULD WRITE THE BEST NOVELS

It is rather curious upon reflection and upon looking over the rank and file of achievement during the period of recorded history, to observe that of all the occupations at first exclusively followed by men, that of writing has been—in all civilizations and among all people—one of the very first to be successfully—mark the qualification of the adverb—to be successfully invaded by women. We hear of women who write poetry long before we hear of women who paint pictures or perform upon musical instruments or achieve distinction upon the stage.

It would seem as if, of all the arts, that of writing is the one to which women turn the quickest. Great success in the sciences or in mercantile pursuits is, of course, out of the question, so that—as at the first—it may be said, speaking largely, that of all the masculine occupations, that of writing is the first to be adopted by women.

If it is the first it must be because it is the easiest. Now to go very far back to the earliest beginnings, all occupations, whether artistic or otherwise, were the prerogative of the male; considering this fact, I say, does it not follow, or would not the inference be strong, that—given an equal start—women would write more readily than men, would do so because they could do so; that writing is a feminine—not accomplishment.merely—but gift?

So that the whole matter leads up to the point one wishes to make, namely, that here, in our present day and time, it should be easier for women to write well than for men. And as writing today means the writing of fiction, we arrive, somewhat deviously and perhaps—after jumping many gaps and weak spots en route—a little lamely, at the very last result of all, which is this: Women should be able to write better novels than men.

But under modern conditions there are many more reasons for this success of women in fiction than merely a natural inherent gift of expression.

One great reason is leisure. The average man, who must work for a living, has no time to write novels, much less to get into that frame of mind or to assume that mental attitude by means of which he is able to see possibilities for fictitious narrative in the life around him. But, as yet, few women (compared with the armies of male workers) have to work for a living, and it is an unusual state of affairs in which the average woman of moderate circumstances could not, if she would, take from three to four hours a day from her household duties to devote to any occupation she deemed desirable.

Another reason is found, one believes, in the nature of women's education. From almost the very first the young man studies with an eye to business or to a profession. In many State colleges nowadays all literary courses except the most elementary—which, indeed, have no place in collegiate curriculums—are optional. But what girls' seminary does not prescribe the study of literature through all its three or four years, making of this study a matter of all importance? And while the courses of literature do not, by any manner of means, make a novelist, they familiarize the student with style and the means by which words are put together. The more one reads the easier one writes.

Then, too (though this reason lies not so much in modern conditions as in basic principles), there is the matter of temperament. The average man is a rectangular, square-cut, matter-of-fact, soberminded animal who does not receive impressions easily, who is not troubled with emotions and has no overmastering desire to communicate his sensations to anybody. But the average woman is just the reverse of all these. She is impressionable, emotional, and communicative. And impressionableness, emotionality, and communicativeness are three very important qualities of mind that make for novel writing.

The modern woman, then, in a greater degree than her contemporaneous male, has the leisure for novel writing, has the education and has the temperament. She should be able to write better novels, and as a matter of fact she does not. It is, of course, a conceded fact that there have been more great men novelists than women novelists, and that to-day the producers of the best fiction are men and not women. There are probably more women trying to write novels than there are men, but for all this it must be admitted that the ranks of the "arrived" are recruited from the razor contingent.

Why, then, with such a long start and with so many advantages of temperament, opportunity, and training, should it be that women do not write better novels than men?

One believes that the answer is found in the fact that life is more important than literature, and in the wise, wise, old, old adage that experience is the best teacher. Of all the difficult things that enter into the learning of a most difficult profession, the most difficult of all for the intended novelist to acquire is the fact that life is better than literature. The amateur will say this with conviction, will preach it in public and practice the exact reverse in private. But it still remains true that all the temperament, all the sensitiveness to impressions, all the education in the world will not help one little, little bit in the writing of the novel if life itself, the crude, the raw, the vulgar, if you will, is not studied. An hour's experience is worth ten years of study—of reading other people's books. But this fact is ignored, and the future writer of what it is hoped will be the great novel of his day and age studies the thoughts and products of some other writer, of some other great novel, of some other day and age, in the hope that thereby much may be learned. And much will be learned—very much, indeed—of the methods of construction; and if the tyro only has wits enough to study the great man's formula, well and good. But the fascination of a great story-writer—especially upon the young, untried little story-writer—is strong, and before the latter is well aware he is taking from the big man that which he has no right to take. He is taking his code of ethics, his view of life, his personality, even to the very incidents and episodes of his story. He is studying literature and not life.

If he had gone direct to life itself, all would have been different. He would have developed in his own code, his own personality, and he would have found incidents and episodes that were new—yes, and strikingly forceful, better than any he could have imagined or stolen, and which were all his own. In the end, if the gods gave him long life and a faculty of application, he would have evolved into something of a writer of fiction.

All this digression is to try to state the importance of actual life and actual experience, and it bears upon the subject in hand in this, that women who have all the other qualifications of good novelists are, because of nature and character that invariably goes with these qualifications, shut away from the study of, and the association with, the most important thing of all for them—real life. Even making allowances for the emancipation of the New Woman, the majority of women still lead, in comparison with men, secluded lives. The woman who is impressionable is by reason of this very thing sensitive (indeed, sensitiveness and impressionableness mean almost the same thing), and it is inconceivably hard for the sensitive woman to force herself into the midst of that great, grim complication of men's doings that we call life. And even admitting that she finds in herself the courage to do this, she lacks the knowledge to use knowledge thus gained. The faculty of selection comes even to men only after many years of experience.

So much for causes exterior to herself, and it is well to admit at once that the exterior causes are by far the most potent and the most important; but there are perhaps causes to be found in the make-up of the woman herself which keep her from success in fiction. Is it not a fact that protracted labor of the mind tells upon a woman quicker than upon a man? Be it understood that no disparagement, no invidious comparison, is intended. Indeed, it is quite possible that her speedier mental fatigue is due to the fact that the woman possesses the more highly specialized organ.

A man may grind on steadily for an almost indefinite period, when a woman at the same task would begin, after a certain point, to "feel her nerves," to chafe, to fret, to try to do too much, to polish too highly, to develop more perfectly. Then come fatigue, harassing doubts, more nerves, a touch of hysteria occasionally, exhaustion, and in the end complete discouragement and a final abandonment of the enterprise: and who shall say how many good, even great, novels have remained half written, to be burned in the end, because their women authors mistook lack of physical strength for lack of genuine ability?

SIMPLICITY IN ART

ONCE upon a time I had occasion to buy so uninteresting a thing as a silver soup-ladle. The salesman at the silversmith's was obliging and for my inspection brought forth quite an array of ladles. But my purse was flaccid, anæmic, and I must pick and choose with all the discrimination in the world. I wanted to make a brave showing with my gift—to get a great deal for my money. I went through a world of soup-ladles—ladles with gilded bowls, with embossed handles, with chased arabesques, but there were none to my taste. "Or perhaps," says the salesman, "you would care to look at something like this," and he brought out a ladle that was as plain and as unadorned as the unclouded sky—and about as beautiful. Of all the others this was the most to my liking. But the price! ah, that anæmic purse; and I must put it from me! It was nearly double the cost of any of the rest. And when I asked why, the salesman said:

"You see, in this highly ornamental ware the flaws of the material don't show, and you can cover up a blow-hole or the like by wreaths and beading. But this plain ware has got to be the very best. Every defect is apparent."

And there, if you please, is a conclusive comment upon the whole business—a final basis of comparison of all things, whether commercial or artistic; the bare dignity of the unadorned that may stand before the world all unshamed, panoplied rather than clothed in the consciousness of perfection. We of this latter day, we painters and poets and writers—artists—must labor with all the wits of us, all the strength of us, and with all that we have of ingenuity and perseverance to attain simplicity. But it has not always been so. At the very earlist, men—forgotten, ordinary men —were born with an easy, unblurred vision that to-day we would hail as marvelous genius. Suppose, for instance, the New Testament was all unwritten and one of us were called upon to tell the world that Christ was born, to tell of how he had seen Him, that this was the Messiah. How the adjectives would marshal upon the page, how the exclamatory phrases would cry out, how we would elaborate and elaborate, and how our rhetoric would flare and blazon till—so we should imagine—the ear would ring and the very eye would be dazzled; and even then we would believe that our words were all so few and feeble. It is beyond words, we should vociferate. So it would be. That is very true—words of ours. Can you not see how we should dramatize it? We would make a point of the transcendent stillness of the hour, of the deep blue of the Judean midnight, of the lip-lapping of Galilee, the murmur of Jordan, the peacefulness of sleeping Jerusalem. Then the stars, the descent of the angel, the shepherds—all the accessories. And our narrative would be as commensurate with the subject as the flippant smartness of a "bright" reporter in the Sistine chapel. We would be striving to cover up our innate incompetence, our impotence to do justice to the mighty theme by elaborateness of design and arabesque intricacy of rhetoric.

But on the other hand—listen:

"The days were accomplished that she should be delivered, and she brought forth her first-born son and wrapped him in swaddling clothes and laid him in a manger, because there was no room for them in the inn."

Simplicity could go no further. Absolutely not one word unessential, not a single adjective that is not merely descriptive. The whole matter stated with the terseness of a military report, and yet —there is the epic, the world epic, beautiful, majestic, incomparably dignified, and no ready writer, no Milton nor Shakespeare, with all the wealth of their vocabularies, with all the resources of their genius, with all their power of simile or metaphor, their pomp of eloquence or their royal pageantry of hexameters, could produce the effect contained in these two simple declarative sentences.

The mistake that we little people are so prone to make is this: that the more intense the emotional quality of the scene described, the more "vivid," the more exalted, the more richly colored we suppose should be the language.

When the crisis of the tale is reached there is where we like the author to spread himself, to show the effectiveness of his treatment. But if we would only pause to take a moment's thought we must surely see that the simplest, even the barest statement of fact is not only all-sufficient, but all-appropriate.

Elaborate phrase, rhetoric, the intimacy of metaphor and allegory and simile is forgivable for the unimportant episodes where the interest of the narrative is languid; where we are willing to watch the author's ingenuity in the matter of scrolls and fretwork and mosaics—rococo work. But when the catastrophe comes, when the narrative swings clear upon its pivot and we are lifted with it from out the world of our surroundings, we want to forget the author. We want no adjectives to blur our substantives. The substantives may now speak for themselves. We want no metaphor, no simile to make clear the matter. If at this moment of drama and intensity the matter is not of itself pre-eminently clear no verbiage, however ingenious, will clarify it. Heighten the effect. Does exclamation and heroics on the part of the bystanders ever make the curbstone drama more poignant? Who would care to see Niagara through colored fire and calcium lights?

The simple treatment, whether of a piece of silversmith work or of a momentous religious epic, is always the most difficult of all. It demands more of the artist. The unskilful story-teller as often as not tells the story to himself as well as to his hearers as he goes along. Not sure of exactly how he is to reach the end, not sure even of the end itself, he must feel his way from incident to incident, from page to page, fumbling, using many words, repeating himself. To hide the confusion there is one resource—elaboration, exaggerated outline, violent color, till at last the unstable outline disappears under the accumulation, and the reader is to be so dazzled with the wit of the dialogue, the smartness of the repartee, the felicity of the diction, that he will not see the gaps and lapses in the structure itself—just as the "nobby" drummer wears a wide and showy scarf to conceal a soiled shirt-bosom.

But in the master-works of narrative there is none of this shamming, no shoddyism, no humbug. There is little more than bare outline, but in the care with which it is drawn, how much thought, what infinite pains go to the making of each stroke, so that when it is made it falls just at the right place and exactly in its right sequence. This attained, what need is there for more? Comment is superfluous. If the author make the scene appear terrible to the reader he need not say in himself or in the mouth of some protagonist, "It is terrible!" If the picture is pathetic so that he who reads must weep, how superfluous, how intrusive should the author exclaim, "It was pitiful to the point of tears." If beautiful, we do not want him to tell us so. We want him to make it beautiful and our own appreciation will supply the adjectives.

Beauty, the ultimate philosophical beauty, is not a thing of elaboration, but on the contrary of an almost barren nudity: a jewel may be an exquisite gem, a woman may have a beautiful arm, but the bracelet does not make the arm more beautiful, nor the arm the bracelet. One must admire them separately, and the moment that the jewel ceases to have a value or a reason upon the arm it is better in the case, where it may enjoy an undivided attention.

But after so many hundreds of years of art and artists, of civilization and progress, we have got so far away from the sane old homely uncomplex way of looking out at the world that the simple things no longer charm, and the simple declarative sentence, straightforward, plain, seems flat to our intellectual palate—flat and tasteless and crude.

What we would now call simple our forebears would look upon as a farrago of gimcrackery, and all our art—the art of the betterminded of us—is only a striving to get back to the unblurred, direct simplicity of those writers who could see that the Wonderful, the Counselor, the mighty God, the Prince of Peace, could be laid in a manger and yet be the Saviour of the world.

It is this same spirit, this disdaining of simplicity that has so warped and inflated The First Story, making of it a pomp, an affair of gold-embroidered vestments and costly choirs, of marbles, of jeweled windows and of incense, unable to find the thrill as formerly in the plain and humble stable, and the brown-haired, grave-eyed peasant girl, with her little baby; unable to see the beauty in the crumbling mud walls, the low-ceiled interior, where the only incense was the sweet smell of the cow's breath, the only vestments the swaddling clothes, rough, coarse-fibred, from the hand-looms of Nazareth, the only pomp the scanty gifts of three old men, and the only chanting the crooning of a young mother holding her firstborn babe upon her breast.

SALT AND SINCERITY

I

IF the signs of the times may be read aright, and the future forecasted, the volume of short stories is in a fair way of becoming a "rare book." Fewer and fewer of this kind of literature are published every year, and only within the last week one of the foremost of the New York publishers has said that, so far as the material success was concerned, he would prefer to undertake a book of poems rather than a book of stories. Also he explains why. And this is the interesting thing. One has always been puzzled to account for this lapse from a former popularity of a style of fiction certainly legitimate and incontestably entertaining. The publisher in question cites the cheap magazines—the monthlies and weeklies—as the inimical factors. The people go to them for their short stories, not to the cloth-bound volumes for sale at a dollar or a dollar and a half. Why not, if the cheap magazines give "just as good"? Often, too, they give the very same stories which, later, are republished in book form. As the case stands now, any fairly diligent reader of two or three of the more important monthlies and weeklies may anticipate the contents of the entire volume, and very naturally he can not be expected to pay a dollar for something he already has.

Or even suppose—as is now generally demanded by the publisher—the author adds to the forthcoming collection certain hitherto unpublished stories. Even this does not tempt the buyer. Turning over the leaves at the bookseller's, he sees two, three, five, half a dozen familiar titles. "Come," says he, "I have read three-fourths of this book already. I have no use for it."

It is quite possible that this state of affairs will produce important results. It is yet, perhaps, too soon to say, but it is not outside the range of the probable that, in America at least, it will, in time to come, engender a decay in the quality of the short story. It may be urged that the high prices paid by periodicals to the important short-story writers—the best men—will still act as a stimulus to production. But this does not follow by any means.

Authors are queer cattle. They do not always work for money, but sometimes for a permanent place in the eyes of the world. Books give them this—not fugitive short stories published here and there, and at irregular intervals. Reputations that have been made by short stories published in periodicals may be counted upon the fingers of one hand. The "life of a novel"—to use a trade term— is to a certain extent indeterminable. The life of a short story, be it never so excellent, is prolonged only till the next issue of the periodical in which it has appeared. If the periodical is a weekly it will last a week, if a monthly a month—*and not a day more.* If very good, it will create a demand for another short story by the same author, but that one particular contribution, the original one, is irretrievably and hopelessly dead.

If the author is in literature "for his own pocket every time," he is generally willing to accept the place of a short-story writer. If he is one of the "best men," working for a "permanent place," he will turn his attention and time, his best efforts, to the writing of novels, reverting to the short story only when necessary for the sake of boiling the Pot and chasing the Wolf. He will abandon the field to the inferior men, or enter it only to dispose of "copy" which does not represent him at his best. And, as a result, the quality of the short story will decline more and more.

So, "taking one consideration with another," it may be appropriate to inquire if it is not possible that the American short story is liable to decline in quality and standard of excellence.

And now comes again this question addressed to certain authors, "Which book do you consider your best?" and a very industrious and painstaking person is giving the answer to the world.

To what end it is difficult to see. Who cares which of the "Waverleys" Sir Walter thought his best? or which of the Rougon-Maquart M. Zola favors the most? The author's point of view is very different from yours—the reader's. Which one do *you* think the best? That's the point. Do you not see that in the author's opinion the novel he is working on at the moment, or which is in press and about to appear—in fine, the last one written—is for a very long time the best he has done? He would be a very poor kind of novelist if he did not think that.

And even in retrospect his opinion as to "his best book" is not necessarily final. For he will see good points in "unsuccessful" novels that the public and critics have never and will never discover; and also defects in what the world considers his masterpiece that for him spoil the entire story. His best novel is, as was said, the last he has written, or—and this more especially—the one he is *going* to write. For to a certain extent this is true of every author, whether fiction writer or not. *Though he very often does better than he thinks he can, he never does so well as he knows he might.*

His best book is the one that he never quite succeeds in getting hold of firmly enough to commit to paper. It is always just beyond him. Next year he is going to think it out, or the next after that, and instead he compromises on something else, and his *chief d'œuvre* is always a little ahead of him. If this, too, were not so, he would be a poor kind of writer. So that it seems to me the most truthful answer to the question, "What is your best book?" would be, "The one I shall never write."

Another ideal that such of the "people who imagine a vain thing" have long been pursuing is an English Academy of letters, and now that "the British Academy for the promotion of Historical, Philosophical and Philological studies" has been proposed, the old discussion is revived, and especially in England there is talk of a British Academy, something on the same lines as the *Académie Française,* which shall tend to promote and reward particularly the production of good fiction. In a word, it would be a distinction reserved only for the worthy, a charmed circle that would open only to the élite upon the vote of those already admitted. The proposition strikes one as pre-eminently ridiculous. Literature is of all arts the most democratic; it is of, by and for the people in a fuller measure than even government itself. And one makes the assertion without forgetting that fine mouth-filling phrase, the "aristocracy of letters." The survival of the fittest is as good in the evolution of our literature as of our bodies, and the best "academy" for the writers of the United States is, after all, and in the last analysis, to be found in the judgment of the people, exercised throughout the lapse of a considerable time. For, give the people time enough, and they will always decide justly.

It was in connection with this talk about an "Academy" that Mr. Hall Caine made the remark that "no academic study of a thing so variable, emotional and independent as the imaginative writer's art could be anything but mischievous." One is inclined to take exception to the statement. Why should the academic study of the principles of writing fiction be mischievous? Is it not possible to codify in some way the art of *construction* of novels so that they may be studied to advantage? This has, of course, never been done. But one believes that, if managed carefully and with a proper disregard of "set forms" and hampering conventions, it would be possible to start and maintain a school of fiction-writing in the most liberal sense of the word "school." Why should it be any more absurd than the painting schools and music schools? Is the art of music, say, any less variable, less emotional, less independent, less imaginative, than the fiction writer's? Heretical as the assertion may appear, one is thoroughly convinced that the art of novel writing (up to a certain point, *bien entendu*) can be acquired by instruction just as readily and with results just as satisfactory and practical as the arts of painting, sculpture, music, and the like. The art of fiction is, in general, based upon four qualities of mind: observation, imagination, invention and sympathy. Certainly the first two are "acquired characters." Kindergarten children the world over are acquiring them every day. Invention is immensely stimulated by observation and imagination, while sympathy is so universally a fundamental quality with all sorts and conditions of men and women—especially the latter—that it needs but little cultivation. Why, then, would it be impossible for a few of our older, more seriously minded novelists to launch a School of Instruction in the Art of Composition—just as Bouguereau, Lefevre, Boulanger and Tony Robert Fleury founded Julien's in Paris?

At present the stimulus to, and even the manner of, production of very much of American fiction is in the hands of the publishers. No one not intimately associated with any one of the larger, more important "houses" can have any idea of the influence of the publisher upon latter-day fiction. More novels are written—practically —to order than the public has any notion of. The publisher again and again picks out the man (one speaks, of course, of the younger generation), suggests the theme, and exercises, in a sense, all the functions of instructor during the period of composition. In the matter of this "picking out of the man" it is rather curious to note a very radical change that has come about in the last five years. Time was when the publisher waited for the unknown writer to come to him with his manuscript. But of late the Unknown has so frequently developed, under exploitation and by direct solicitation of the publisher, into a "money-making proposition" of such formidable proportions that there is hardly a publishing house that does not now hunt him out with all the resources at its command. Certain fields are worked with the thoroughness, almost, of a political canvass, and if a given State—as, for instance, Indiana—has suddenly evolved into a region of great literary activity, it is open to suspicion that it is not because there is any inherent literary quality in the people of the place greater than in other States, but that certain firms of publishers are "working the ground."

It might not have been altogether out of place if upon the Victor Hugo monument which has just been unveiled in Paris there had been inscribed this, one of the most important of the great Frenchman's maxims:

"Les livres n'ont jamais faites du mal;"

and I think that in the last analysis, this is the most fitting answer to Mr. Carnegie, who, in his address before the Authors Club, put himself on record as willing to exclude from the libraries he is founding all books not three years old. No doubt bad books have a bad influence, but bad books are certainly better than no books at all. For one must remember that the worst books are not printed —the really tawdry, really pernicious, really evil books. These are throttled in manuscript by the publishers, who must be in a sense public censors. No book, be assured, goes to press but that there is—oh, hidden away like a grain of mustard—some bit, some modicum, some tiny kernel of good in it. Perhaps it is not that seed of goodness that the cultured, the fastidious care much about. Perhaps the discriminating would call it a platitude. But one is willing to believe that somewhere, somehow, this atom of real worth makes itself felt—and that's a beginning. It will create after a while a taste for reading. And a taste for reading is a more important factor in a nation's literary life than the birth of a second Shakespeare.

It is the people, after all, who "make a literature." If they read, the few, the "illuminati," will write. But first must come the demand—come from the people, the Plain People, the condemned *bourgeoisie*. The select circles of the élite, the "studio" hangers-on, the refined, will never, never, clamor they never so loudly, toil they never so painfully, produce the Great Writer. The demand which he is to supply comes from the Plain People—from the masses, and not from the classes. There is more significance as to the ultimate excellence of American letters in the sight of the messenger boy devouring his "Old Sleuths" and "Deadwood Dicks" and "Boy Detectives," with an *earnest, serious* absorption, than in the spectacle of a "reading circle" of dilettanti coquetting with Verlaine and *pretending* that they understand.

By the same token, then, is it not better to welcome and rejoice over this recent "literary deluge" than to decry it? One is not sure it is not a matter for self-gratulation—not a thing to deplore and vilify. The "people" are reading, that is the point; it is *not* the point that immature, untrained writers are flooding the counters with their productions. The more the Plain People read the more they will discriminate. It is inevitable, and by and by they will demand "something better." It is impossible to read a book without formulating an opinion upon it. Even the messenger boy can tell you that, in *his* judgment, No. 3,666, "The James Boys Brought to Bay," is more or less—as the case may be—exciting than No. 3,667, "The Last of the Fly-by-Nights." Well, that is something. Is it not better than that the same boy should be shooting craps around the corner? Take his dime novel from him, put him in the "No Book" condition—and believe me, he will revert to the craps. And so it is higher up the scale. In the name of American literature, let the Plain People read, anything—anything, whether it is three days or three years old. Mr. Carnegie will not educate the public taste by shutting his libraries upon recent fiction. The public taste will educate itself by *much* reading, not by *restricted* reading. "Books have never done harm," Victor Hugo said it, and a bad book—that is to say, a poor, cheap, ill-written, "trashy" book—is not after all so harmful as "no book" at all.

Later on, when the people have learned discrimination by much reading, it will not be necessary to bar fiction not three years old from the libraries, for by then the people will demand the "something better," and the writers will have to supply it—or disappear, giving place to those who can, and *then* the literary standards will be raised.

II

In a recent number of his periodical, the editor of "Harper's Weekly" prints a letter received from a gentleman who deplores the fact that the participants in the Harvard-Yale track teams are given a great place in the daily newspapers while—by implication—his son, an arduous student and winner of a "Townsend prize," is completely and definitely ignored. "I could not but think of my son," writes the gentleman, "a Yale Senior who, as one of the results of nine years' devotion to study, won a Townsend prize." One will ask the reader to consider this last statement. The publicity of the college athletes is not the point here. The point is "nine years' devotion to study" and—"a Townsend prize." Nine years—think of it—the best, the most important of a boy's life given to devoted study!—not of Men, not of Life, not of Realities, but of the books of Other People, mere fatuous, unreasoned, pig-headed absorption of ideas at second hand. And the result? Not a well-ordered mind, not a well-regulated reasoning machine, not a power of appreciation, not an ability to create. None of these, but— Great Heavens!—a *Townsend Prize,* a rectangular piece of the skin of a goat, dried and cured and marked with certain signs and symbols by means of a black pigment; this and a disk of the same metal the Uganda warrior hangs in his ears. A Townsend Prize. And for this a young American living in the twentieth century, sane, intelligent, healthful, has pored over Other People's books, has absorbed Other People's notions, has wearied his brain, has weakened his body, has shut himself from the wide world, has denied himself, has restrained himself, has stultified emotion, has in a word buried his talent in the earth wrapped carefully in a napkin. "And," comments the editor, "the boy who won the Townsend prize for scholarship, if he keeps on, will some day be honored by his fellow-men, when the athletic prize-winner, if he does nothing else, will be a director of a gymnasium. The serious worker comes out ahead every time." But winning Townsend prizes by nine years of study is, we submit, not serious work, but serious misuse of most valuable time and energy. Scholarship? Will we never learn that times change and that sauce for the Renaissance goose is *not* sauce for the New Century gander? It is a fine thing, this scholarship, no doubt; but if a man be content with merely this his scholarship is of as much use and benefit to his contemporaries as his deftness in manicuring his finger nails. The United States in this year of grace nineteen hundred and two does not want and does not need Scholars, but Men—Men made in the mold of the Leonard Woods and the Theodore Roosevelts, Men such as Colonel Waring, Men such as Booker Washington. The most brilliant scholarship attainable by human effort is not, to-day, worth nine years of any young man's life. I think it is Nathaniel Hawthorne who tells the story of a "scholar" who one day, when a young man, found the tooth of a mammoth. He was a student of fossil remains, and in his enthusiasm set out to complete the skeleton. His mind filled with this one idea, to the exclusion of all else, he traveled up and down the world, year after year, picking up here a vertebra, here a femur, here a rib, here a clavicle. Years passed; he came to be an old man; at last he faced death. He had succeeded. The monstrous framework was complete. But he looked back upon the sixty years of his toil and saw that it was a vanity. He had to show for his life-work—the skeleton of a mammoth. And, believe this implicity: if—as the editor and commentator remarks—the Townsend prize-winner *keeps* on, this will be the result, a huge thing no doubt, a thing that looms big in the eye and in the imagination, but an empty thing, lifeless, bloodless, dead; yes, and more than dead—extinct; a mere accumulation of dry bones, propped up lest it fall to the ground, a thing for the wind to blow through and the vulgar to gape at.

But in connection with this subject one may cite so high an authority as Doctor Patton of Princeton, who has recently said that nowadays men do not go to colleges to become scholars, and that it was time and money wasted to try to make them such. This is a good saying and should be taken to heart by every college faculty between the oceans. Sooner or later there is bound to come a fundamental change in the mode of instruction now in favor in most American colleges. The times demand it; the character of the student body, the character of the undergraduate, is changing. One chooses to believe that the college of the end of the present century will be an institution where only specialized work will be indulged in. There will be courses in engineering, in electricity, in agriculture, in law, in chemistry, in biology, in mining, etc., and the so-called general "literary" or "classical" courses will be relegated to the limbo of Things No Longer Useful. Any instructor in collegiate work will tell you to-day that the men in the special courses are almost invariably the hardest, steadiest, most seriour workers. The man who studes law at college finishes his work a lawyer, he who studies engineering ends an engineer, the student of biology graduates a biologist, the student of chemistry a chemist. But the student in the "literary" course does not—no, not once in a thousand instances—graduate a literary man. He spends the four years of his life over a little Greek, a little Latin, a little mathematics, a little literature, a little history, a little "theme" writing, and comes out—just what it would be difficult to say. But he has in most cases acquired a very profound distaste for the authors whose work he has studied in class and lecture-room. Great names such as those of Carlyle, Macaulay, and De Quincey are associated in his mind only with tedium. He never will go back to these books, never read with enjoyment what once was "work." Even his conscientiousness—supposing him to be animated with such a motive— will trap him and trick him. I do not think that I shall ever forget the spectacle and impression of a student in my own Alma Mater— a little lass of seventeen (the college was co-educational), with her hair still down her back and her shoes yet innocent of heels, rising in her place in the classroom to read before a half-hundred of raw boys and undeveloped girls—not three months out of the high school —a solemn and quite unintelligible "theme" on "The Insincerity of Thomas Babington Macaulay."

Just at the time of the present writing a controversy has been started in London literary circles as to the legitimacy of a reviewer publishing the whole or parts of the same unsigned article in two or more periodicals. Mr. Arthur Symons is the reviewer under fire, and his article a *critique* of the dramas of Mr. Stephen Phillips. It was Mr. Phillips, so we are told, who first started the protest, and he has found followers and champions. And on first consideration there does seem to be ground for complaint here. It has been assumed that the first publisher of the article has a right to expect that for the money he pays to the writer this latter shall give to him all he has to say upon the subject. If he has very much to say— enough for another article—is it not the duty of the scribe to condense and compact so that the matter may be represented as a unit and not as a fragment? Moreover, does it seem fair to Mr. Phillips that three reviews—as was the case—all unfavorable, should appear in as many publications, thus giving to the public the impression that a *group* of critics, instead of merely one, was hostile to his work? Lastly, it has been urged that it is not honest to sell a thing twice—that if a horse has been sold by A to B, A can not sell it again to C.

But none of the objections seems valid. If the space allotted to the article in the paper is not sufficient, that is the fault of the editor, not the writer. The editor pays only for what he prints: the surplusage is still the author's property and can be by him disposed of as such. As for the public considering the single—unfavorable—review as the opinions of three men, and as such unfair to Mr. Phillips, this as well is inadequate and incompetent. Another critic, reviewing Mr. Phillips *favorably*, is just as much at libery to split up his work as the adverse reviewer. Last of all, it *is* under certain circumstances perfectly honest to sell the same thing twice. Articles, stories, poems and the like are continually syndicated in hundreds of newspapers simultaneously, and in this sense are sold over and over again. The analogy between the sale of a horse and the sale of a bit of literature is quite misleading. For the matter of that, the writer does not sell the actual concrete *manuscript* of his work, but merely the right to print it, and unless the word "exclusively" is understood in the agreement he is in no wise bound. The writer is not selling his copy as the owner sells his horse. The analogy would be true if A sold to B the *use* of the horse. When B had got the "use" out of the animal no one will deny the right of A to sell the same "use" to C, D, E, and so on through the whole alphabet. The reviewer of books has a hard enough time of it as it is. It is only fair to give him the same freedom as a livery stable keeper.

It has often occurred to me as a thing of some importance and certain significance that all great travelers are great writers. And the fact is so well established, the effect flows so invariably from the cause, that there would seem to be here a matter for reflection. One affirms and will maintain that the one is the direct result of the other, that the faculty of adequate expression, of vivid presentation, of forceful and harmonious grouping of words, is engendered and stimulated and perfected by wide journeying.

This is not at all an orthodox view, not at all the theory cherished by our forebears. The writer, according to unvarying belief, is the man of the closet, the bookish man, a student, a sedentary, a consumer of kerosene, a reader rather than a rover. And the idea is plausible. The nomad, he without local habitation, has no leisure, no opportunity, nor even actual concrete place to write. Would it not seem that literature is the quiet art, demanding an unperturbed mind, an unexcited, calm, reposeful temperament? This is a very defensible position, but it is based upon a foundation of sand. It assumes that the brain of the writer is a jar full of a precious fluid —a bottle full of wine to be poured out with care and with a hand so quiet, so restful and unshaken that not a drop be spilled. Very well. But when the jar, when the bottle is emptied—then what? Believe me, the gods give but one vintage to one man. There will be no refilling of the vessel; and even the lees are very flat, be the wine ever so good. The better the grape, the bitterer the dregs; and the outpouring of the "best that is in you" in the end will be soured by that brackish, *fade* sediment that follows upon lavish expenditure, so that the man ends ignobly and because of exhaustion and depletion, with all the product of his early and mature richness making more prominent and pitiful the final poverty and tenuity of his outgiving—ends the butt of critics, the compassion of the incompetent, a shard kicked of every scullion.

And in all the world there is nothing more lamentable than this —the end of a man once strong who has used himself up, but who decants lees and not wine. Even when the lees are spent he absorbs them once more and once more gives them forth, each time a little staler, a little thinner, a little feebler, realizing his exhaustion, yet— urged by some whip of fortune—forced to continue the miserable performance till the golden bowl be broken and the pitcher shattered at the fountain.

But suppose the productive power of the writer be considered not as a golden bowl to be emptied and in the end broken, but as a silver cord of finest temper that only needs to be kept in tune. True, the cord may be stretched to the breaking point. But its end comes at the very height and in the very consummate fulness of its capacity, and oh, the grand world-girdling Note that it sends forth in the breaking!—the very soul of it at mightiest tension, the very spirit of it at fiercest strain. What matter the loosening or the snapping when so noble an *Amen* as that vibrates through the nations to sound at once the Height and the End of an entire Life—a whole existence concentrated into a single cry!

Or it may become out of tune. But this is no great matter, because so easily remedied. The golden bowl once emptied there will be no refilling, but by some blessed provision of heaven nothing is easier than to attune the cords of being which are also the cords—the silver singing cords—of expression.

But—and here we come around once more to the *point de depart*—the silver cords once gone *dis*cordant, once jaded and slack, will not, can not be brought again to harmony in the closet, in the study, in the seclusion of the cabinet. Tinker them never so cunningly, never so delicately, they will *not* ring true for you. Thought will avail nothing, nor even rest, nor even relaxation. Of one's self, one can not cause the Master-note to which they will respond to vibrate. The cords have been played on too much. For all your pottering they will yet remain a little loose, and so long as they are loose the deftest fingering, the most skilful touch, will produce only false music.

And the deadly peril is that the cords of Life and the cords of expression lie so close together, are so intricately mingled, that the man can not always tell that the cords of expression are singing out of tune. Life and expression are two parts of the same instrument. If the whole life be out of tune, how can the man distinguish the false music from the true? There is a danger here, but it is not great. Sooner or later the conviction comes that the productive power is menaced. A little frankness with one's self, a little uncompromising testing of the strings, and the dissonance begins to impress itself.

And—as was said—the remedy is not to be found by the taking of thought, but by a heroic, drastic thrusting out from the grooves and cogs of the life of other men—of the life of the city and the comfortable stay-at-home, hour-to-hour humdrum, and a determined journeying out into the great wide world itself.

The further afield the better. The Master-note will not be heard within "commuting distance of the city." The whir of civilization smothers it. The click of the telegraph, the hiss of steam and the clatter of the printing-press drown it out. It is not always and of necessity a loud note. Though Nansen heard it in the thunder of the pack-ice of the Furthest North, it came to the ear of Stevenson in the lap of lazy wavelets in the hushed noonday of a South Sea strand.

Travel is the only way. Travel in any direction, by any means, so only it be far—very, very far—is the great attuner of the listless cords of the writer's instrument. For again and again and again his power is *not* a bowl to be emptied, but an instrument to be played on. To be of use it *must* be sensitive and responsive and true. And to be kept sensitive and responsive and true it must go once in so often to the great Tuner—to Nature.

We speak of the Mountains, the Rivers, Deserts and Oceans as though we knew them. We know the Adirondacks from a fortnight in a "summer camp"; the Rivers and the Deserts in kinetoscopic glimpses from the Pullman's windows; the Ocean—God forgive us!—from the beach of a "resort" or the deck of an Atlantic "greyhound." And I think the gods of the Mountains, Rivers, Deserts, and Oceans must laugh in vast contempt of our credulity to suppose that we have found their secrets or heard their music in this timid, furtive peeping and pilfering. For such little minds as these the gods have inexhaustible stores of tinkling cymbals and sounding brasses—Brummagem ware that they sell us for the price of "commutation tickets" and mileage books.

The real knowledge, the real experience that tautens and trims the fibres of being, that tunes the cords, is a very different matter. The trail and the tall ship lead to those places where the Master-note sounds, lead to those untracked, uncharted corners of the earth, and dull indeed must be the tympanum that once within ear-shot can not hear its majestic diapason. It sounds in the canyons of the higher mountains, in the plunge of streams and swirling of rivers yet without names—in the wildernesses, the plains, the wide-rimmed deserts. It sings a sonorous rhapsody in the rigging of the clipper ship driven by the trade winds, in the ratlines and halyards of South Sea schooners, and drums "reveille" on the tense, hard sails of the fishing-boats off the "Banks." You can hear it in the cry of the lynx, the chant of the wild goose, the call of the moose, and in the "break" of the salmon in the deeper pools below the cataract. It is in the roar of the landslide and in the drone of the *cicada;* in the war-whoop of the savage and in the stridulating of crickets; in the thunder of the tempest and in the faintest breath of laziest zephyrs.

And the silver cord of our creative faculty—the thing nearest to perfection in all the make-up of our imperfect human nature—responds to this Master-note with the quickness and sensitiveness of music mathematics; responds to it, attunes itself to it, vibrates with its vibration, thrills with its quivering, beats with its rhythm, and tautens itself and freshens itself and lives again with its great pure, elemental life, and the man comes back once more to the world of men with a true-beating heart and a true-hearing ear, so that he understands once more, so that his living, sensitive, delicately humming instrument trembles responsive to the emotions and impulses and loves and joys and sorrows and fears of his fellows, and the Man writes true and clear, and his message rings with harmony and with melody, with power and with passion of the prophets interpreting God's handwriting to the world of men.

III

THERE can be no question nor reasonable doubt that the "language, institutions, and religion" of fiction writers are at present undergoing the most radical revolution in the history of literature. And I mean by that that the men themselves are changing—their characters, their attitudes toward life; even the mode and manner of their own life. Those who are not thus changing are decaying. And those others, the Great Unarrived who do not recognize the Change, who do not acknowledge the Revolution, will never succeed, but will perish untimely almost before they can be said to have been born at all.

Time was when the author was an aristocrat, living in seclusion, unspotted from the world. But the Revolution of which there is question here has meted out to him the fate that Revolutions usually prepare for Aristocrats, and his successor is, must be, *must be*— if he is to voice the spirit of the times aright, if he is to interpret his fellows justly—the Man of the People, the Good Citizen.

How the novelists of the preceding generation played the Great Game is no matter for discussion here. Times were different then. One shut one's self in the study; one wore a velvet coat; one read a great deal and quoted Latin; one knew the classics; one kept apart from the vulgar profane and never, never, never read the newspapers. But for the novelist of the next fifty years of this twentieth century these methods, these habits, this conception of literature as a cult, as a refinement to be kept inviolate from the shoulderings and elbowings of the Common People is a clog, is a stumbling-block, is a pitfall, a bog, mire, trap—anything you like that is false, misleading and pernicious.

I have no patience with a theory of literature—and, oh, how often one hears it preached!—that claims the Great Man belongs only to the cultured few. "You must write," so these theorists explain, "for that small number of fine minds who because of education, because of delicate, fastidious taste are competent to judge." I tell you this is wrong. It is precisely the same purblind prejudice that condemned the introduction of the printing-press because it would cheapen and vulgarize the literature of the day. A literature that can not be vulgarized is no literature at all and will perish just as surely as rivers run to the sea. The things that last are the understandable things—understandable to the common minds, the Plain People, understandable, one is almost tempted to say, to the very children.

It is so in every branch of art: in music, painting, sculpture, architecture. The great monuments of these activities, the things that we retain longest and cherish with the most care, are plain almost to bareness. The most rudimentary mind can understand them. All the learning, all the culture, all the refinement in the world will not give you a greater thrill on reading your "Iliad" than the boy of fifteen enjoys. Is the "Marseillaise" a thing of sublety or refinement? Are the Pyramids complex? Are Angelo's Sibyls involved? But the "Iliad," the "Marseillaise," the Pyramids, the Sibyls will endure and endure and endure while men have eyes to see, ears to hear and hearts to be moved. These great things, these monuments were *not* written nor composed, nor builded, nor painted for the select, for the cultured. When Homer wrote there were no reading circles. Rouget de Lisle gave no "recitals." One does not have to "read up" to understand the message of Cheops, nor take a course of art lectures to feel the mystery of the Delphic Sibyl.

And so to come back to the starting place, the Revolution in the character of the writer of fiction. If the modern novelist does not understand the Plain People, if he does not address himself directly to them intelligibly and simply, he will fail. But he will never understand them by shutting himself away from them. He must be —and here one comes to the conclusion of the whole matter—a Man of the World. None more so. Books have no place in his equipment, have no right to be there; will only cumber and confuse him. His predecessor never read the newspapers, but for him the newspaper is more valuable than all the tomes of Ruskin, all the volumes of Carlyle. And more valuable than all are the actual, vital Affairs of Men. The function of the novelist of this present day is to comment upon life as he sees it. He can not get away from this; this is his excuse for existence, the only claim he has upon attention. How necessary then for him—of all men—to be in the midst of life! He can not plunge too deeply into it. Politics will help him, and Religious Controversies, Explorations, Science, the newest theory of Socialism, the latest development of Biology. He should find an interest in Continental diplomacy and should have opinions on the chances of a Russo-Japanese war over the Corean question.

He should be able to tell why it is of such unusual importance for Queen Wilhelmina of Holland to give birth to an heir, and should know who ought to be nominated for Governor of his native State at the next convention.

No piece of information—mere downright acquisition of fact—need be considered worthless. Nothing is too trivial to be neglected. I know a novelist of international reputation who told me that the following little bits of knowledge (collected heaven knows where and stored up for years in some pigeon-hole of his memory) had been of use to him in the composition of a novel he is now at work upon: That great cities tend to grow to the westward; that race-horses are shod with a long and narrow shoe; and that the usual price charged by an electrician for winding an armature is four dollars. And he seemed prouder of the fact that he had these tiny odds and ends at his command, when needed, than he was of the honorary degree just conferred upon him by Harvard University.

I suppose this is an exaggerated case, and it is not to be denied that it is better to have a Harvard degree than to know the shape of a race-horse's shoe, but it surely goes to prove the point that, as far as actual material worth and use were concerned, the fugitive foolish memory-notes were of more present help than the university degree, and that so far as information is concerned the novelist can not know too much.

In a recent number of "The Bookman" there appears an able article under the title "Attacking the Newspapers." The title is a trifle misleading, since the author's point and text are a defence of modern journalism, or rather let us say an apology. The apology is very well done. The manner of presentation is ingenious, the style amusing, but none the less one can not let the article pass without protest or, at the least, comment.

The original function of a newspaper was, and still should be, to tell the news—and, if you please, nothing more than that. The "policy" of the paper was (before the days of the yellow press) advocated and exploited in the editorial columns.

The whole difficulty lies in the fact that nowadays the average newspaper is violently partisan and deliberately alters news to suit its partisanship. "Not a very criminal procedure," I hear it said; "for by reading the opposition papers the public gets the other side." But one submits that such a course *is* criminal, and that it can be proved to be such. How many people do you suppose read the "opposition" papers? The American newspaper readers have not time to read "both sides" unless presented to them in one and the same paper.

Observe now how this partisanship works injustice and ruin. Let us suppose a given newspaper is hostile to the Governor of the State. Now every man—even a journalist—has a right to his opinions and his hostilities, and important men in public life must expect to be abused. There are for them compensations; their position is too high, too secure to be shaken by the vituperation of malevolent journals. But these journals have one favorite form of attacking important public men which, though it does not always harm the personage assaulted, may easily ruin the subordinates with which he surrounds himself. This is the habit of discrediting the statesman by defaming his appointees. The Governor, we will say, has appointed John Smith to be the head of a certain institution of the State. But the Governor has incurred the enmity of the "Daily Clarion"—the leading newspaper. Promptly the "Clarion" seizes upon Smith. His career as head of the institution has been a record of misrule (so the "Clarion" reads), has been characterized by extravagance, incompetency, mismanagement, and even misappropriation of the State's money. And here begins the cruel injustice of the business. The editor of that paper will set no bounds upon the lengths to which he will urge his reporters in their vilification of Smith. The editor knows he is a liar, the reporters know they are liars, but the public, ninety-nine times out of a hundred, ignoring motives, unable to see that the real object of attack is the Governor, unable to understand the brute callousness and wretched hypocrisy of the whole proceeding, *believes the calumny,* believes that Smith is an incompetent, a spendthrift, even a thief. And even the better class of readers, even the more intelligent who make allowances for the paper's political prejudices, will listen to the abuse and believe that there "must be some fire where there is so much smoke." Do you suppose for one moment that Smith will ever get a hearing in that paper? Do you suppose its reporters will ever credit him with a single honest achievement, a single sincere effort? If you do, you do not understand modern journalism.

Ah, but the opposition papers! They will defend Smith. They will champion him as vehemently as the "Clarion" attacks. That is all very well, but suppose there are no opposition papers. Politics are very complicated. The press of a given community is not always equally divided between the Republican and Democratic parties. Time and time again it happens that all the leading newspapers of a city, a county, or even a State, Democratic, Republican, Independent, etc., are banded together to oppose some one Large Man.

Where then will Smith get his hearing? He can not fight all the newspapers at once. He is not strong enough to retaliate even upon the meanest. The papers are afraid of nothing he can do. They hold absolute power over his good name and reputation. And for the sake of feeding fat the grudge they bear the Great One they butcher the subordinate without ruth and without reproach Believe me, it has been shown repeatedly that, placed in such a position, the modern newspaper will check at no lie however monstrous, at no calumny however vile. If Smith holds a position of trust he will be trumpeted from end to end of the community as a defaulter, gambling away the public moneys intrusted to his care. He will be pictured as a race-track follower, a supporter of fast women, a thief, a blackguard, and a reprobate. If he holds an administrative office, it will be shown how he has given and taken bribes; how he has neglected his duties and ignored his responsibilities till his office has engendered calamity, ruin, and even actual physical suffering. If his work is in the nature of supervision over one of those State institutions where the helpless are cared for—the infirm, the imbecile, the aged, or sick, or poor—his cruelty to his wards will be the theme, and he will be written of and pictured as whipping or torturing old men and little children, imprisoning, tormenting, making a hell of what was meant to be a help.

And the man once blackened after this fashion will never again rehabilitate himself in the eyes of the public. The people who read newspapers always believe the worst, and when an entire press, or even the major part of it, unite to defame a man there is no help or redress possible. He is ruined, ruined professionally and financially, ruined in character, in pocket, and in the hopes of ever getting back the good name that once was his.

And all this is done merely as a political move, merely to discredit the Big Man who put Smith in his place, merely to hurt his chances of renomination, merely to cut down the number of his votes. It is butchery; there is no other word than this with which to characterize the procedure, butchery as cruel, as wanton and as outrageous as ever bloodied the sands of the Colosseum. It is even worse than this, for the victim has no chance for his life. His hands are tied before the beasts are loosed. He is trussed and downed before the cages are opened, and the benches thunder for his life, not as for a victim to be immolated, but as a criminal to be punished. He is getting only his deserts, his very memory is an execration, and his name whenever mentioned is a by-word and a hissing.

And this in face of the fact that the man may be as innocent of the charges urged as if he had never been born.

Yet Doctor Colby in "The Bookman" article writes: "If we must attack the newspapers let it be as critics, not as crusaders, for the people who write for them are under no stricter obligations than ourselves." What! the reporter or the editor who by some fillip of fortune is in a position to make public opinion in the minds of a million people under no more obligations than you and I! If ever obligation bore down with an all but intolerable weight it is in just his case. His responsibility is greater than that of the Pulpit, greater than that of the Physician, greater than that of the Educator. If you would see the use to which it is put, you have only to try to get at the real truth in the case of the next public character assailed and vilified in the public prints.

Doctor Colby is wrong. It *is* a crusade and *not* a criticism that will put down the modern yellow newspaper from the bad eminence to which the minds of the hysterical, of the violent, of the ignorant, brutal and unscrupulous have exalted it.

IV

THERE is a certain journal of the Middle West of the United States which has proclaimed, with a great flourish of trumpets, that Mme. Humbert of Paris would have made a great "fictionist" if she had not elected to become a great swindler. This is that Mme. Humbert who cheated a number of bankers, capitalists and judges out of a great deal of money with a story of $20,000,000 in a safe which for certain reasons she could not open. Very naturally, when her hand was forced the safe was empty. And this person, the Middle West paper claims, is a great novelist *manquée,* "a female Dumas or Hugo." The contention would not be worthy of notice were it not for the fact that it is an opinion similar to that held by a great number of people intelligent enough to know better. In a word, it is the contention that the personal morality of the artist (including "fictionists") has nothing to do with his work, and that a great rascal may be a good painter, good musician, good novelist. With painters, musicians and the like this may or may not be true. With the novelist one contends, believes and avers that it is absolutely and unequivocally false, and that the mind capable of theft, of immorality, of cruelty, of foulness, or falseness of any kind is incapable, under any circumstances, or by any degree of stimulation, of producing one single important, artistic or useful piece of fiction. The better the personal morality of the writer, the better his writings. Tolstoi, for instance: it is wholly and solely due to the man's vast goodness and philanthropy that his novels carry weight. The attitude of the novelist toward his fellow-men and women is the great thing, not his inventiveness, his ingenuity, his deftness, or glibness, or verbal dexterity. And the mind wholly mean, who would rob a friend of $40,000 (after the manner of the Humbert person), or could even wilfully and deliberately mar the pleasure of a little child, could never assume toward the world at large that attitude of sympathy and generosity and toleration that is the first requisite of the really great novelist. Always you will find this thing true: that the best, the greatest writers of fiction are those best loved of troops of friends; and for the reason that, like the Arab philosopher of the poem, they, first of all, have "loved their fellow-men." It is this that has made their novels great. Consider Stevenson, or our own "Dean," or Hugo, or Scott, men of the simplest lives, uncompromising in rectitude, scrupulously, punctiliously, Quixotically honest; their morality—surely in the cases of Stevenson and Hugo—setting a new standard of religion, at the least a new code of ethics. And thus it goes right down the line, from the greater lights to the lesser and to the least. It is only the small men, the "minor" people among the writers of books who indulge in eccentricities that are only immoralities under a different skin; who do not pay their debts; who borrow without idea of returning; who live loose, "irregular," wretched, vicious lives, and call it "Bohemianism," and who believe that "good work" can issue from the turmoil, that the honeycomb will be found in the carcass, and the sweet come forth from the putrid. So that in the end one may choose to disagree with the Middle West editor and to affirm that it is not the ingenious criminal who is the novelist *manqué*, but the philanthropist, the great educator, the great pulpit orator, the great statesman. It is from such stuff that the important novels are made, not from the deranged lumber and disordered claptrap of the brain of a defective.

In the course of a speech made at a recent dinner given in London, Sir Donald Mackenzie Wallace has deplored the fact that our present generation of English writers has produced no worthy successors to the great men of the mid-Victorian period—that there are no names to place beside Scott, Dickens, Thackeray, Browning, or Keats. But he also brought forward extenuating circumstances, chief among which was the fact that the novelists of to-day were working overtime to supply the demands of an ever-increasing public, and that, by implication, their work was therefore deteriorating. One does not believe that this is so. Rapid work may cause the deterioration of a commercial article, but it by no means follows that the authors who are called upon to produce a very large number of books are forced into the composition of unworthy literature. The writer's brain does *not* hold the material for his books. It is not like a storehouse, from which things may be taken till nothing remains. The writer's material is life itself, inexhaustible and renewed from day to day, and his brain is only the instrument that adapts life to fiction. True, this instrument itself may wear out after a while, but it usually lasts as long as the man himself, and is good for more work than the unthinking would believe possible. As a matter of fact, the best novelists have, as a rule, been the most prolific, have been those who had to write rapidly and much to satisfy, if not the demands of the public, then at least other more personal demands, none the less insistent. Scott and Dickens were unusually prolific, yet the rapidity with which they accomplished their work did not hurt the quality of the work itself. Balzac and Dumas produced whole libraries of books and yet kept their standards high. As one has urged before, it is the demand of the People that produces the great writer, not *re*duces the quality and fineness of his work. If he has the "divine spark," the breath of the millions will fan rather than extinguish it.

One does not choose to believe that the art of fiction nor the standards of excellence have deteriorated since the day of Scott, Dickens and Thackeray. True, we have no men to equal them as yet, but they are surely coming. Time was, at the end of the seventeenth century, when the dearth of good fiction was even more marked than at present. But one must bear in mind that progress is never along a direct line, but by action and reaction. A period will supervene when a group of geniuses arise, and during the course of their activities the average of excellence is high, great books are produced, and a whole New Literature is launched. Their influence is profound; the first subschool of imitators follow good enough men but second-rate. These in turn are followed by the third-raters, and these by the fourth-raters, and no one is found bold enough to strike out for himself until the bottom is reached. Then comes the reaction, and once more the group of giants towers up from out the mass. We are probably living through the era of the fourth-raters just now, and one believes that we are rather near to the end even of that. The imitators of the romantic school have imitated to ten places decimals and have diluted and rediluted till they can hardly go further without producing something actually and really new. At any rate, the time is most propitious for a Man of Iron who can be bent to no former shape nor diluted to no old-time essence. Then will come the day of the New Literature, and the wind of Life itself will blow through the dry bones and fustian and sawdust of the Imitation, and the People will all at once realize how very far afield the fourth-raters have drawn them and how very different a good novel is from a bad one.

For say what you will, the People, the Plain People who Read, do appreciate good literature in the end. One must keep one's faith in the People—the Plain People, the Burgesses, the Grocers—

else of all men the artists are most miserable and their teachings vain. Let us admit and concede that this belief is ever so sorely tried at times. Many thousands of years ago the wisest man of his age declared that "the People imagine a vain thing." Continually they are running away after strange gods; continually they are admiring the fake and neglecting actual worth. But in the end, and at last, they will listen to the true note and discriminate between it and the false. *In the last analysis the People are always right.* Somehow, and after all is said and done, they will prefer Walter Scott to G. P. R. James, Shakespeare to Marlowe, Flaubert to Goncourt. Sometimes the preference is long in forming, and during this formative period they have many reversions, and go galloping, in herds of one hundred or one hundred and fifty thousand (swelling the circulations), after false gods. But note this fact: that the fustian and the tinsel and the sawdust are discovered very soon, and, the discovery once made, the sham idol can claim no single devotee.

In other words, it is a comfort to those who take the literature of the American—or even of the Anglo-Saxon—seriously to remember, in the long run and the larger view, that a circulation of two hundred, three hundred or four hundred thousand—judging even by this base-scale of "copies sold"—is not so huge after all. Consider. A "popular" novel is launched and sells its half-million. Within a certain very limited period of time, at most five years, this sale stops definitely and conclusively. The People have found out that it is not such a work of genius after all, and will have no more of it.

But how about the circulation of the works of the real Masters, Scott and Dickens, say—to be more concrete, let us speak of "Ivanhoe" and "David Copperfield"—have not each of these 'sold" more than two hundred thousand since publication? Is not two hundred million nearer the mark? And they are still selling. New editions are published every year. Does not this prove that the People are discriminating; that they are—after all—preferring the best literature to the mediocre; that they are not such a mindless herd after all; that in the end, in fine, they are always right? It will not do to decry the American public; to say that it has no taste, no judgment; that it "likes to be fooled." It may be led away for a time by clamorous advertising and the "barking" of fakirs. But there comes a day when it will no longer be fooled. A million dollars' worth of advertising would not to-day sell a hundred thousand copies of "Trilby." But "Ivanhoe" and "Copperfield," without advertising, without *réclames* for exploitation, are as marketable this very day as a sack of flour or a bag of wheat.

Mr. Metcalfe, in a recent issue of "Life," has been lamenting the lack of good plays on the American stage during the past season, and surely no one can aver that the distinguished critic is not right. One can not forbear a wince or two at the thought of what future art historians will say in their accounts of the American drama at the beginning of the twentieth century. Frankly and unreservedly the native American drama is just about as bad as it can be, and every intelligent-minded person is quite willing to say so. The causes are not difficult to trace. Two come to the mind at once, which in themselves alone would account for the degeneracy—*i. e.*, the rage for Vaudeville and the exploitation of the Star. The first has developed in the last ten years, an importation from English music halls. Considered at first as a fad by the better class of theatre-goers, a thing to be countenanced with amused toleration like performing bears and the animal circus, it has been at length boosted and foisted upon the public attention till, like a veritable cancer, it has eaten almost into the very vitals of the Legitimate Comedy (using the word in its technical sense). Continually nowadays one may see a "specialty"—generally in the form of a dance—lugged in between the scenes of a perfectly sober, perfectly sane Comedy of Manners. The moment any one subordinate feature of a dramatic action is developed at the expense of *vraisemblance* and the Probabilities, and for the sake of amusing the galleries, there is the first bacillus of decay. Vaudeville is all very well by itself, and one will even go so far as to admit that it has its place as much as an Ibsen problem-play. But it should keep to that place. It is ludicrously *out* of place in a comedy—quite as much so as the "Bible Incident" in "Ebbsmith" would be in a Hoyt farce. But because the "specialty" because Vaudeville, will "go" with the "gallery" at any time and at any place, the manager and—the pity of it!—the author, too, will introduce it whenever the remotest possibility occurs, and by just so much the tone of the whole drama is lowered. It has got to such a pass by now, however, that one ought to be thankful if this same "tone" is not keyed down to the specialty.

But the exploiting of the Star, it would seem, is, of all others, the great cause of the mediocrity of present-day dramatic literature. One has but to glance at the theatre programmes and bills to see how matters stand. The name of the leading lady or leading man is "scare-headed" so that the swiftest runner can not fail to see. Even the manager proclaims his patronymic in enormous "caps." But the author!—as often as not *his* name is not discoverable at all. The play is nothing—thus it would seem the managers would have us believe—it is the actress, her speeches, her scenes, her gowns, her personality, that are the all-important essentials. It is notorious how plays are cut, and readjusted, and dislocated to suit the Star. Never mind whether or not the scene is artistic, is vivid, is dramatic. Does the Star get the best of it? If not, write it over. The Star must have all the good lines. If they can not be built into the Star's part, cut 'em out. The Probabilities, the construction, artistic effect, climax, even good, common, forthright horse sense, rot 'em! who cares for 'em? Give the Star the lime-light—that's the point.

If the audience is willing to pay its money to see Miss Marlowe, Miss Mannering, or Mrs. Carter put through her paces, that's another thing; but let us not expect that good dramas will issue forth from this state of affairs.

Where are the Books for Girls? Adults' books there are and books for boys by the carload, but where is the book for the young girls? Something has already been said about literature for the amiable young woman, but this, now, is a very different person. One means the girl of fourteen to eighteen. The boy passing through this most trying formative period finds his literature ready to hand. Boys' books, tales of hunting, adventure and sport abound. They are good books, too, sane, "healthy," full of fine spirit and life. But the girl, where does she read? Surely the years between fourteen and eighteen are even more trying to a young girl than to a boy. She is not an active animal. When the boy is out-of-doors, pitching curves or "running the ends," the girl (even yet in the day and age of "athletics for women") is in the house, and, as like as not, reading. And reading what, if you please? The feeblest, thinnest, most colorless lucubrations that it is given to the mind of misguided man to conceive or to perpetuate. It must be this or else the literature of the adult; and surely the novels written for mature minds, for men and women who have some knowledge of the world and powers of discrimination, are not good reading, in any sense of the word, for a sixteen-year-old girl in the formative period of her life.

Besides Alcott, no one has ever written intelligently for girls. Surely there is a field here. Surely a Public, untried and unexplored, is waiting for its author; nor is it a public wanting in enthusiasm, loyalty or intelligence.

But for all this great parade and prating of emancipated women it nevertheless remains a fact that the great majority of twentieth-century opinion is virtually Oriental in its conception of the young girl. The world to-day is a world for boys, men and women. Of all humans, the young girl, the sixteen-year-old, is the least important—or, at least, is so deemed. Wanted: a Champion. Wanted: the Discoverer and Poet of the Very Young Girl. Unimportant she may now appear to you, who may yet call her by her first name without fear and without reproach. But remember this, you who believe only in a world of men and boys and women; the Very Young Girl of to-day is the woman of to-morrow, the wife of the day after, and the mother of next week. She only needs to put up her hair and let down her frocks to become a very important person indeed. Meanwhile, she has no literature; meanwhile, *faute de mieux,* she is trying to read Ouida and many other books intended for maturer minds; or, worse than all, she is enfeebling her mind by the very thin gruel purveyed by the mild-mannered gentlemen and ladies who write for the Sunday-school libraries. Here is a bad business; here is a field that needs cultivation. All very well to tend and train the saplings, the oaks and the vines. The flowers—they have not bloomed yet—are to be thought about, too.

All the more so that the young girls takes a book to heart infinitely more than a boy. The boy—*his* story once read—votes it "bully," takes down his cap, and there's an end. But the average Very Young Girl does not read her story: she lives it, lingers over it, weeps over it, lies awake nights over it. So long as she lives she will never quite forget the books she read when she was sixteen. It is not too much to say that the "favorite" books of a girl at this age become a part of her life. They influence her character more than any of us, I imagine, would suspect or admit. All the more reason, then, that there should not only be good books for girls, but plenty of good books.

THE END

AMERICAN CENTURY SERIES